VISUAL DESIGN FUNDAMENTALS:
A DIGITAL APPROACH

VISUAL DESIGN
FUNDAMENTALS:
A DIGITAL APPROACH

ALAN HASHIMOTO

CHARLES RIVER MEDIA, INC.

Hingham, Massachusetts

Publisher: Jenifer Niles
Production: Publishers' Design and Production Services, Inc.
Cover Design: The Printed Image
Cover Images: Alan Hashimoto, Bob Winward, Phillip Kesler
Contributing Writer and Technical Advisor: Mike Clayton

CHARLES RIVER MEDIA, INC.
10 Downer Avenue
Hingham, Massachusetts 02043
781-740-0400
781-740-8816 (FAX)
info@charlesriver.com
www.charlesriver.com

This book is printed on acid-free paper.

Alan Hashimoto. Visual Design Fundamentals: A Digital Approach.
ISBN: 1-58450-259-2

Library of Congress Cataloging-in-Publication Data

Hashimoto, Alan.
    Visual design fundamentals : a digital approach / Alan Hashimoto.
        p.   cm.
    ISBN 1-58450-259-2
    1. Computer-aided design.   2. Image processing—Digital techniques.
    3. Graphic arts.   I. Title.
    TA174.H313 2003
    745.4—dc22

                            2003021249

Printed in the United States of America
03 7 6 5 4 3 2 First Edition

To my greatest creation, Oliver, who was born when I started this book and may wonder someday what his father was doing the first year of his life.

CONTENTS

ACKNOWLEDGMENTS

First I would like to thank Mike Clayton for his great contributions to this book. I'd also like to include his patient wife, Mindy, and his children, Aaron and Aimee, who made such good models for the last tutorials.

I want to thank the many talented artists, designers, and students who permitted me to use their great work. I would also like to acknowledge the graphics students and faculty at The University of the Incarnate Word and Utah State University for their participation and artwork.

Special thanks to Adam Watkins for his advice and help; Ryan Morishita, an intellectual properties genius; Jon Anderson and Glen Edwards, my first design instructors; and the many artist agents, art directors, and clients who put up with me through the years and gave me the wisdom to write this book.

I would like to personally thank my wife, Amy Hopkins, and her mother, Kathy, for keeping me sane and healthy throughout this whole process and to my parents, Shigeru and Miekowho will always be part of everything I accomplish.

. . . and last but not least many thanks to the greatest editor and Coach of the Year, Jenifer Niles at Charles River Media for taking a chance on a kid.

INTRODUCTION

Digital technology has become integrated into every aspect of visual communications. New digital techniques and tools for designers and artists are being invented every day. Many more options and solutions for design and art projects can be explored in greater detail and in less time. The ease of use and inexpensive cost of hardware and software has given the public the ability to create computer-generated graphics and artwork. However, the availability of technology and the advances in imaging and production techniques will not cover what is essentially a bad design. The history of design teaches us that the same elements and principles of design have always existed regardless of medium or technique. As the marketplace and exhibition rooms become saturated with digitally produced images, knowledge of the fundamentals of design becomes even more important. To create sophisticated visuals, which entertain and communicate effectively, an artist or designer cannot ignore what defines design. The intent of this book is to provide a basic understanding of design and how to integrate this knowledge into digitally produced two-dimensional images.

PURPOSEFUL ORGANIZATION

Design can be defined as "purposeful organization." As it relates to this book, the term "design" will be narrowed to include only the visual aspect of design and more specifically to those visuals that can be represented two-dimensionally.

So what is meant by "purposeful organization of visuals represented two-dimensionally"? "Purposeful organization" is the opposite of chance. Everything is thought out, planned, and placed or arranged with reason.

"Visuals" are things we can see. They consist of one or more of the following elements: line, shape, space, volume, value, color, and texture. These elements are organized using the "principles" of design. Design principles are concepts and ideas that use the elements of design to create visuals. A design that both communicates and is aesthetically pleasing is dependent on a clear understanding and effective application of these principles.

"Two-dimensional" refers to height and width. The images contained in this book are reproduced on paper or observed on a monitor. They are all examples of two-dimensional visuals. One-dimensional design would refer only to length. A true one-dimensional design could not be seen because it has no width. A line is often referred to as one-dimensional; however, a line has width and is in reality two-dimensional. This book will look past this fact and define lines as one-dimensional. Three-dimensional visuals have length and width but also depth. Examples of three-dimensional designs are packaging, industrial design, sculpture, interiors, and architecture.

HOW TO USE THIS BOOK

There are two primary concepts of design: content and form. The designs and format of this book will follow these ideas. Content is the subject matter, concept, or solution to a design problem. Form is the actual visual that is created. Not all art is created using both of these ideas. Some visuals are purely conceptual with no need to be presented in form. Some visuals are created only for visual pleasure without subject matter or a problem to be solved. The focus of this book is on visuals that communicate, which extend beyond art that is created solely for aesthetic purposes. Each chapter examines and explains important content, outlines, and gives instruction on process. Digital prints demonstrating specific content will be the final form resulting from the understanding of fundamental design theory and use of digital tools and techniques.

Classic art combined with contemporary design and illustration will be combined to explore the classic nature of the concepts in this book. To aid in the practical usage of the fundamentals of design there will be a series of projects designed to inform and expand the knowledge and experience of the reader. These projects will also encourage the exploration of alternative creative options. Accompanying these projects will be tutorials detailing classic digital techniques and procedures. These tutorials will give the reader the basic tools to complete each project.

BACKGROUND AND TECHNOLOGY REQUIREMENTS

Specific subject matter and personal expression will not be a necessary part of these projects, making it easier to focus on the specific element or principle being discussed. Because of the universal nature of these exercises, they will be applicable across a variety of design areas. Readers who are well trained in software will discover the classic art of design behind all the technology. Others who have art training, but little experience in the area of digital tools, will begin to see the relationship between art and technology by completing digitally produced design projects.

DESIGN ELEMENTS

INTRODUCTION

Line, shape, negative space, volume, value, color, and texture are the elements of design. These elements, called the "principles of design," are used either together or separately to create all visuals. To a visual designer, the elements of design are the same as notes to a musician or words to a writer. They are the tools used to create their masterpieces. Similarly, design principles can be compared to the rules that apply to composing a musical score, or the grammatical structure and rules required for writing a novel. Chapter 2 discusses the many ways a designer can use the elements and principles of design. For now, let's look at defining each of the elements.

LINE

Lines are the most basic element of design. They are a child's first visual means of expression and the foundation for most works of art. Many designers use lines to think through concepts and create preliminary sketches that communicate their ideas quickly (see Figures 1.1 & 1.2).

The emotional expression and communicative quality of lines are often underestimated. Lines can be either thin and delicate or thick and

1

FIGURE 1.1   Example of a concept sketch beginning the process of creating characters for an animation project. *Thumbnail Sketches* © 2003. Reprinted with permission from Nathan Tufts.

FIGURE 1.2   Example of a preliminary drawing and the final illustration that was created from this drawing. *Informatics Poster* © 2003. Reprinted with permission from Alan Hashimoto.

strong. They are either curved and organic or sharp and mechanical (see Figure 1.3).

A line might define the outside contours of a shape, whereas multiple lines can create value and repeated lines might produce patterns and textures (see Figures 1.4 & 1.5).

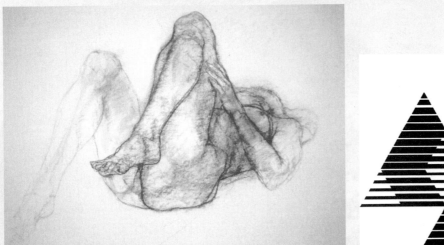 

FIGURE 1.3   Example on the left is a drawing that uses thin and delicate organic lines. *Reclining Figure* © 2003. Reprinted with permission from Adrian Van Suchtelen. The design on the right is an example of lines that use thick mechanical lines. *The Avant Group Trademark* © 2003. Reprinted with permission from Alan Hashimoto.

FIGURE 1.4   Example of a design that uses lines as the outside contours of a shape. The shirt is described by lines that follow the contour, and the hand and face in contrast are created with form. *Vincent* © 2003. Reprinted with permission from Adrian Van Suchtelen.

FIGURE 1.5   The design on the left is an example of an illustration that uses multiple lines to create value. *Camera Guy* © 2003. Reprinted with permission from Alan Hashimoto. The design on the right is an example of an illustration that uses line to describe a variety of patterns. *Yard Sale* © 2003. Reprinted with permission from Alan Hashimoto.

On the left side of Figure 1.5, notice how the subtle differences in cross-hatching or use of the direction of the lines creates different visual textures and values in the sweater, hat, face, hands, and camera.

Line and Design

Line can be defined as having only length or one dimension. There are two types of lines: *visual lines* and *implied lines*. The more commonly used—visual line—is defined as a line that can be seen. Figures 1.1 through 1.5 are examples of visual lines. In mathematical terms, a line is the distance between two points. A true one-dimensional line cannot be seen, because it has length but no visible width. This type of line is called an *implied* line. An implied line forms an invisible connection between other elements to form a line (see Figure 1.6).

Line Direction

One of the most important characteristics of a line is direction. Line direction is the feeling of movement created by the structure and placement of elements in a composition. This feeling of motion, or lack of motion, is based on our experiences with gravity. For example, vertical lines suggest stability, because when we stand up perfectly straight and well balanced we feel stable. A soldier standing at attention is a good example. Large

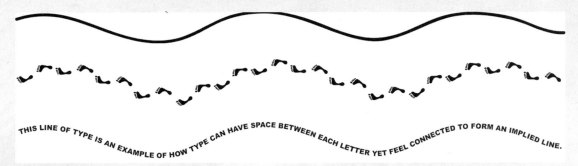

FIGURE 1.6   The line at the top is an example of a visual line. The line in the middle is an example of an implied line. Notice how the footprints do not touch but seem to connect to form a line. The line at the bottom is an example of an implied line using type. Notice how each letter is separate but seems to connect to form a line.

buildings surging straight up into the sky also seem well planted and powerful. Figure 1.7 with the vertical line direction diagrammed is a good example of vertical line direction.

FIGURE 1.7   Example of vertical line direction. Notice the how the vertical beam of light and tall doors express the feeling of power and stability. *Is there a Future in Education?* © 2003. Reprinted with permission from Alan Hashimoto.

Horizontal lines create a feeling of stability and also give a sense of calmness, whereas vertical lines do not. Think about how landscapes and seascapes stretching out horizontally seem relaxed and soothing. When we are at rest, our bodies are usually horizontal, providing the sense of calm required for sleep. Figure 1.8 is an example of a horizontal line direction that gives the painting a tranquil feeling.

Diagonal lines communicate motion and tension. When we are running or participating in any physical sport our body is usually angled forward. Likewise, an object that is tilting and about to fall gives us a tense feeling as we anticipate the action. See an example of this in Figure 1.9.

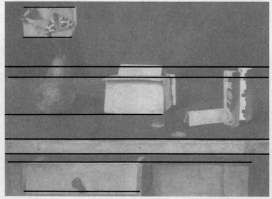

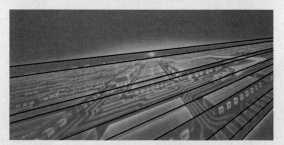

FIGURE 1.8   Example of horizontal line direction. The horizontal line direction is identified more clearly in the lower composition. *Vanitas: House of Cards* © 2003. Reprinted with permission from Adrian Van Suchtelen.

FIGURE 1.9   Example of a composition using diagonal line direction to communicate action. The diagonal line direction is identified more clearly in the lower composition. *Racing to Find the Solution* © 2003. Reprinted with permission from Alan Hashimoto.

Figure 1.10 is a perfect example of how line direction affects the mood and feeling of a design. The top design is a painting that has been cropped to show a horizontal line direction. The lower design is the same painting in its original state. Notice how different each composition feels even though the colors and objects are basically the same.

FIGURE 1.10   The top composition is cropped, giving it a horizontal line direction. The lower composition is the original painting with a diagonal line direction. *Shallow Water* © 2003. Reprinted with permission from Glen Edwards.

SHAPE

Shape is defined as having both length and width. It is two-dimensional without having mass or depth.

When we see an object at a great distance, the first thing we notice is its shape. We do not see specific lines, values, or colors, because details at a distance blend together to form a basic shape. From far away we can only recognize the basic shape of a person. As they approach, we will be able to discern their gender or basic attire, because more details will come into focus. Shape is the element that communicates the identity of objects most immediately and directly. We usually do not need to see every line, value, color, or texture to recognize an object. We identify objects by their shapes.

The main objective of any successful graphic designer is to communicate visual information in a unique and efficient way. The competition for visual attention in an environment bombarded by images, coupled with the public's short attention span, makes the understanding and creative use of shapes a necessity. Shapes have the ability to communicate visual messages quickly and directly.

Shape and Design

There are several different ways shapes can be designed: They can be realistic, distorted, abstract, stylized, and non-objective.

Realism

Realism is the way we observe images in nature with all the proportions and dimensions of the natural world. Figure 1.11 is an example of realism. All the objects are represented in a way we would expect to see them without distortion or exaggeration. The object placement is natural and not unusual. The textures and lighting obey the laws of nature and do not seem to be manipulated.

FIGURE 1.11   Example of a painting using realism. *Requiem* © 2003.
Reprinted with permission from Chris Terry.

Realism is used to accurately communicate a visual image to the largest audience possible. Everyone can relate to the images seen in real life. A well-drafted painting or drawing of a mountain can be easily understood as a mountain to almost anybody. Most designs for mass communication use realism to ensure that the visual message is understood with little or no doubt. Realism may not be the most unique or efficient way of using shape, but the images will be interpreted with little effort.

Distortion

When realistic shapes are manipulated or changed, but are still recognizable as natural objects, it is called *distortion*. Distortion can be used to either emphasize or de-emphasize a natural shape to aid in expressing a particular feeling or idea. The legs of an athlete are drawn extremely long to emphasize his ability to run. The head of a person may be painted larger in proportion to his or her body to inform us they are either really smart or extremely thick headed. These are all examples of distortion (Figure 1.12).

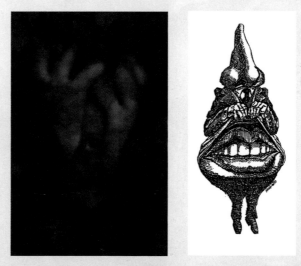

FIGURE 1.12   Examples of designs that use distortion. The illustration on the left was created using digital photography and computer manipulation. *Young Goodman Brown* © 2003. Reprinted with permission from Bob Winward. The illustration on the right is a traditional pen and ink drawing. *Nosey Gossip* © 2003. Reprinted with permission from Alan Hashimoto.

Abstraction

Another way designers and artists use shape and distortion is through *abstraction*. Abstraction is the process of reducing natural shapes to their simplest form.

Trademarks and other commercial symbols use abstraction to communicate the maximum amount of visual information delivered through a minimal amount of shapes. Pictographs or information symbols are examples of how abstraction is used. Road signs, buttons on a DVD player, and Website navigation symbols must be simple and read quickly. Trademarks are another example of how abstracted symbols deliver information simply and directly. In a glance, the aspirations, products, services, and integrity of a company are being represented in a single image. Figure 1.13 shows five symbols that communicate using abstracted shapes. In Figure 1.13, notice how these five simple graphic examples express the essence of what might be very complex objects or ideas. The top-left design is a label and trademark for clothing. The top-right design is a trademark for an interactive media company. The lower-left trademark communicates grilling using abstracted steam and eating utensils. The lower-middle trademark is used for a greenhouse and nursery. The lower-right design is a trademark for a chiropractor.

FIGURE 1.13   Examples of simple graphics that express the essence of objects or ideas. Top: *Work Zone* © 2003 and *Horizons* © 2003. Reprinted with permission from Jerry Skaggs. Bottom, left, and middle: *Vino Bistro* © 2003 and *Red Leaf Nursery* © 2003. Reprinted with permission from Meliza Aaron. Bottom, right: *Chiropractor Trademark* © 2003. Reprinted with permission from Nancy Wride.

Stylization

There are varying degrees of abstraction depending on the amount of visual information needed to communicate the content of a design. If there is a need for more realism and the abstraction is slight, it is called *stylization*. Many artists and illustrators use stylization to give their work a unique look. Their simplified images may also be interpreted with less effort, thus making the specific visual message more obvious (Figure 1.14).

FIGURE 1.14   Example of a magazine cover illustration using stylized shapes. *Wasatch Yard and Garden Olympic Edition*
© 2003. Reprinted with permission from Alan Hashimoto.

Non-Objective

When shapes in a design do not have a recognizable visual representation to anything in nature, they are defined as *non-objective* (Figure 1.15).

Because there is no distracting subject matter in a non-objective design, elements and principles of design are isolated and observed clearly. It is necessary to rely on the element or principle itself to begin to understand and appreciate these types of compositions.

A successful non-objective design can still carry emotional content. In fact, it may be easier to recognize emotional content because we are not trying to find meaning in "real" objects or concerning ourselves with how the subjects are being represented or presented. We can simply see the color blue and feel cool or look at a large shape next to a small shape and sense the contrast.

Rectilinear Shapes

There are two very different types of shapes, rectilinear and curvilinear. Rectilinear shapes are sharp and angular. They often reflect the charac-

FIGURE 1.15 Example of a composition using non-objective shapes. *April Morning* © 2003. Reprinted with permission from Adrian Van Suchtelen.

FIGURE 1.16 Example of composition using rectilinear shapes. The angular and mechanical quality of the shapes in this illustration gives the feeling of organization and structure, typical of designs using rectilinear shapes. *Getting to Seven* © 2003. Reprinted with permission from Alan Hashimoto.

teristics of man-made mechanical objects that are rigid and geometric in nature (Figure 1.16).

Around the turn of the century, during the Industrial Revolution, rectilinear shapes were commonly seen in design as well as in fine art. They reflected the new mechanized world and related social issues that dominated society at that time. Futurism, Constructivism, Cubism, and Art Deco were a few of the art and design movements that were influenced by the new world of mass production and machines. These movements are still very popular and often imitated by contemporary designers involved in every facet of design, from graphic design to architecture.

The following is a brief description of a few of the historic design styles and art movements, still relevant to contemporary design, that use rectilinear shapes.

Cubism

Cubism was developed in Paris and can be described as the breaking up of space and realism into abstract or non-objective shapes or forms. Cubists created this effect by overlapping or connecting rectilinear shapes. Multiple points of view being presented at one time is also characteristic of Cubism.

Futurism

Futurism began in Italy and was based on the glorification of the machine and denunciation of classical art and culture of the past. Aggressive praise of new technology led to violent manifestos. Motion, dynamics, and speed are characteristics of Futurism. Many of the Futurist attitudes and beliefs are the beginnings of the more contemporary cyber punk movement (see Figure 1.17).

FIGURE 1.17 Example of a contemporary book design about Futurism. This cover, etched on a copper plate, uses typography design influenced by the Futurists. *Futurista* © 2003. Reprinted with permission from Holly Craven.

Constructivism

Constructivism in relationship to art is a movement that incorporated minimal geometric and orderly non-objective shapes with an idealistic attitude that tried to find a new approach to art and architecture that could deal with the social and economic problems of the day. The early principles of Constructivism began in Russia and were heavily influenced by both the Cubist and Futurist art movements. Constructivism is still used today in industrial, interior, and graphic design (Figure 1.18).

FIGURE 1.18   The design on the left is a Constructivist-influenced trademark. *Van Doesburg* © 2003. Reprinted with permission from Mike Clayton. The example on the right is a contemporary title design dealing with Constructivism, which uses typography design from the period. The larger design at the top is the main title. The three designs below are minor titles. *Constructivism Titles* © 2003. Reprinted with permission from Nancy Wride.

Art Deco

Geometric, simple shapes and streamlined design of machines characterize Art Deco. Art Deco began in Europe as an ornament and surface decoration style based on the concepts of Art Nouveau. Art Deco gained popularity in the United States in interior design and architecture. The Chrysler Building and Empire State Building in New York City are examples. Theaters, restaurants, hotels, ocean liners, furniture, sculpture, clothing, jewelry, and graphic design became heavily influenced by Art Deco (Figure 1.19).

FIGURE 1.19   The two fonts on the left reflect the simple geometric shapes characteristic of Art Deco. The illustrations on the right are contemporary examples of Art Deco influence. *Road Rally and Speak* © 2003. Reprinted with permission from Patrick Wilkey, *www.visiocommunications.com.*

Curvilinear Shapes

In contrast, shapes that are organic, curved, and round are called curvilinear. They are based on life forms that exist in nature (Figure 1.20). *Art Nouveau*, and some of the psychedelic art of the sixties are just two examples of art and design movements that use curvilinear shapes.

The following is a brief description of design styles and art movements, still relevant to contemporary design, that use curvilinear shapes.

FIGURE 1.20   Example of composition using curvilinear shapes. The flowing organic shapes give the feeling of lively motion commonly found in designs using curvilinear shapes. *Four Seasons Illustration* © 2003. Reprinted with permission from Patrick Wilkey, *www.visiocommunications.com*.

Art Nouveau

Art Nouveau is a decorative art style characterized by detailed patterns of curving lines and shapes. The Art Nouveau artists wanted to unify all arts and center the arts around man and his life. This movement had many names in other countries based on the major artists', magazine, or firm names. In France this movement was know as "Style Guimard," in Germany as "Jugendstil," and in Italy as "Stile Liberty"(Figure 1.21).

Psychedelic Art

The hippie culture is represented by the style of Psychedelia. It borrowed from past art movements such as Art Nouveau, Op Art, and Pop Art.

 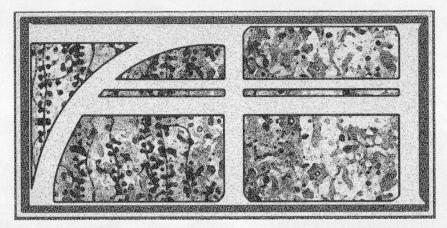

FIGURE 1.21   The illustration on the left and trademark on the right are contemporary examples of the organic, free-flowing shapes characteristics of Art Nouveau. *Vinegar Label and AH Design Trademark* © 2003. Reprinted with permission from Alan Hashimoto.

Bright colors, organic shapes, and decorative typefaces make up the major forms of psychedelic art. Graffiti artists and Gen-X designers use images and designs based on psychedelic art to speak to another generation looking to break the rules (Figure 1.22).

FIGURE 1.22   The left design is a proposed symbol for Utah State University art department based on type design of Art Nouveau. *Proposed University Symbol* © 2003. The design on the right is a contemporary example of a logo influenced by psychedelic art and design. *Ashbury Pub* © 2003. Reprinted with permission from Alan Hashimoto.

There are many more historic art and design movements that contributed to the contemporary design of rectilinear and curvilinear shapes. Some of these are Arts and Crafts, Baroque, Bauhaus, De Stijl, Pre-Raphaelites, and Rococo.

NEGATIVE SPACE

Negative space is the empty area surrounding a positive shape. When designing with recognizable subject matter it is very easy to identify what is a positive shape and what is a negative space. The term *figure/ground* is given this relationship. The figure is the positive shape and the background the negative space (Figure 1.23).

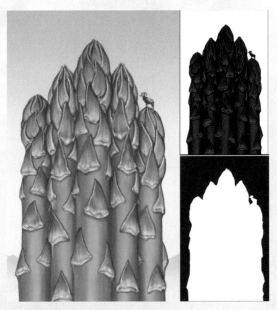

FIGURE 1.23   The larger image to the left is the original illustration as it was published. The smaller darkened image at the top right is indicating the figure or positive shape. The darkened background image at the bottom right is indicating the ground or negative space. *Asparagus and Mountain Goat* © 2003. Reprinted with permission from Alan Hashimoto.

When a design is composed of non-objective shapes this term (figure/ground) does not necessarily apply. Any non-objective shape may be viewed as either a positive shape or a negative space. This becomes important because it emphasizes the fact that as we design positive shapes we are also designing negative space.

In some designs the negative space is confused with the positive shape and vice versa. This technique adds interest to designs and reminds us that negative space is a design element not to be ignored (See Figure 1.24).

To understand negative space fully, the surface boundaries around a design must be defined. This area is called the *picture frame*. The picture frame will aid in creating and defining those areas that are positive shapes

FIGURE 1.24   The example on the left is a design composed of non-objective shapes. Which is the figure? Which is the ground? *The Four Seasons: Autumn* © 2003. Reprinted with permission from Adrian Van Suchtelen. The example on the right is a design where the positive shape and negative space are interchangeable and confused, adding interest to the design. *Zoo Figure Ground Tee-Shirt Illustration* © 2003. Reprinted with permission from Bob Winward.

or negative spaces. Figure 1.25 shows examples of how the picture frame affects these elements. Notice how the absence of a picture frame in the top-left design makes the positive shape feel like part of the entire

FIGURE 1.25   Examples of the importance of the picture frame and how it affects the entire design. *Beethoven* © 2003. Reprinted with permission from Alan Hashimoto.

page. The picture frames in the other examples illustrate the change in negative space and how different formats can affect the entire design. The upper-right design feels much more active because there is less negative space. The lower-left design is more tranquil because of the horizontal line direction and added negative space. The lower-right design is more powerful in nature because of the added vertical negative space and line direction.

VOLUME

Volume defines three-dimensional visuals that have length and width and also depth. Images of this element can be represented two-dimensionally in this book, but realistically volume would have to be observed from an assortment of angles in an actual environment. This could be done virtually using a time-based medium such as a CD-ROM, DVD, or video. However, because the image would be viewed on a monitor, it would still technically be a two-dimensional image. This book will deal with volume indirectly and attempt to include three-dimensional examples when discussing the elements and principles. Interior design, architecture, industrial design, and sculpture share the same basic principles of design as two-dimensional shapes.

VALUE

Value describes light and dark. It is dependent on light, without which value does not exist. Light permits us to see the contrast of values that make up shape and form. Extreme contrast of values in a design gives a sense of clarity and depth as seen in the painting on the left in Figure 1.26. Similar values may give a sense of subtlety and shallowness as seen in the design on the right in Figure 1.26.

Value and Design

When values are very light, the term *high key* is used. Lighter values suggest a brighter, happier mood as seen in the painting on the left in Figure 1.27. Conversely, values that are dark are called *low key*. They usually feel somber and serious as seen in the design on the right in Figure 1.27.

FIGURE 1.26   The watercolor on the left uses strong light and shadow to emphasize the dynamics of the landscape. *Afternoon Stage* © 2003. Reprinted with permission from Glen Edwards. Because of the similar values used in the design on the right, the mood is very solemn with many subtle details that can only be seen upon close inspection. *Morcote* © 2003. Reprinted with permission from Bob Winward.

FIGURE 1.27   The painting on the left is an example of a high-key design. The light values reinforce the subject matter made up mostly of spring flowers. *In Celebration of Spring* © 2003. Reprinted with permission from Adrian Van Suchtelen. The illustration on the right is an example of a low-key design. *Vertical Fields* © 2003. Reprinted with permission from Bob Winward.

Value is also used to describe volume two-dimensionally by imitating the way light reveals a form or object. The lightest values are in the direct line of light whereas the darker values are in shadow, as seen in Figure 1.28.

FIGURE 1.28   Example of a composition using light to reveal form. The light coming from the right side emphasizes the form of the swans and castle in the background. *Montreux* © 2003. Reprinted with permission from Bob Winward.

There will be more information concerning value and design in Chapter 8, including a project that analyzes value as a design element.

COLOR

Color is essentially an element of light. If you have ever looked at natural light shining through a prism you can see how light can be broken down into various colors. A surface that is painted red reflects only the red rays and absorbs the rest of the colored rays. Green paint absorbs all the rays except the green rays, which are reflected. This kind of color produced from reflected light is called *subtractive*. Color that is made from emitted light, such as a computer monitor, is light that is combined to make that color and is referred to as *additive*. When discussing color mixing, these two systems are very different from each other. If you combine the primary subtractive colors of yellow, red, and blue, you will get a muddy gray. If you combine the primary additive colors of red, green, and blue you will get a white light.

There are many other theories associated with color that will be discussed in Chapter 9. Color as a design element will also be included in design projects from Chapters 9, 10, and 11.

TEXTURE

Texture is the surface quality of an object. There are two types of texture: *implied* and *tactile*. Implied texture is texture that can be seen but not felt or touched. Technically, implied texture is not texture at all: it is the illusion of texture. Tactile texture is texture that can actually be felt and touched (see Figure 1.29).

FIGURE 1.29 The painting on the left uses implied textures on almost every object in the painting. *Like a Ripe Watermelon* © 2003. Reprinted with permission from Greg Schulte. The bowl on the right is an example of tactile texture. The interesting surface quality is very evident. *Nawame Bowl* © 2003. Reprinted with permission from John Neely.

SUMMARY

Now that the elements have been identified, you should be able to point out many examples of these elements in the art and design you observe every day. Look at the type and images in a printed poster, art book, or design magazine. What kind of line direction is being used for the image? What kind of line direction is being used for the layout? What kinds of shapes are being used? Are the shapes examples of realism, non-objective, distortion, abstraction, or stylization? Are the shapes organic or mechanical or are they a mixture of both?

Look at examples of trademarks. Are they using abstraction or stylization to communicate the identity of their business? Is the negative shape or space being used as an example of figure/ground to increase the communicative content of their identity?

Take a closer look at your own photographs or photographs in a book or magazine. What kind of value is being used? Is it high key or low key? Are the values contrasting or similar? Try to find examples of tactile texture and implied texture. Observe the difference.

As a visual designer you should try to increase your observation skills by looking more carefully at images. In many ways this is like physical exercise. If you practice, it becomes more natural. The more you observe the broader your visual vocabulary will become. The more images you have in your vocabulary the more options you will have to create your own original art and design.

2

PRINCIPLES OF DESIGN

INTRODUCTION

The "elements" of design are "what" are used and the "principles" of design are "how" they are used. The use of each principle is specific to the individual problem to be solved. Once the problem is researched and well defined, the elements can be selected and the principles can be applied. Design is about making these visual choices. This chapter will concentrate on the many ways design elements can be used and what to be aware of when creating and analyzing successful design projects.

GESTALT

Understanding how the eye and mind work together to perceive and organize visuals is an absolute necessity for any designer. The principles of design outlined in this chapter use results from psychological studies based on human perception of visual elements. The most widely accepted study on this subject is included in the Gestalt theory of visual perception. Generally speaking, it states that humans inherently look for order or a relationship between various elements. People observe and analyze individual parts of an image as separate components and have the tendency to group these parts into a larger, greater image that may be very different from the components (see Figure 2.1).

The design on the left in Figure 2.1 is an example of how similar shapes group themselves to form a diamond. This diamond shape is clearly evident to a viewer and can be seen with little effort on the viewer's part. The design on the right is an example of how shapes that are not physically connected form a relationship between each other and become a greater shape, different from its parts.

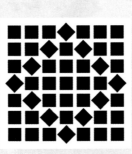 

FIGURE 2.1 Examples of Gestalt theory. Left: *Gestalt Example* © 2003. Reprinted with permission from Alan Hashimoto. Right: *Transcendental Birthday Party* © 2003. Reprinted with permission from Brisida Magro.

The two examples in Figure 2.1 represent just a few of the many fundamental ideas associated with Gestalt theory. The following sections will explore the relationship between the elements and principles of design using Gestalt theory as evidence of how people naturally organize images.

UNITY OR HARMONY

Unity expresses the idea that things belong together. Harmony is another word that might be used in place of unity. The idea that we tend to visually group similar elements and try to find the relationships that exist between them is an example of how the design principle of unity is incorporated into the Gestalt theory of visual perception. A design that is void of unity is usually chaotic and uncomfortable to view (see Figure 2.2).

Unity can be accomplished in many different ways, including: placement, repetition, rhythm, and continuation. Each of these principles can be applied to any element of design including line, shape, and value. These ideas will be defined and discussed in the following sections. Unity and color will be discussed in Chapter 9.

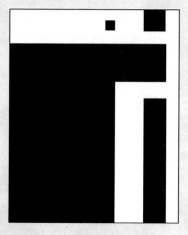

FIGURE 2.2   The simple design on the left is an example of unity. Notice how the similarity of shapes and their placement creates unity throughout the entire composition even though the sizes or the shapes vary. In contrast, the simple design on the right is void of unity. Notice how the lack of unity between shapes causes the composition to feel chaotic.

Unity and Placement

Unity and Placement Using Line

The placement of elements next to each other is one way to create unity. In creating text for a layout, notice how lines of type are organized to group information that is related (see Figure 2.3).

The placement of lines of type in relationship to each other can affect the entire look of the shape, value, and legibility of a paragraph. The space between each line of type is referred to as *leading*. The shape of a paragraph appears dark and dense when less leading is used and the lines of type are close together. Figure 2.4 illustrates a paragraph with less leading and a paragraph with more leading.

Placing lines of type *flush* (vertically lined up to one side) or *justified* (vertically lined up on both sides) is a way of giving unity to a block of text. Notice in Figure 2.5 how flush and justified arrangements of type give the paragraph unity. Figure 2.5 also shows an example of the same information arranged randomly, making the paragraph less readable and more chaotic.

Unity and Placement Using Shape

Notice the relationship between the shapes in Figure 2.6. All the shapes in the left design are placed far apart and all are too close to the *picture*

FUNDAMENTALS OF DESIGN
A DIGITAL APPROACH

Digital technology has become integrated into every aspect of visual communications. New digital techniques and tools for designers and artists are being invented every day. Many more options and solutions for design and art projects can be explored in greater detail and in less time. The ease of use and inexpensive cost of hardware and software has given the public the ability to create computer generated graphics and artwork. However, the availability of technology and the advances in imaging and production techniques will not cover up what is essentially a bad design. The history of design teaches us that the same elements and principles of design have always existed regardless of medium or technique. As the market place and exhibition rooms become saturated with digitally produced images, knowledge of the fundamentals of design becomes even more important. To create sophisticated visuals, which entertain and communicate effectively, an artist or designer cannot ignore what defines design. The intent of this book is to provide a basic understanding of design and how to integrate this knowledge into digitally produced two-dimensional images.

So what is meant by "purposeful organization of visuals represented two-dimensionally"? "Purposeful organization" is the opposite of or chance. Everything is thought out, planned and placed or arranged with reason. "Visuals"

are things we can see. They consist of one or more of the following elements: line, shape, space, volume, value, color, and texture. These elements are organized using the "principles" of design. Design principles are concepts and ideas that use the elements of design to create visuals. A design that both communicates and is aesthetically pleasing is dependent on a clear understanding and effective application of these principles.

Design can be defined as "purposeful organization". As it relates to this book, the term "design" will be narrowed to include only the visual aspect of design and more specifically to those visuals that can be represented two-dimensionally.

"Two-dimensional" refers to height and width. The images contained in this book are reproduced on paper or observed on a monitor. They are all examples of two-dimensional visuals. One-dimensional design would refer to only length. A true one-dimensional design could not be seen because it has no width. A line is often referred to as one-dimensional, however, a line has width and is really two-dimensional. This book will look past this fact and define lines as one-dimensional. Three-dimensional visuals have length and width but also depth. Examples of three-dimensional designs are packaging, industrial design, sculpture, interiors, and architecture.

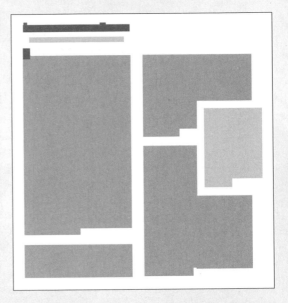

FIGURE 2.3   Example of lines of type organized to group information. The design on the left is a page from an article that uses the placement of lines of type and surrounding space to create a relationship between various forms of information. The design on the right emphasizes the shapes and values that are formed by these lines of type.

Digital technology has become integrated into every aspect of visual communications. New digital techniques and tools for designers and artists are being invented every day. Many more options and solutions for design and art projects can be explored in greater detail and in less time. The ease of use and inexpensive cost of hardware and software has given the public the ability to create computer generated graphics and artwork. However, the availability of technology and the advances in imaging and production techniques will not cover up what is essentially a bad design. The history of design teaches us that the same elements and principles of design have always existed regardless of medium or technique. As the market place and exhibition rooms become saturated with digitally produced images, knowledge of the fundamentals of design becomes even more important. To create sophisticated visuals, which entertain and communicate effectively, an artist or designer cannot ignore what defines design. The intent of this book is to provide a basic understanding of design and how to integrate this knowledge into digitally produced two-dimensional images.

Digital technology has become integrated into every aspect of visual communications. New digital techniques and tools for designers and artists are being invented every day. Many more options and solutions for design and art projects can be explored in greater detail and in less time. The ease of use and inexpensive cost of hardware and software has given the public the ability to create computer generated graphics and artwork. However, the availability of technology and the advances in imaging and production techniques will not cover up what is essentially a bad design. The history of design teaches us that the same elements and principles of design have always existed regardless of medium or technique. As the market place and exhibition rooms become saturated with digitally produced images, knowledge of the fundamentals of design becomes even more important. To create sophisticated visuals, which entertain and communicate effectively, an artist or designer cannot ignore what defines design. The intent of this book is to provide a basic understanding of design and how to integrate this knowledge into digitally produced two-dimensional images.

FIGURE 2.4   Example of a paragraph with less leading and a paragraph with more leading. Notice the relationship between the lines of type. Can you see the differences in value? Which is easier to read?

Placing lines of type flush (vertically lined up to one side) or justified (vertically lined up on both sides) is a way of giving unity to a block of text. Notice in Figure 2.7 how flush and justified arrangements of type give the paragraph unity. Figure 2.7 also shows an example of the same information arranged more randomly making the paragraph less readable and chaotic. Figure 2.7 Example of type arrangement that is flush to the right and type arrangement that is justified, and a type arrangement that is random, less readable, and chaotic.

Placing lines of type flush (vertically lined up to one side) or justified (vertically lined up on both sides) is a way of giving unity to a block of text. Notice in Figure 2.7 how flush and justified arrangements of type give the paragraph unity. Figure 2.7 also shows an example of the same information arranged more randomly making the paragraph less readable and chaotic. Figure 2.7 Example of type arrangement that is flush to the right and type arrangement that is justified, and a type arrangement that is random, less readable, and chaotic.

Placing lines of type flush (vertically lined up to one side) or justified (vertically lined up on both sides) is a way of giving unity to block of text.

Notice in Figure 2.7 how flush and justified arrangements of type give the paragraph unity. Figure 2.7 also shows an example of the same information arranged more randomly making the paragraph less readable and chaotic.

Figure 2.7 Example of type arrangement that is flush to the right and type arrangement that is justified, and a type arrangement that is random, less readable, and chaotic.

FIGURE 2.5   Example of type arrangement that is flush to the left, type arrangement that is justified, and a type arrangement that is random.

frame (outside boundaries of a design). When shapes are placed closer to the *picture frame* and further away from each other, they will form a strong relationship to the picture frame and a weak relationship to each other. When this happens, the edges of the composition will receive the attention leaving the middle feeling open and empty. Figure 2.7 shows an example of a title set closer together (tight) and an example of the same title set further apart (loose).

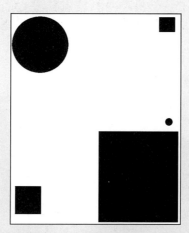 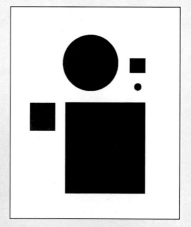

FIGURE 2.6   The design on the left is an example of shapes placed too close to the picture frame leaving the middle of the composition open and empty. The design on the right places the same shapes closer to each other, creating a more unified relationship between each shape.

THE MULTIMEDIA MARCHING BAND

T H E   M U L T I M E D I A   M A R C H I N G   B A N D

FIGURE 2.7   Example of type set close together, which creates a fast-paced feeling. The bottom line of type is an example of the same type set loose, creating a title that must be read at a slower pace.

This idea may be useful when designing type for titles or headlines. A fast-paced feeling can be achieved by setting type closer together. In contrast, a slower, calmer feeling is created when type is set further apart. In visual design, distance is equal to time. This means that the larger the distance between elements of a design the more time it will take for the viewer to recognize the relationship. Titles with type spaced far apart can still feel unified by using letters from the same font as well as by placing the letters on the same line, commonly called a baseline.

Designs that use shapes placed randomly can seem active and fun. If the visual message is short and simple these designs can be effective; however, most designs demand a more complex and detailed visual message that needs to be communicated very quickly. Creating easy to recognize relationships between visuals becomes absolutely necessary. Similar line directions, related shapes, and lining up edges of shapes and lines of type can help in unifying a design. Figures 2.8 and 2.9 illustrate how the same shapes may be organized differently to create either chaos or stability.

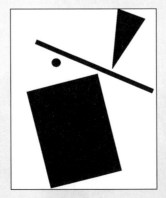 

FIGURE 2.8   Shapes in the left design are placed at random and seem chaotic. In the right design the same shapes are placed together, taking advantage of similar line direction and related aspects of the shapes themselves. Notice how the triangle feels less tense when placed with the heavier, more stable side face down. This occurs because of our relationship to gravity.

VISUAL DESIGN
FUNDAMENTALS:
A Digital Approach

VISUAL DESIGN
FUNDAMENTALS:
A Digital Approach

FIGURE 2.9   The left design illustrates how neglecting to establish unity between type and lines of type can make reading a message difficult. The design on the right uses the same type but delivers the visual message quickly and more effectively.

Unity and Repetition

Unity and Repetition Using Line

Repetition is also a characteristic of unity that can be applied to any element of design. It is the idea that a part of a design repeats somewhere else in a composition to create unity. Figure 2.10 is an example of how repetition of a line can unify a composition. Another example of repetition and line creating unity can be seen in Figure 2.11.

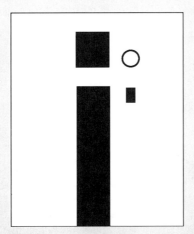 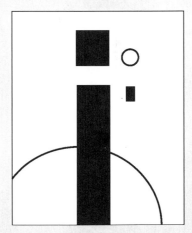

FIGURE 2.10   The simple design on the left is made up of three shapes and one contour line describing the outside of a circle. The shapes seem to feel unified but the circle seems out of place. The design on the right illustrates how repeating a line similar to the circle can make the entire composition more harmonious. The newly added line is larger to give the design variety and interest.

FIGURE 2.11   Example of an illustration that uses a consistent repeated line width in conjunction with shape to create unity. *Eye in Hand Illustration* © 2003. Reprinted with permission from Patrick Wilkey, *www.visiocommunications.com.*

As stated earlier in Chapter 1, direction is a characteristic of lines. Repetition of a common line direction can help relate all parts of a design. Figure 2.12 is an example of how repeating the vertical line directions of primary shapes unifies a design. Figure 2.13 is an example of how a diagonal line direction unifies all the elements into a harmonic, dynamic design.

 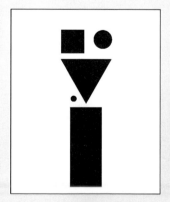

FIGURE 2.12   The design on the left contains shapes that seem unrelated. Through the use of a vertical line direction, the shapes in the right design appear to be more unified.

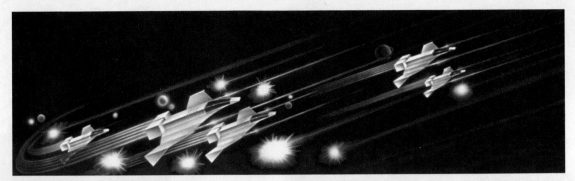

FIGURE 2.13 This illustration for an electronic jukebox is an example of diagonal line direction creating unity between all the shapes. *Space Jet Jukebox* © 2003. Reprinted with permission from Alan Hashimoto.

Unity and Repetition Using Shape

As discussed earlier there are two different types of shapes, rectilinear and curvilinear. Designs that consist of the same or similar types of shapes are usually harmonious. Figure 2.15 shows a design with similar rectilinear shapes and a design with similar curvilinear shapes. Both feel very unified. A third design makes use of both shapes in one composition illustrating the idea that both types of shapes can be present in a unified design. The idea that these shapes are different from each other but can exist in the same design is a good example of balancing unity with variety.

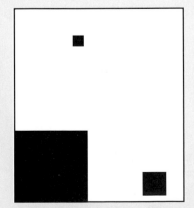

FIGURE 2.14 Example of a simple design with similar rectilinear shapes is located on the left. The design in the middle is an example of a design using curvilinear shapes. Both shapes are combined and unified in the design on the right.

Many designs that emphasize unity usually use either curvilinear or rectilinear shapes. The two type designs in Figure 2.15 use both of these types of shapes but allow one or the other to dominate. The focus on the design on the left is mainly on curvilinear shapes. The design on the right uses primarily rectilinear shapes.

FIGURE 2.15   These two greeting cards use shapes that are curvilinear and rectilinear. The one on the left emphasizes curvilinear shapes and the design on the right uses rectilinear shapes for unification. Diagonal line direction helps both designs feel more dynamic and harmonious. *For You* © 2003. *Merry Christmas* © 2003. Reprinted with permission from Alan Hashimoto.

Unity and Rhythm

Another design principle closely related to repetition is rhythm. Rhythm creates unity by repeating exact or slightly different elements in a predictable manner. It differs from repetition in the degree of duplication of elements and a feeling of pacing. Rhythm depends on a more exact duplication of elements as seen in Figure 2.16.

There are two other types of rhythm, *alternating rhythm* and *progressive rhythm*. In alternating rhythm, two contrasting elements are created. These two elements are repeated over and over, one right after the other. Progressive rhythm relies on a progressive change in a series of elements that are repeated. These elements change from one element to the next in increasing or diminishing size or weight. Figure 2.17 will help define these types of rhythm as well as illustrate a few concepts associated with

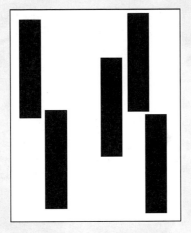
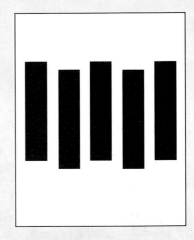

FIGURE 2.16   The design on the left is an example of a design that uses repetition of shapes, not rhythm. The design on the right is an example of rhythm.

them. The first design on the left is an example of alternating rhythm. The second design from the left is an example of progressive rhythm. Notice how your eye follows the design downward until it almost leaves the picture frame. This is not what a designer wants if the point is to keep the viewer's interest. The third design from the left solves this problem by creating a shape at the bottom that stops the progressive rhythm. This bottom shape feels unified because it is aligned with another shape located near the top. Notice how your eye is stopped from going out of the picture frame and back up to the top. The design farthest to the right is an example of progressive rhythm that progresses in two different directions. It is also an example of alternating rhythm because of the alternating thick and thin shapes.

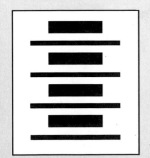

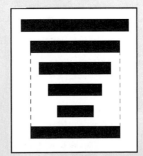

FIGURE 2.17   Illustrates alternating and progressive rhythm and related concepts.

The illustration on the left in Figure 2.18 uses alternating rhythm to create a unified composition. The most obvious example is the cat and circle shapes alternating vertically with the red division symbols and green rectangles. Notice how repetition unifies this entire composition and rhythm gives a sense of movement. The illustration on the right uses progressive rhythm. Notice how the repeated shapes located near the bottom force you to look progressively upward where your eye stops and focuses on the concentric circles inside the monitor screen. The concentric circles add contrast, creating a *focal point*.

FIGURE 2.18   Alternating rhythm is exemplified in the design on the left. Progressive rhythm is used in the illustration on the right. *Division One* © 2003. *Computerscape* © 2003. Reprinted with permission from Alan Hashimoto.

Unity Using Value

Unity can be achieved through the use of repeated values in a design. Through the use of value, unrelated shapes may be designed into a unified composition. Figure 2.19 illustrates an example of how this can be done. Figure 2.20 shows illustrated examples of how similar values can be used to create unity.

Unity and Continuity

Another less obvious way to create unity is continuity. Continuity uses the idea that something is carried over or connected to another element. A grid, or guides, to organize information and images in magazines, books,

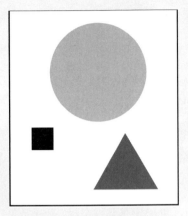 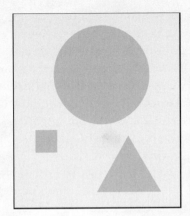 

FIGURE 2.19   The example on the left shows several unrelated shapes. Similar values create unity between these shapes in the middle design. If placement and line direction were also considered these shapes would have an even greater sense of harmony, as exemplified in the design on the right.

FIGURE 2.20   The illustration on the left uses lighter values that help create the feeling of harmony between the various elements. Repetition of similar plant shapes organized throughout the entire composition also aid in unifying this design. *Spring Anxiety* © 2003. Reprinted with permission from Alan Hashimoto. The illustration on the right uses similar dark values to create unity. This design also incorporates progressive rhythm to achieve harmony. Notice how the apple shapes are prevented from progressively leaving the composition through the use of the silhouetted tree line. *After Apple Picking* © 2003. Reprinted with permission from Bob Winward.

and Web sites is a common example of how continuity is achieved. Grids are used to make reading and viewing large amounts of material easier by creating a rhythm and consistent structure so the eye and mind do not have to work to adjust to unexpected changes and unorganized information. Figure 2.21 uses vertical and horizontal guides to indicate where visuals and text can be placed. Notice how the repetitious grid is broken by a few images to give the layout interest through variety. If the placement of images is carefully thought out, the continuity of the grid can be broken but the basic rhythm will still exist. Compare this to a simple piece of music. You can hear a consistent rhythm even though the melody might not always follow every beat. Some notes will be held for more than one count yet the rhythm is not affected.

Continuity can apply to any series of art or design projects. The element or elements that are being carried over can be related to line, line direction, shapes, values, colors, forms, or texture. Figure 2.22 is an example of how the principle of continuity can be observed in the relationship between photographic images.

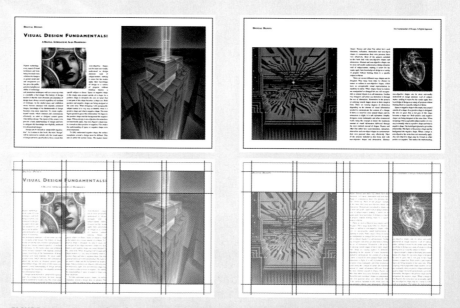

FIGURE 2.21   Example of a basic grid structure used for a simple double-page spread layout. Notice how the two-column vertical grid structure and horizontal flow lines are carried over to the next page. The two double-page spreads at the bottom make the grid structure more obvious and easier to see.

Continuity is used in establishing corporate identities. Trademarks, product labels, equipment, packaging, business literature, and other promotional and associated material must be consistent to ensure that the

FIGURE 2.22   Example of two photographs that illustrate continuity. The theme, color, values, and basic composition are very similar, which creates continuity. These collaged photographs are good examples of the design project detailed in Chapter 11. *Shovel* © 2003. *Rake* © 2003. Reprinted with permission from Jim Godfrey.

identity of a company is reinforced and remembered. Figure 2.23 is an example of how continuity is used to create a corporate identity for a packet of promotional materials.

FIGURE 2.23   Example of promotional materials that support a corporate identity using the principle of continuity. *Visio Communications Project Estimate Packet* © 2003. Reprinted with permission from Patrick Wilkey. *www.visiocommunications.com.*

VARIETY

When everything is overly structured and unified the result can be so predictable and repetitive that it becomes boring. Variety introduces interest through contrast. Contrast is the difference between elements. Unity attempts to accomplish the opposite by establishing similarity between elements.

Although they are very different from each other, unity and variety have two things in common 1) they can both be applied to any or all elements of design, and 2) most successful designs are composed of a balance between these two principles. Too much variety causes chaos. Too much unity is boring (see Figure 2.24).

 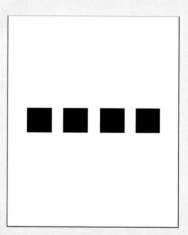

FIGURE 2.24   The example on the left illustrates too much variety. The example on the right illustrates too much unity. Find the perfect balance and you may have created a masterpiece.

Variety and Line

To create variety, line can be used as a contrasting design element. Contrasting thick and thin lines as well as different line directions create interest and add more variety to overly unified designs. Figure 2.25 illustrates the use of contrasting lines to create variety.

Figure 2.26 is a composition that uses contrasting line directions to create variety. Notice how the main line direction is horizontal and the diagonal line directions, although still very noticeable, are less important. The random diagonals give this illustration contrast and help the calm horizontal design to become very active.

FIGURE 2.25   Example of a composition that
incorporates contrasting widths of lines to create
interest. *Sunflowers* © 2003. Reprinted with permission from
Adrian Van Suchtelen.

FIGURE 2.26   Example of a music compact disc package insert is located at the top. A
diagram pointing out line directions is located just below. *Marc Aramian Music* © 2003.
Reprinted with permission from Alan Hashimoto.

Variety and Visual Weight

Shapes may contrast in a variety of ways to create interest. They can vary in size or visual weight. Visual weight is the feeling that a design element is heavy or light depending on the attention that element is given. This term usually applies to the size of a shape. Large shapes seem heavier than small shapes.

Visual weight is most commonly related to visual size but it can also be applied to the value of a shape. If the value of a shape has little contrast with the background, the visual weight will seem light. The same shape may seem heavier if the values are more contrasted. Figure 2.27 uses simple shapes to make this point obvious. Notice how the value contrast of the shape and background seems to feel heavier than the same shape of less contrasted value.

 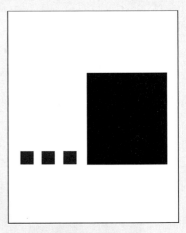

FIGURE 2.27   Example of simple designs that illustrate how visual weight is influenced by value. The design on the left shows a large shape that is closer in value to the background, giving the feeling of less visual weight. The same shape in the design on the right feels heavier because of the contrast in value. The three smaller shapes are used to emphasize and give reference to the large shape's visual weight in both designs.

Variety and Contrasting Types of Shapes

Another way shape can be used to create variety is to contrast different types of shapes. Thick and thin shapes, tall and short shapes, and rectilinear and curvilinear shapes. Both images in Figure 2.28 use a variety of different types of shapes to create interest through contrast.

If all elements have variety and are different from one another, the result is chaos and disorder. Variety must be used with unity to create a

FIGURE 2.28 The design on the left uses a variety of lines and shapes to create action and activity. These shapes contrast the unified shapes at the bottom of the composition. *Dreams Illustration* © 2003. Reprinted with permission from Patrick Wilkey. *www.visiocommunications.com.* The design on the right creates contrast between the organic shapes of the lilies and the geometric pattern placed behind them. Each lily is in a different position, which adds more variety. The color of this composition unifies both the background and foreground shapes, creating a relationship between all the elements. This painting is a good example of achieving balance between variety and unity. *Easter Lillies* © 2003. Reprinted with permission from Adrian Van Suchtelen.

successful design. There must be similarity and harmony as well as variety to add interest. It is up to the designer to balance these two principles. A design can emphasize unity or variety, but both principles should be present. Figure 2.29 uses simple shapes to illustrate this concept.

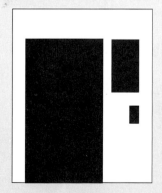 

FIGURE 2.29 The design on the left emphasizes unity over variety. All the shapes are similar but there is variation in the size of each shape. The design on the right emphasizes variety over unity. There are a variety of shapes and sizes unified by placement and repetition of each shape placed throughout the entire design.

FOCAL POINT AND VISUAL HIERARCHY

A focal point is an element that is given emphasis so it will attract attention. It is a way to catch viewers' attention and make them look deeper into a design. Contrast is one way to create a focal point by making an element different from its surroundings; however, unity must be part of a focal point to ensure that the focal point will still fit into the overall composition (see Figure 2.30).

 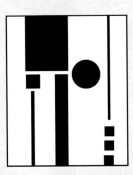 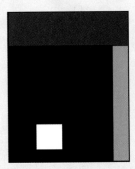 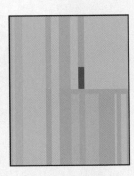

FIGURE 2.30   Beginning with the simple design on the left and continuing to the design on the right, a focal point is created using line direction, different types of shapes, contrasting values, and contrasting color.

Another way of creating a focal point is by the positioning of an element. If a shape, value, or color is isolated and positioned away from the majority of the other elements, it will receive more attention and become a focal point (See Figure 2.31).

Many designs have several focal points. These must be organized carefully. They cannot all command attention at the same time. When a design consists of many different areas of emphasis, the concept of hierarchy must be introduced. The idea of visual hierarchy is to organize each area of emphasis so that it does not conflict or take away attention from another area of emphasis. Focal points must be viewed one at a time in stages. One focal point will get the most attention. The viewer's eye will then move to another subtler focal point and from there to another. The careful staging of focal points and areas of emphasis will lead the viewer from one part of a design to the next until the entire design has been viewed in detail. Areas of lesser emphasis are called accents. They keep the viewer's attention in the subtlest areas of a design. Figure 2.32 is a good example of visual hierarchy. The main focal point is the title of this book cover. There are other less important focal points. From the title,

FIGURE 2.31 Example of an illustration that creates a focal point using placement. Unity is still maintained through the use of harmonious color. *Alone* © 2003. Reprinted with permission from Glen Edwards.

the two distorted eyes will become the next focal point because of their position next to the title, similar color, and value contrast. The next logical focal point would be the mouth shape. It is one of the larger, warm-colored shapes contrasted by the large surrounding dark green, blue, and black shapes. The progressive pattern of orange square shapes below the mouth and down the neck make the viewer's eye follow down to the bottom where there is an area of warmer, dark yellow backlit shapes. The backlit, dark, and diagonal shapes push the eye back up to the top—where the whole process of eye movement can begin again.

Not all designs have focal points. Generally speaking, the absence of a focal point usually results in the entire composition being seen as a pattern. A pattern is a repetition of a similar or exact element of design. Patterns do not communicate individual elements as quickly as a design using visual hierarchy because there are no beginning or ending points of interest. Figure 2.33 shows two examples of designs that do not have focal points.

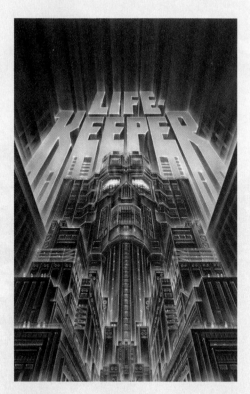

FIGURE 2.32 Example of a design that emphasizes visual hierarchy. *Life Keeper* © 2003. Reprinted with permission from Alan Hashimoto.

FIGURE 2.33 The painting on the left is an example of a composition with no specific focal point. *Halves and the Halve-Nots* © 2003. Reprinted with permission from Greg Schulte. The design on the right is a pattern created for a quilt. *Max's Quilt* © 2003. Reprinted with permission from Amy Hopkins.

BALANCE

The visual principle that a design should be weighted equally is called *balance*. Visual balance gives a natural feeling that is achieved by distributing weight equally on both sides of a composition. Things that are tipped, leaning, or heavy to one side or the other exemplify *imbalance*. Figure 2.34 shows both a diagram of a balanced design and a diagram of an imbalanced design.

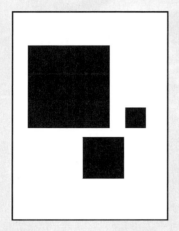 

FIGURE 2.34   These two diagrams illustrate balance in the left design and imbalance in the right design.

When one side of a design is exactly the same as the other side it is called *symmetrical balance*. It is also referred to as *classical balance* because of the historical significance of symmetry in Greek and Roman architecture. *Formal* is another term given to symmetrical balance. It is based on the fact that symmetrical designs give the feeling of stability and permanence. Figure 2.35 is an example of symmetrical balance.

Balanced designs that use elements that are very different from each other are referred to as *asymmetrically balanced*. The weight of the design is distributed unevenly but balance is still maintained. Architecture is usually associated with symmetrical balance, whereas paintings are generally asymmetrical in nature. The reason might be that many paintings are trying to capture a real-life scene and architecture is concerned with building a structure. Figure 2.36 is an example of a painting that uses asymmetrical balance. Notice how the partial glimpse of the doorway balances the larger shape of the table. The rectilinear shapes of the doorway, molding, and floor are contrasted by the curvilinear shapes of the

FIGURE 2.35   Example of a design that is symmetrically balanced. *Looking for a Job* © 2003. Reprinted with permission from Alan Hashimoto.

tablecloth, tabletop, and bowl. A small part of the molding can be seen on the right side of the painting, unifying that portion of the composition with the molding and corner of the room's left side.

FIGURE 2.36   Example of a design that is asymmetrically balanced. *Water Offering* © 2003. Reprinted with permission from Chris Terry.

Both symmetrical and asymmetrical designs use a fulcrum or center balancing point to achieve balance. The fulcrum for symmetry is in the center of a composition as seen. In asymmetry, the fulcrum is shifted to one side or the other to maintain the balance between dissimilar elements. Figure 2.37 shows the location of the fulcrum for a symmetrical design and the location of the fulcrum for an asymmetrical design.

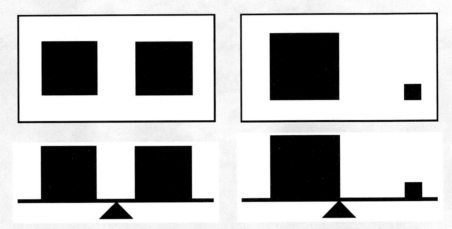

FIGURE 2.37   Diagram illustrating the location of the fulcrum for a symmetrical design on the left and the location of the fulcrum for an asymmetrical design on the right.

Radial balance is another kind of balance. It can be described as balance that radiates out from a central focal point. It can be either symmetrical or asymmetrical depending on the location of its focal point. This type of balance is commonly used when a dynamic focal point is required. All the attention from anywhere in the design will lead back to a single source. Advertising and packaging use radial balance to attract and hold a viewer's attention in a single spot so a visual message has time to be delivered. The design on the left in Figure 2.38 is an example of a software package that uses symmetrical radial balance. The design on the right is an example of a magazine cover that uses asymmetrical radial balance.

FIGURE 2.38   Example of symmetrical radial balance on the left. Example of asymmetrical radial balance on the right. *Finding Wisdom in a Digital Age* © 2003. *Games* © 2003. Reprinted with permission from Alan Hashimoto.

SUMMARY

The concepts and ideas associated with Gestalt theories and the principles of design can apply to many different forms of design other than two-dimensional design. Take a closer look at a piece of furniture or an example of industrial design and see if you can identify the harmony and variety in its design. Do any of these examples make use of continuity, repetition, rhythm, or contrast? Are they asymmetrically balanced or symmetrically balanced?

The design principles can be found in the organization and design of almost anything. Have you ever organized a party? You assumed that for a successful social function everyone should have something in common. You also knew that the party would be boring if everyone had the exact same experiences, interests, and hobbies. This is an example of balancing harmony with variety. Can you think of any experiences that are good examples of continuity, repetition, rhythm, contrast, and balance?

The elements and principles of design are the foundation for every project in this book. These concepts are universal, but the specifics of how they will be used are dependent on the design problem to be solved. The next step and chapter deal with the procedures associated with defining design problems and creating visual solutions using the elements and principles of design.

3

INTRODUCTION TO CONTENT AND FORM: PROBLEM SOLVING AND DIGITAL PROCESS

INTRODUCTION

Now that the elements and principles of design have been defined, the next step is to make this information relevant to each individual by solving specific design problems and creating original designs digitally. This chapter will introduce you to the steps involved in conceptualization and give basic information concerning digital tools and their use.

To begin, there are two primary concepts dealing with visual design: content and form. Content is the subject matter, concept, or solution to a design problem. Form is the actual physical visual created as a final finished object or image.

Another concept that is related to both content and form is *process*. *Process* is the procedure and steps necessary for the creation of a visual. It can be divided into two very different ideas; conceptual process and production process. *Conceptual process* is the "thinking" part of design *content*. It involves the organization of a series of steps that will lead to the idea and solution to a visual problem. Once the conceptual process is completed, the process of *production* may begin. The *production process* deals with "doing." It is the organization and implementation of the steps involved with the physical creation of the visual *form*.

All the following chapters have been designed to take advantage of these universal and classic design concepts. Each chapter will deal with specific design elements and principles. A design project will be presented for you to solve, followed by a tutorial that will help you to complete this project digitally.

The following section will explain the general ideas and procedures associated with each of these concepts as they relate to the seven projects in this book. Each project will be discussed in more detail in the following chapters.

INTRODUCTION TO DESIGN PROJECTS

The previous two chapters were concerned with the general content that makes up most visual designs. With the exception of color, which will be discussed in Chapter 11, these chapters covered the basic elements and principles of design that should be evident when designing any visual. Each of the following chapters introduces an element or principle that requires the reader to create an original design following basic rules. Beginning with a simple designed shape using elementary digital techniques and tools, each project builds from the preceding chapter, adding a new design element, principle, digital technique, or tool. The final project uses all the elements and principles to create a very involved design. The following is a brief description of the seven projects included in this book. You should get a basic idea of how these projects build onto one another to create an increasingly more difficult and sophisticated design. The final form of each of these designs will be a tabloid-size digital print.

1. The first project is divided between Chapters 4 and 5. It involves using Gestalt theory to structure a series of asymmetrically balanced non-objective shapes. Non-objective shapes are used as design elements to avoid distracting subject matter. The focus can then be isolated to the study of universal principles of harmony and variety. After the introduction to content and process in this chapter, you will be introduced to some of the basic tools and techniques that Adobe Illustrator® uses to create simple designs.

2. The second project deals with examining letterforms as shapes. As an example of shape, letterforms will be designed using the same design principles associated with any element of design. How to use and

design simple letterforms and apply them to the principles of design will be introduced. The type capabilities and new drawing tools of Illustrator will be used to create this second design.

3. Project three is also about shape as a design element subject to the principles of harmony and variety. Stylized figures will be abstracted and distorted to demonstrate the principles of continuity, symmetrical balance, and open versus closed form. More involved digital tools and techniques will be introduced.

4. Value as a design element is the main topic of the fourth project. A basic value study of photographic composition is the basis for this project. Examining the basic design of photographs and understanding how to create value digitally will be the main topics.

5. This next project combines all the design principles associated with shape and value but will be expanded to include the element of color. Color theory and color schemes are used to create designs from multiple sources. Digital color and how to mix and apply color will be studied for this project.

6. Project six deals with the relationship between value, shape, letterforms, and type used as text. Text type, as a design element, and its association with pattern and implied texture are emphasized. More information concerning digital type and how to create and manipulate type will be discussed in the tutorials accompanying this chapter.

7. A collage using photography, and illustrated images are the elements that make up this next project. Color, value, shape, and line will be used to create a composition that will demonstrate all the principles associated with design. Digital paint programs, tools, and techniques will make up most of the tutorials.

CONCEPTUAL PROCESS

As mentioned earlier, conceptual process is the "thinking" part of designing. The following procedures should aid you in this first part of the design process.

Step One: Research and Define the Problem

The first step in the conceptual process is to ask questions and gather as much information and research about the design project as possible. After examining all of this material, parameters and guidelines are created to make the design problem easier to define. Once the problem to be solved is clear, the process of focusing in on a solution can begin.

Step Two: Preliminary Solutions, Organized List of Options, and Thumbnail Sketches

There are an infinite number of solutions for a single problem. These solutions may be narrowed through a process of objective reasoning, close observation, and educated guessing. You might want to organize options by writing them down in lists. This will make your ideas more concrete and easier to examine and compare. Think about the specific reasons why one design choice may be better than another. If there are no specific reasons to explain your choice it is highly possible it is not the best pick. The definition of design is "planned organization." If a design is "planned" then decisions concerning design choices should be clear.

After exploring all your preliminary alternatives, give them a visual representation by creating small, quick sketches called thumbnails. Thumbnails should be concerned with only the most basic information. To allow for the maximum amount of ideas using the least amount of time, thumbnails should not be detailed. By quickly getting these visuals onto paper using traditional tools such as a pencil or pen, thumbnails allow for more intuitive thinking and make it easier to quickly change direction to explore more alternative views and approaches to visual problem solving. Figures 3.1 shows examples of some selected thumbnail sketches used to visualize characters for an animation. These very simple preliminary drawings were created quickly, but communicate clearly the basic characteristics of each figure or model. Notice the emotional quality of line and how drawing style can vary and reflect the personality of each character, even at this preliminary stage.

FIGURE 3.1   Examples of a variety of quickly drawn thumbnail character sketches. Top two rows of thumbnail sketches: © 2003. Reprinted with permission from Nathan Tufts. Bottom row of thumbnail sketches: © 2003. Reprinted with permission from Jon Pitcher.

You do not need drawing experience to create thumbnails. Simple lines and shapes can represent objects and object placement. Details can be added later using other tools or the computer. Figure 3.2 is a good example of how simple lines abstractly represent placement of subject matter in an illustration.

FIGURE 3.2   Example of a thumbnail sketch and the finished illustration it inspired. Notice how the simple lines represent subject matter placement. *Barrel Pond Romance* © 2003. Reprinted with permission from Alan Hashimoto.

Step Three: Roughs. Refined Preliminary Visual Design Solutions and Alternatives

Once a decision concerning several design solutions has been reached, these solutions should be expanded and refined as "roughs." Roughs are preliminary options of a design that communicate in more detail than thumbnails. Roughs are placed side-by-side so they can be compared, contrasted, and analyzed. Decisions concerning specific design options can then be made (see Figure 3.3).

Roughs help the designer focus on alternatives without having to commit to a final decisive solution. Roughs should clearly communicate problem-solving concepts; position and proportions of shapes and objects; value and color; and general composition.

If necessary, experimentation with new methods for creating the final project can be tested and developed at this stage.

Step Four: Composites or Comps. The Final Preliminary Step in the Design Process

Comps are the final preliminary step before the finished design is created. A final concept or concepts should be chosen and all the elements involved

FIGURE 3.3   The two designs located on the top row and the bottom-left design are examples of just three rough alternatives for an advertising campaign dealing with education and the future. The lower-right design is the final design that was selected. *The Future of Education* © 2003. Reprinted with permission from Alan Hashimoto.

put into position. Tools and techniques should have been thoroughly tested and chosen. The comp should be as similar to the final solution as time and resources permit.

Many times the comp will follow the exact techniques of the final design and may even appear to have all the details and refinements of a finished design. The main purpose of a comp is for presentation and discussion of last-minute changes before expensive and time-consuming production begins. Figures 3.4 and 3.5 are examples of rough comps and the final art that was created.

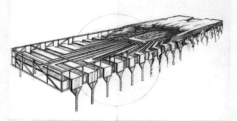

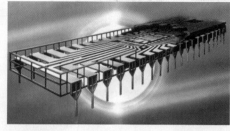

FIGURE 3.4   Example of a comp created with a drafting pen and ink and the finished art made from this rough. *Chip Off the Old Block* © 2003. Reprinted with permission from Alan Hashimoto.

FIGURE 3.5   Example of a comp created with light-colored pencils on textured black paper and the finished art created from these comps. Because the final solution would be a dark background, using light-colored pencils on black board seemed to duplicate the effects of the finish accurately and efficiently. There is an emotional quality to the high contrast of light colors on black that needed to be captured without spending too much time. This comp was created in less than an hour. *Hierarchy Search* © 2003. Reprinted with permission from Alan Hashimoto.

Step Five: The Final Design or Finish

After the completion of all the preliminary steps, final decisions are made. The final or finish is the result. This is the last step of the conceptual process. The production process may now take place. Mass production processes such as printing will use the finish as a guide to compare the actual product or print with the finished design. When dealing with animation, textures, models, environments, and sound can now be edited together into the final video or film.

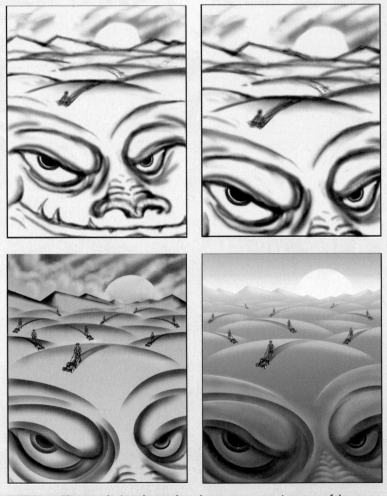

FIGURE 3.6   The two designs located on the top row were just two of the many alternative ways this design could have been cropped in the rough step of the illustration. The bottom-left design is an example of a comp or composite. The lower-right design is the final design. *Lawn Monster* © 2003. Reprinted with permission from Alan Hashimoto.

The final phase of the conceptual process as it relates to the projects in this book will lead to a two-dimensional design created digitally as a print. Figure 3.6 illustrates the various steps involved in the conceptual process. The section on Production Process in this chapter examines the basic concepts of digital hardware and software necessary for the production part of the process.

PRODUCTION PROCESS

The projects in this book are to be created using a computer and related software. The following is an introduction to the most basic digital concepts dealing with the production process. Each chapter will introduce new and increasingly advanced digital production concepts, tools, and techniques.

Computer Applications Used in Design

If you look back through the history of graphic design, each era had its own unique set of tools. Some had letterpresses, some had drafting tools, and some were designed by collage. Over the last 30 years, computers have been a key component in the world of art and design.

For the past two decades, people have used computers to create all sorts of digital imagery. It made setting type easier, correcting photographs simpler, and gave us a three-dimensional space to work in.

Over the years, the computer has evolved and many companies have come and gone. The two types of computers that have stood the test of time (so to speak) are the Microsoft Window® personal computer (PC) and the Apple Macintosh® computer (Mac). What makes these two computers quite different is their operating systems (OS). These are the software that run the whole show. The operating system allows all the parts of the computer to talk to each other. Both PCs and Macs have their own operating systems.

When a computer is turned on (booted up), the OS is started and the machine responds to its commands. It launches the basic software that becomes the "environment" that you work in. The OSs are written in different code, allowing some to excel over others. Different OSs may require their own version of software. For instance, an application written for Windows cannot be installed on a Macintosh and vice versa.

On the computer (separate from the OS), software applications are installed that allow you to do a variety of tasks. You can use one piece of software to surf the Internet, another to check your e-mail, and yet another to write papers. There is software that lets you listen to music, make a movie, do your taxes, or play video games. There are also applications that you purchase that will allow you to begin your dream of being a successful digital artist and designer.

Software Applications for Graphics

Software applications used in creating images can be divided into two main categories: paint programs and object-oriented (vector) programs. Each type of software is unique and has its own distinct purpose in creating and modifying visuals. Paint programs, like Adobe Photoshop®, create a variety of bitmap (pixel-based) images, whereas object-oriented programs, such as Adobe Illustrator® and Macromedia Freehand®, create vector (mathematically based) images.

For the purposes of this book, industry standard in software will be represented: For bitmap images: Adobe Photoshop, and for vector graphics: Adobe Illustrator.

Paint Programs: Bitmap Graphics

Look at a painting. If you look closely you will see that every bit of the canvas is covered with bright hues and tempered shadows. The artist's brush has passed over each and every inch of that canvas. Imagine that canvas in your head and divide the picture into little squares of single colors. Can you see the individual colors? How tiny are they? It is those little squares that make up the image.

Each of those little squares of color is called a pixel. A bitmap is an image made up of dozens of millions of those little pixels. Look at the ever-lovable "smilie" in Figure 3.7. He is made up of 256 pixels (16 rows of 16 pixels). It is obvious to see the little squares that make up this image. In Figure 3.8, it is harder to see the pixels because there are so many. The more pixels an image has, the higher the quality of the image. This is called resolution, or a ratio of pixels per inch.

Web images are bitmaps that have a resolution of 72 pixels per inch. It is usually possible to see the pixels in a Web image. These images are not meant to be of a high quality because they are only to be viewed on the screen.

In a magazine, newspaper, book, or anything printed, this is a different story. The quality of the image needs to be higher in printed works. Some magazines and high-end publications use images that have 2,400 pixels per inch (ppi). That's a little less that 5.8 million pixels per square inch (5,760,000 pixels to be exact).

FIGURE 3.7   The smilie is made up of 256 pieces of information or bits.

FIGURE 3.8   A detail from the bitmap image reveals that the image is made up of many pixels.

Each pixel (or piece of information) takes up space. Images that have a high ppi tend to have very large file sizes and require lots of disk space.

Images can be created directly into paint programs using the drawing tools. Images may also be scanned. The computer rewrites the image as pixels, allowing you to take the image into a program such as Photoshop for modification.

After an image is created, there are many formats in which a file can be saved for later use. Each format has its own unique qualities. A TIFF (Tagged Image File Format) is a cross-platform graphic that can be read on both PCs and Macs. These images are meant for printing because they have a large tolerance for color depth. As you scan your images for the projects you will do in this book, save the files as TIFF for the best results.

Object-Oriented Programs: Vector Graphics

Vector-based images are defined by mathematical equations. In Figure 3.9, on the left, we see the vector image and on the right, the lines that were used to create it.

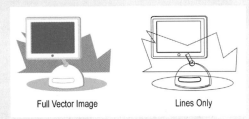

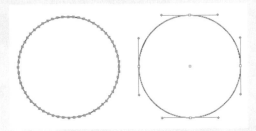

FIGURE 3.9   The image on the left is the vector illustration. The image on the right is the points and lines it took to create the drawing.

FIGURE 3.10   The principle of point, curve, and line is demonstrated with these two circles.

Images are drawn using the point and line system. In order to draw a straight line, all you need are two points and the line in between. It is with those points and lines that simple or complex images can be drawn. In Figure 3.10, there are two circles. The circle on the left is made up of 60 points and 60 lines. The circle on the right uses 4 points and 4 curved lines. These curved lines, called Bézier Curves, can be used to simplify the path and the object.

Vector drawings normally have small file sizes because they only contain mathematical data about the placement of the points and the angles of the curves. Illustrator saves files with the extension .ai (for Adobe Illustrator).

HOW TO USE DESIGN APPLICATIONS AND THIS BOOK

This text contains many assignments, projects, and tutorials to help you learn the basics of these types of software.

We will begin with the object-oriented program, Adobe Illustrator, using the tools to create and modify basic shapes. Step-by-step tutorials are included to show you how to use the different tools, palettes, and settings available in this program.

Toward the end of this text, your attention will turn to bitmap files and paint programs. For this section, Adobe Photoshop will be used. Again, there are tutorials that will show you the basic tools and concepts that can be used.

Along the way you will be introduced to new tools, commands, and palettes. Each of these can be accessed using palettes and menus and the file menu along the top of the screen. These will be written in such a way that they can be easily identified. For example:

```
To open a new document, choose File > New.
```

The ">" indicates that a menu or submenu is available under that option. To open a new document, you would select File from the top menu and then New (see Figure 3.11).

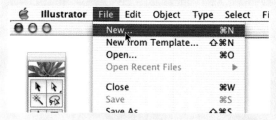

FIGURE 3.11   Choose File from the main menu, and then New to open a new document.

Some menus hold submenus.

```
To move this object to the back, select Object > Arrange > Send to
Back.
```

To access the previous example, you would select the Object menu, then mouse down to Arrange, and then over to the Send to Back option (Figure 3.12).

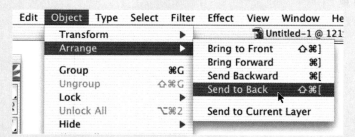

FIGURE 3.12   Choose Object from the main menu, then Arrange, and then Send to Back from the submenu.

Simple keyboard combinations (called shortcuts) can access most tools. These shortcuts will follow the name of the tool of the menu option and will be flanked by parentheses (). For example:

```
To open a new file, choose File > New (PC: control + N; Mac:
command + N).
```

The keyboard shortcuts are different for the PC and Mac, but normally only differ by one key (Figure 3.13). On the PC, the primary key for a shortcut is the control key. On the Mac, it's the command (or Apple) key. In this case, to open a new document on a PC, you would hold down the control key and press "N." On the Mac, the command key and the "N" key would be pressed.

FIGURE 3.13 Location of the "control" key on the PC (left) and the "command" key on a Macintosh (right).

Some tools in the toolbar can be accessed, switched, or activated with a simple key press.

```
Select the Direct Selection Tool (A).
```

In this example, pressing the "A" key on the keyboard would switch the current tool to the desired tool (Figure 3.14).

FIGURE 3.14 Pressing the "A" key can activate the Direction Selection Tool without physically selecting the tool in the toolbar.

By using these software applications on your computer coupled with this book, you will have a tool that can become very powerful and pivotal in your becoming a designer. Not only will you learn the software, but you will also gain an understanding of the thought process involved in creating great designs.

SUMMARY

Design is about making decisions with purpose and organizing or placing elements in the most appropriate manner. These actions require a thorough knowledge of the elements and an extremely well-planned procedure. Try to fix a car or put together a barbecue without knowing what a car or barbecue is used for. Take a trip to the downtown area of a large unfamiliar city in Poland without a map to find a shop that sells fresh blintzes. You can quickly see how important knowledge and research are if you are trying to find a solution to a problem and develop a plan to get it done.

4

DESIGN PROJECT ONE:
MODULAR DESIGN PROJECT
PART ONE

INTRODUCTION

The Modular Design Project is divided into two parts covering two chapters. This is the only project that will span two chapters. The reason for this is that many fundamental design concepts and digital techniques might be unfamiliar to some readers. More time and space in this book will be dedicated to these chapters to ensure a firm foundation necessary for the successful completion of future projects.

Part one of the project (Chapter 4) will discuss unity and the underlying grid. Part two (Chapter 5) will use this grid to create a series of designs that emphasizes variety through contrast and distortion. Both parts deal with the element of shape and its relationship to the Gestalt theory of visual design. Non-objective shapes are used as design elements to avoid distracting subject matter. This will also force the focus to be placed solely on the aesthetic use of design principles.

CONTENT

The Basic Problem Defined

Using the digital production process explained later in the "Production Process" section of this chapter, you will create four basic patterns as seen in Figure 4.1. These grids and circles should be created using the application program Adobe Illustrator. This will give you practical experience and familiarity with this program's basic tools and techniques.

Each of these four basic patterns seen in Figure 4.1 may be referred to as a grid. The four different patterns have been selected to create a set of underlying structures to help develop different ways to create shapes. The grid on the upper left is the simplest way of creating unity by using a simple square or rectilinear shape. The grid on the upper right introduces diagonals and should help give the resulting shapes more contrast and dynamics. The grid on the bottom left suggests the shapes designed following this grid will have variety through contrasting shapes. Round or curved shapes contrast with sharp or flat shapes. The grid on the lower right consists of mostly curvilinear shapes, the opposite of the shapes on the grid on the upper left.

Using the four grids as guides, create four asymmetrically balanced shapes. Figure 4.2 is an example of asymmetrically balanced shapes created in a lighter tone so that the underlying structure can be observed. Figure 4.3 is an example of asymmetrically balanced shapes filled in black and ready to be used for part two of the project, found in Chapter 5.

Be sure each design is not symmetrically balanced if a 45-degree angle or a horizontal midway line is used as a centerline (see Figure 4.4). The grid in these examples has not been completely discarded to help you see the parts of the grid that have been filled in. The upper-left design is just one alternative to creating an asymmetrically balanced design that can be used for part two of this project. The upper-right design is an obvious example of symmetrical balance and should not be used. The lower-left design is symmetrically balanced if a 45-degree line is used for a centerline as demonstrated. The lower-right design is also symmetrically balanced if a horizontal midway line is used for a centerline. Only an asymmetrically balanced shape exemplified by the example in the upper-left design can be used for part two of the project.

Remember these are just examples. You should try to create your own. These designs will be used later as a beginning point for further distortion and manipulation in Chapter 5.

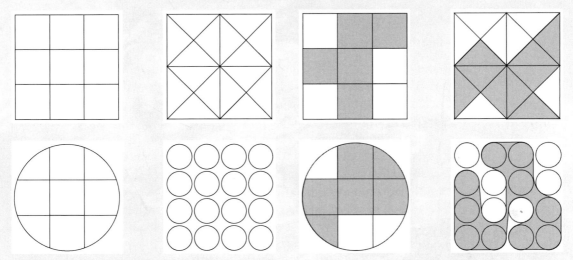

FIGURE 4.1 Basic grids for Chapter 4 Modular Design Project, part one.

FIGURE 4.2 Example of asymmetrically balanced shapes created in a lighter tone so that the underlying structure can be observed.

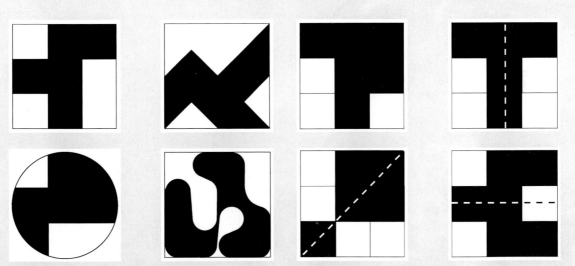

FIGURE 4.3 Example of asymmetrically balanced shapes created in black discarding the grid for use in the next part of the project found in Chapter 5.

FIGURE 4.4 These designs observed from any direction should indicate they are asymmetrical.

In the next section, a thorough background into the significance of each objective and concept related to this project will be discussed. This will be followed by a description of the conceptual and production processes demonstrating how to create part one of the project.

Background

Designs Created from Grids

One of the main objectives of this project is to understand unity and the underlying structure of design through the use of grids and other related principles dealing with harmony. Gestalt theories of visual design, first introduced in Chapter 2, states that humans inherently look for order between various elements. It is the designer's job to make reading and understanding both written and visual information as easy as possible. Organizing and structuring information and images is made simpler by using unifying elements such as grids, similarity, repetition, and continuity.

By creating four designs from the four grid structures, a demonstration of Gestalt theory will be put into practice. A big part of Gestalt theory states that individual parts of an image can be analyzed and seen as separate components but that people have the tendency to group these parts into a larger, greater image that may be very different from the components. By using the grids as guides, individual shapes will be filled in and designed together as one "larger, greater image."

In Chapter 2, grids were used to aid in creating continuity between text and images for layouts. They can also give continuity and unity to other types of visuals. Figures 4.5 and 4.6 are examples of complex grid structures that are used to organize a multitude of shapes.

Asymmetrical Balance

Asymmetrical balance is used to begin the design process for the Modular Design Project for several reasons. The first reason is that it can be more of a challenge to create asymmetrically because, as humans, most of us are symmetrical and naturally create symmetrically balanced, functional things. Automobiles, kitchen utensils, beds, bathroom fixtures, entertainment devices, and furniture are usually symmetrical. It is more of a challenge to create using asymmetrical balance.

Asymmetry is used mainly for designs that are represented two dimensionally. Paintings and photographs are more commonly asymmetrical in their composition. This type of balance can also be more difficult for designers because every shape must be examined on its own and not merely reflected on both sides of a centerline. In addition, asymmetrical balance is more dependent on negative space that must be taken into consideration when shapes of different weight are balanced by placement.

It is not to say that symmetrical balance is extremely simple to create or that it is not important. Classical art, trademarks, packaging, signs, symbols, posters, industrial designs, and architecture are mostly symmetrical. Symmetrically balanced compositions have their own challenges, which are explored in Chapter 6.

FIGURE 4.5   Example of a complex grid that structures mainly horizontal and vertical shapes. Notice there are also diagonal and circular shapes that are part of a contrasting grid structure that introduces contrast or variety in a more subtle way. *Gated Community* © 2003. Reprinted with permission from Alan Hashimoto.

FIGURE 4.6   The design on the left is the original magazine illustration of an article on communism and extra sensory perception. The design on the right points out the curvilinear shapes that create the underlying structure. Notice how there are also rectilinear shapes that are used in lesser amounts to create good hierarchy and contrast. *Communism and Extra Sensory Perception* © 2003. Reprinted with permission from Alan Hashimoto.

Non-Objective Shapes

To avoid subject matter that may distract from focusing on the universal study of the principles of harmony and variety, non-objective shapes are used as design elements for this first project. There are other reasons non-objective shapes are used. The relationship between figure and ground become nonexistent if there is no identifiable subject to act as a figure. The positive and negative shapes become more equally observed and the element of space can be easier to recognize as a design element. In addition, if there is no object to identify with, shapes themselves will have to elicit abstract feelings or impressions. Line direction becomes very important to the feeling of the entire composition, as well as using both harmonizing and contrasting types of shapes. The lack of representational reference forces us to interpret shapes abstractly with more immediacy and spontaneity.

Figure 4.7 is an example of some of the concepts we have discussed so far in this chapter. It illustrates unifying shapes through implied grids; asymmetrical balance related to painting; and creating interesting non-objective shapes to examine the composition of a design. This is a good example of what part two of the Modular Design Project, and to some degree part one, will be expressing in terms of asymmetrically balanced shapes that have both harmony and variety.

CONCEPTUAL PROCESS

As stated earlier, the conceptual process is the "thinking part of design." This first part of the Modular Project deals with creating a simple structure and forming shapes that must follow a set grid. This should be a fairly easy task without much "thinking" or need to follow the five steps of the conceptual process outlined in Chapter 3. Part one is mainly concerned with what lies beneath the design, a set structure and knowledge of tools to build on that structure. Part two will include more of the "thinking" part of design. Each project will become progressively more concerned with content and conceptual process.

This first project may not seem as creative as other projects in this book. In fact it's fairly simple to understand. Beginning to use the principles of unity through structure however is very difficult. Creating images on the computer is fun until you want to do something challenging or involved. This first chapter is all about the basics. Think of it as the first day on the court and you're learning to put a backspin on the ball or trying to boil water, figuring out basic measurements, and selecting vegetables for your first spaghetti dinner.

FIGURE 4.7   The example of the upper left is the original painting. The example on the upper right shows lines that produce a grid that points out the many relationships that exist between the shapes in the painting. The black shape on the bottom left illustrates the basic shape created by the background. The design on the bottom right isolates this shape so we can see it clearly. *Eye Chart* © 2003. Reprinted with permission from Chris Terry.

The next chapter will be more fun because you will have completed the background study in digital tools and basic design structure. The simple unified shapes will be manipulated and distorted using variety to create a design that is more expressive and individual.

PRODUCTION PROCESS

Using the object-oriented program, Adobe Illustrator, four grid and circle patterns will be created. These patterns will be used as guides to design an asymmetrically balanced shape. Later, in Chapter 5, part two of the Modular Project, these shapes will be manipulated and distorted into more interesting and unique designs using the principles of harmony and variety. The balance of the chapter consists of tutorials that go through the various steps involved in creating grid and circle patterns and then creating shapes using the grid and circle patterns as guides.

| TUTORIAL | ## STEPS IN CREATING THE GRID AND CIRCLE PATTERNS |

CREATING A NEW DOCUMENT

1. Launch Adobe Illustrator and create a New Document by selecting `File > New` (PC: control + N; Macintosh: command + N). Make sure that the Artboard Setup is set to Letter, Inches, and has an Orientation of Portrait (Figure 4.8).

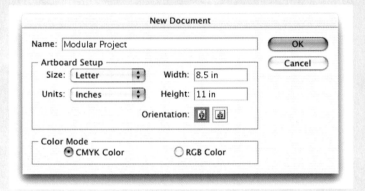

FIGURE 4.8   Adobe Illustrator: New Document Dialog Box.

2. Show your Rulers by selecting `View > Show Rulers` (PC: control + R; Macintosh: command + R). A horizontal and vertical ruler, showing inches, will appear.
3. View the grid by selecting `View > Show Grid` (PC: control + "; Macintosh: command + "). Because "inches" was selected as the unit of measurement, the grid is divided using the same. Each grid section is .25" by .25", with the heavy gray grid lines showing 1" by 1".
4. Turn on the Snap to Grid by selecting `View > Snap to Grid` (PC: control + shift + "; Macintosh: command + shift + "). This will allow all points drawn to "snap" to the grid.

CREATING THE GRID #1: THE 3 X 3 SQUARE GRID

1. With the Rectangle tool (M), click in the work area once. In the Rectangle dialog box enter a width and height of 1 inch. Click OK (Figure 4.9).

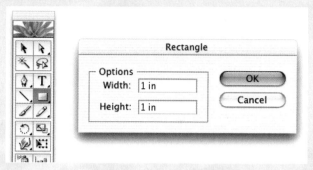

FIGURE 4.9   The Rectangle Dialog Box.

2. Illustrator then creates a square that is 1" by 1". Using the Selection tool (V), click within the center of the square shape and move it so that it is one inch from the left and one inch from the top.

3. With the square in its proper place and selected, select Edit > Copy (PC: control + C; Macintosh: command + C) to copy the shape to the clipboard.

4. Select Edit > Paste (PC: control + V; Macintosh: command + V) to paste a copy of the square into the Artboard. Use the Selection tool (V) and move the new square to the immediate right next to the first square. Because "snapping" is turned on, it will be easy to get the squares to align correctly.

5. Using the same steps as previously shown, paste another square into the Artboard area and likewise move that square to the right of the second square, making three in a row. Repeat these steps until you have created a 3 x 3 grid using the square shapes (Figure 4.10).

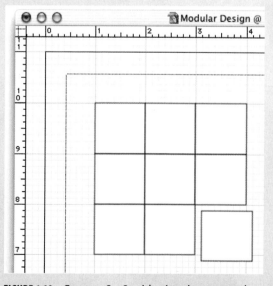

FIGURE 4.10   Create a 3 x 3 grid using the square shapes.

6. Select `Select > All` (PC: control + A; Macintosh: command + A) to select all the objects on the Artboard (in this case the nine squares).
7. With the objects selected, choose `View > Guides > Make Guides` (PC: control + 5; Macintosh: command + 5). This step changes the grid from an object to a guide, making it easier for you to draw your first design.

Using the Pen tool

The process of using the Pen tool is simple. To draw using the Pen tool is as simple as click, click, click. To draw, click once to insert a point and then move the mouse and click again. You have now recreated the simplest form of drawing, the line. By subsequently moving the mouse and clicking you can add more points and lines to your shape. If you bring the cursor back over the first point, a small circle will appear next to the pen cursor, allowing you to close the line.

CREATING THE GRID #2: THE TRIANGLE GRID

1. By studying the image of the second grid (the triangle one), you see it is constructed of 16 right triangles (a right triangle contains one right angle, or a 90° angle). To create this first right triangle, use the Pen tool (P) and draw a right triangle that has one side that is 1.5" and has a height of .75" (Figure 4.11). Make sure that the triangle is a complete (closed) path.

FIGURE 4.11   Example of a right triangle, point by point.

2. Using the Selection tool (V), select the triangle and position it so that it is 1" from the top of the page and .5" from the right of the square grid.
3. Copy the triangle and paste it. Rotate the triangle 90° clockwise by selecting the triangle and choosing `Object > Transform > Rotate`. In the Rotate dialog box (Figure 4.12), type "90" in the Angle field, then click OK.

FIGURE 4.12   The Rotate dialog box.

4. Move the triangle so that it fits underneath the first. Repeat the process until you have a square of triangles (Figure 4.13).

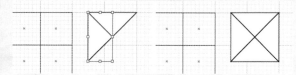

FIGURE 4.13   Position the triangle underneath the first triangle (left). The finished square is comprised of four right triangles (right).

5. Select all the triangles (`Select > All`).
6. Group the four triangles together by selecting `Object > Group`.
7. Copy and paste the group of triangles three times and position them so that they form a grid that is two units by two units (Figure 4.14).

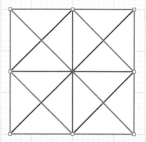

FIGURE 4.14   The groups arranged in two rows of two.

8. Select all four groups and convert them to guides by choosing `View > Guides > Make Guides`.

CREATING THE GRID #3: THE SQUARE AND CIRCLE GRID

1. As in Grid #1, create a series of squares that is three units high by three units wide. Position these squares so they are 1" below the first grid (Figure 4.15).
2. Next, select the Ellipse tool (L).

Hidden Tools

In Illustrator, as well as in other applications, there are dozens and dozens of tools that can be used. If they were all displayed at the same time, our

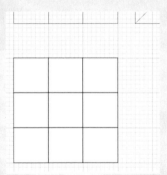

FIGURE 4.15   The second set of nine squares

screens would be crowded. A way has been developed to "hide" certain tools until you need them. If you take a close look at the Tool palette in Illustrator, you will see that some of the tools have a small triangle in the bottom right-hand corner; this is a visual clue to let the user know that there are other tools nested under that tool. To reveal those tools, click and hold down your mouse button until the tools pop up. Then, with your mouse still pressed, drag over to the desired tool and release the mouse. The tool will now be selected. For example, under the Rectangle tool in Illustrator 10 are five other tools: the Rounded Rectangle tool, the Ellipse tool, the Polygon tool, the Star tool, and the Flare tool.

3. With the Ellipse tool now selected, click on the Artboard area once to open the Ellipse dialog box. Enter "3" into both the width and height fields. Click OK.
4. Using the Selection tool (V), select the circle and position it over the top of the squares (Figure 4.16).

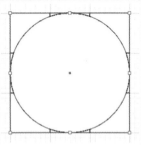

FIGURE 4.16   Position the circle over the squares.

5. Select all the squares and the circle (Select > All) and convert them to Guides (View > Guides > Make Guides).

CREATING THE GRID #4: THE CIRCLES

1. With the Ellipse tool (L) selected, click once in the work area. In the Ellipse dialog box, enter a "0.7" into the width and the height fields. This is the correct size for all the circles that constitute this grid.
2. Position the circle so that it is 1" from the bottom of the triangle grid and 0.5" from the circle and square grid.
3. Copy and paste the circle. Position the second circle so that its right side is 1" from the right edge of the document and 1" from the bottom of the grid (Figure 4.17).

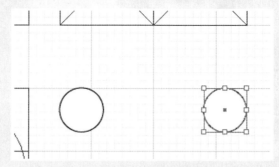

FIGURE 4.17   Position the second circle.

4. Paste two more circles and place them in between the two existing circles.
5. Select the four circles, this time using the Selection tool (V). While holding down the Shift key, select the first circle and then each subsequent circle. Holding the Shift key while selecting allows you to select more than one object at a time.
6. Open the Align palette by selecting `Window > Align`. The Align palette allows you to line objects up or distribute them according to top, middle, bottom, left, center, right, and so on.
7. Select Vertical Align Top (image) from the Align palette. This step aligns all the circles along the top (Figure 4.18).

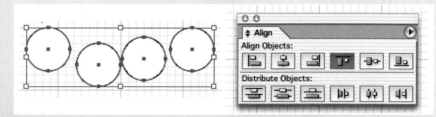

FIGURE 4.18   Align the shapes according to their tops.

8. Select Horizontal Distribute Center (image) from the Align palette. This step spaces the center of the selected objects evenly (Figure 4.19).

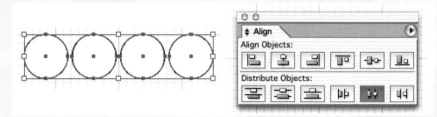

FIGURE 4.19   Distribute the shapes according to their centers.

9. Group the four circles together.
10. Copy this group and paste them three times, one under the other, to create four rows.
11. Place the bottom row so that it is even with left of the row above (4.5" vertical) and the bottom of the grid to its left (3.5" from the bottom of the page; Figure 4.20).

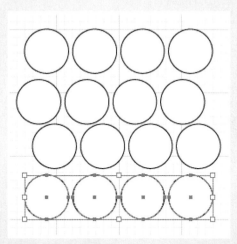

FIGURE 4.20   Position of the bottom row.

12. Select all four rows and select Horizontal Align Left (image) from the Align palette.
13. Select Vertical Distribute Center (image) from the Align palette. The four rows should now be evenly spaced.
14. Group the four rows together. Reposition the new group so that it is 5" from the top and 4.5" from the left.
15. With the four rows selected, make them into guides (Figure 4.21).

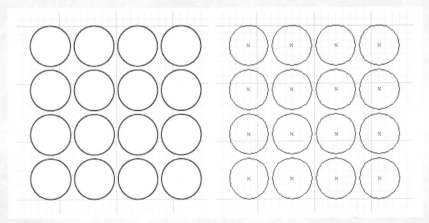

FIGURE 4.21   Make the shapes into guides.

| TUTORIAL | ### STEPS IN CREATING SHAPES USING THE GRID AND CIRCLE PATTERNS AS GUIDES |

Now that the grids have been created we can begin to create our designs. You will start with the first grid you created: the squares. Using the Pen tool (P) you can easily draw these basic shapes (Figure 4.22).

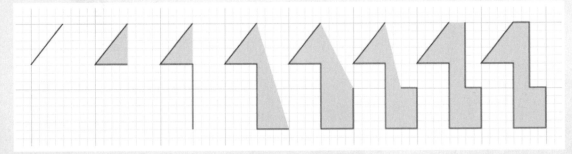

FIGURE 4.22   Use the Pen tool to create a shape by using simple clicks.

USING THE PEN TOOL

The process of using the Pen tool can be either simple or complicated. To draw using the Pen tool is as simple as click, click, click.

To draw, click once to insert a point and then move the mouse and click again. You have now recreated the simplest form of drawing, the line. By subsequently moving the mouse and clicking you can add more points and lines to your shape. If you bring the cursor back over the first point, a small circle will appear next to the pen cursor, allowing you to close the line (Figure 4.22).

THE FIRST DESIGN

Follow these directions to create the following design (Figure 4.23).

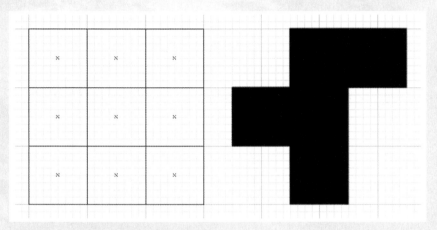

FIGURE 4.23   The grid and the final shape.

1. Select the Pen tool (P) from the toolbar.
2. Click once in the upper right-hand corner of the first square of the grid to place a point (Figure 4.24).

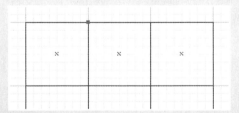

FIGURE 4.24   Place the first point.

3. Click 2" to the right of that point.
4. Click 1" below that point. Now you have created three points and two lines. Illustrator automatically fills the shape in at this stage. The path is not a complete path; the shape is not closed.
5. Continue to place points until the shape you create looks like the one shown in Figure 4.25.

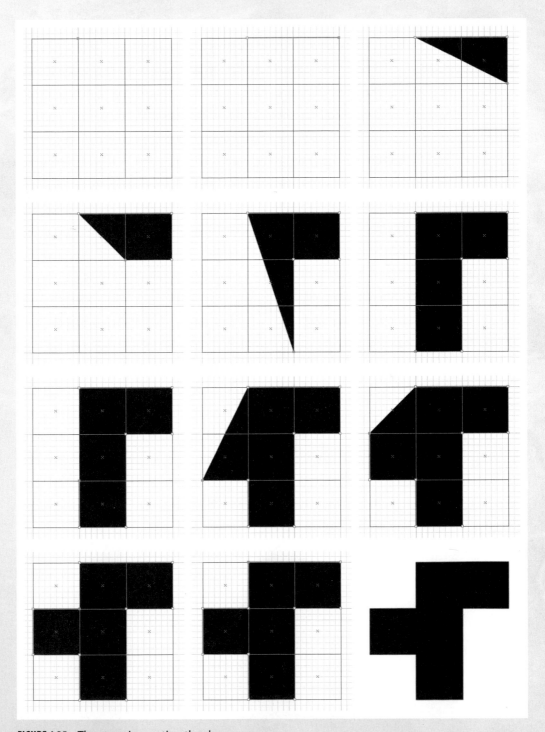

FIGURE 4.25   The steps in creating the shape.

THE SECOND DESIGN

Much in the same way that you created the shape for the first grid, the second grid is just as simple: click, click, click (Figure 4.26).

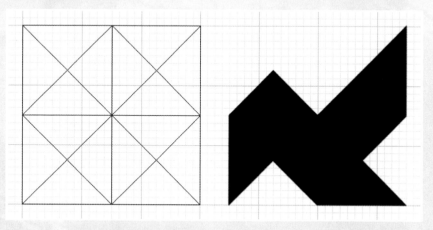

FIGURE 4.26 The grid and the final shape.

1. Select the Pen tool (P) from the toolbar.
2. Click once in the lower left-hand corner of the grid to place a point (Figure 4.27).

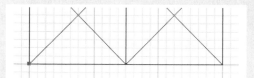

FIGURE 4.27 Place the first point.

3. Click again 1.5″ above that point.
4. Click again up and to the right, in the middle of the upper-left group of triangles. Now you have created three points and two lines. Again, Illustrator auto-fills the shape in at this stage. Remember, the path is still open.
5. Continue to place points until the shape you create looks like the one shown in Figure 4.28.

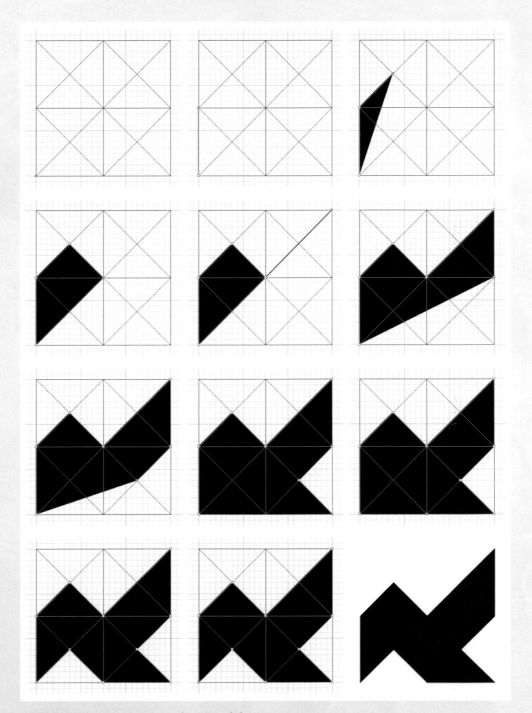

FIGURE 4.28 The steps to create the second shape.

THE THIRD DESIGN: USING THE PATHFINDER PALETTE

Using the third grid (squares and circle), create the following shape (Figure 4.29).

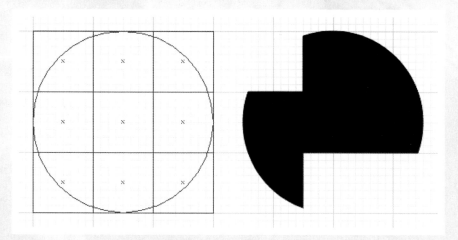

FIGURE 4.29   The third grid and the shape.

To complete this task successfully, you have to be introduced to the Pathfinder palette. The Pathfinder is used to create complex shapes by simply merging, cropping, adding, and subtracting the areas of different shapes.

1. Open the Pathfinder palette by selecting `Window > Pathfinder`.

The Pathfinder Palette

The Pathfinder can do just about anything when it comes to combining the area of two or more shapes. The following is a list of buttons included in the Pathfinder and how they effect shapes. There are two types of tools included in the Pathfinder: the Shape Modes and the Pathfinders.

THE SHAPE MODES

When using the Shape Mode option, the objects themselves do not combine; but, rather, are shared in creating the new shape. To combine them into one continuous path, select the shape and click on the Expand button in the Pathfinder palette. This will merge the paths into one.

Add to Shape Area: This function combines the areas of the shapes into one shape.

Subtract from Shape Area: This function subtracts the shape in the front from the shape behind it.

Intersect Shape Areas: This function leaves behind only the areas of the shape that share the same space.

Exclude Overlapping Shape Areas: This function is the opposite of the Intersect operation. It deletes the area that shapes share.

THE PATHFINDER TOOLS

When using these operations, the integrity of the shapes is altered, resulting in one or more paths (both complete and incomplete). By default, these resulting shapes are grouped together and can be moved individually by either ungrouping the objects or using the Direct Selection (A) tool.

Divide: This operation separates all overlapped areas into their own shape. If two shapes are overlapped, then the result is three shapes.

Trim: In this function, the shape on top subtracts its area from the image behind, while leaving the shape intact. This results in two shapes, the image in front (untouched) and the image behind (with the overlapping area cropped out). Both shapes are complete paths.

Merge: Like the aforementioned Add to Shape Area mode, this function joins the two shapes into one shape with one complete path.

Crop: Like the aforementioned Intersect Shape Areas mode, this function leaves behind only the overlapped areas of the shapes, resulting in one complete path.

Outline: When you use this operation on two overlapping shapes, the result is three paths. The overlapped areas are rendered as a complete path, with the two outlying paths left open, but intact.

Minus Back: Instead of subtracting the shape in front from the one behind, this function does just the opposite. It subtracts the area of the overlapping shape in the back from the one in the front, resulting in a complete path (Figure 4.30).

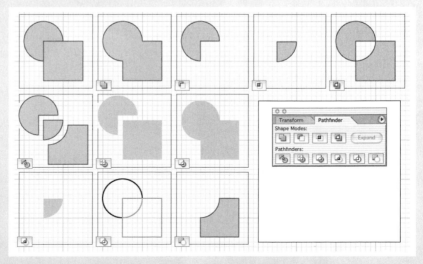

FIGURE 4.30   The Pathfinder (top row) original shapes, Add to Shape Area, Subtract from Shape Area, Intersect Shape Areas, Exclude Overlapping Shape Areas, (middle row) Divide, Trim, Merge, (bottom row) Crop, Outline, and Minus Back.

2. On the third grid, use the Ellipse tool (L) to draw a circle, the same size as the circle in the grid. Make sure that both the fill and stroke are black (Figure 4.31).

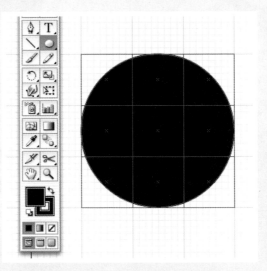

FIGURE 4.31 Draw a circle the same size as the guide.

3. With the Rectangle tool (M), draw a square in the upper left-hand corner (1" wide by 1" high). Then draw a second rectangle in the lower right-hand corner (2" wide by 1" high; Figure 4.32).

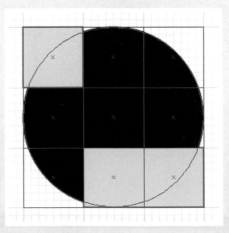

FIGURE 4.32 Draw a square and a rectangle as shown.

4. Using the Selection tool (A), press the Shift key and select all three shapes.

5. With the shapes selected, click on the Subtract from Shape Area button in the Pathfinder palette (first row, second button). This function subtracts the overlapping areas from the shape behind (Figure 4.33).

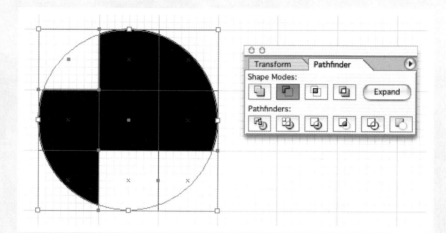

FIGURE 4.33   The Subtract from Shape Area mode gives you the following result.

6. With the new shape still selected, click the Expand button in the Pathfinder, converting the three paths into one closed path that you can modify later (Figure 4.34).

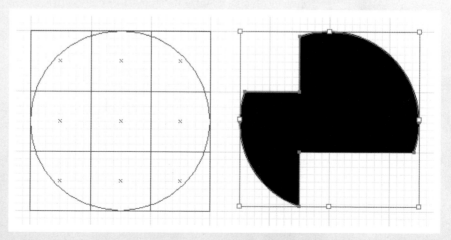

FIGURE 4.34   The completed shape from the squares and circle grid.

THE FOURTH DESIGN

The most difficult of the grids is the fourth one, the grid that is made up of circles. Before now, the Pen tool (P) has been used to make simple point-by-point polygonal shapes. It is now time to expand your knowledge (Figure 4.35).

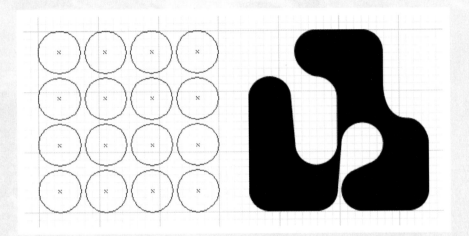

FIGURE 4.35   The fourth grid and the resulting shape.

Bézier Curves

To draw a straight line in Illustrator using the Pen tool (P), start by clicking the mouse to place a point. After releasing the mouse, move the cursor to the desired location for the end of the line and click again. This time, do not release the mouse button. Simply drag the mouse slowly in any direction. Watch the line between the points as it bends in a slight curve. This is called a Bézier curve.

French mathematician Pierre Bézier developed the curve in the 1970s for use with CAD (Computer-Aided Drafting) programs. There are at least three points used to define the curve (Figure 4.36). The two endpoints of the curve are called the anchor points, while the other point (or points) defines the actual curvature. That point is called a handle (which is also referred to as a tangent point or node). By moving the handles you can modify the shape of the curve.

THE BASICS OF BÉZIER CURVES

1. With the Pen tool (P) selected, click once somewhere on the document.
2. Move the mouse about two inches to the right of that line and press the mouse button, but do not release it yet. With the mouse button pressed, slowly drag the mouse up about one inch. The line that is usually

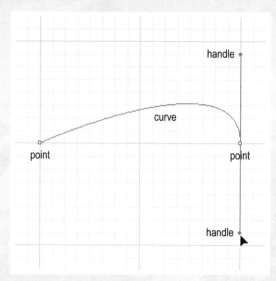

FIGURE 4.36   The basic parts of a Bézier curve are point, curve, and handle. The distance and angle of the handle in relationship to the point create the curve.

straight is now curved. By dragging the handle below the point, the curve is the top. Likewise, if you move the mouse up, the curve bends down. The further away from the point you go, the more intense the curve (Figure 4.37).

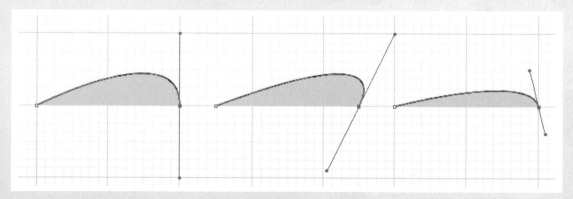

FIGURE 4.37   As you create the curve, move the mouse back and forth to see what kind of a curve you are drawing.

Dragging the cursor is often called "pulling." By pulling the cursor after placing a point, you are creating a curve. "Pulling" is a term that will be used quite frequently in this text.

Take some time and experiment with these tools. Attempt to draw a path with multiple points and varying curves, by clicking and dragging the mouse. As you make a handle, move the mouse around freely and watch the blue preview line show you how the curve would be if you were to let go of the mouse button. By alternating curve direction and angles see if you can recreate any of the paths shown in Figure 4.38. Remember that Illustrator still auto-fills the path even though it is not complete. To turn off the auto fill, simply change the Fill Swatch to "None."

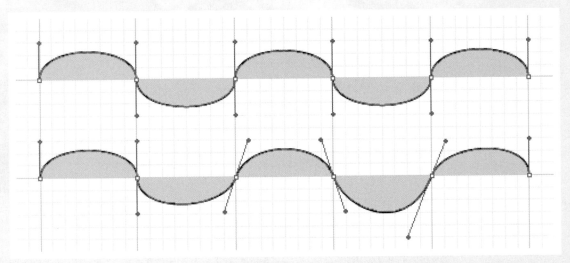

FIGURE 4.38   Examples of complex paths that show variations in handle length and angle. All the points and handles are shown for your reference.

Alternating between clicking points and clicking and dragging points can give you a combination of straight and curved lines. Simply click and click to create straight-line segments, and alternately click and drag to create curved lines (Figure 4.39).

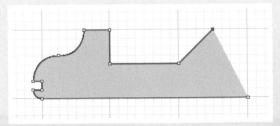

FIGURE 4.39   You can draw objects that contain both straight and curved lines. To close a path, simply click on the first point of your path to complete it.

Modifying Curves by "Pulling" Handles

As you use the Pen tool (P) to draw, along the way you might make mistakes and need to go back and modify the curves. Because the handles control the curve, you can move the handle using the Direct Selection tool (A)—sometimes referred to as the "Open Arrow"—and change the curve. By moving the handle's angle, the direction of the curve can be changed. By increasing and decreasing the distance from the handle and the point, you can change the height of the curve.

1. Using the Pen tool (P), create a curve similar to the one pictured in Figure 4.40. Place a point, without dragging, and then place another point two inches away, but drag the mouse so that the curve appears.

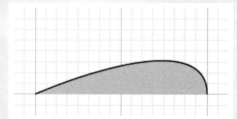

FIGURE 4.40   A simple Bézier curve.

2. Using the Direct Selection tool (A) select the top handle (Figure 4.41) and click and drag it to the left. Watch the blue preview of the curve move to the left and become more even (Figure 4.42). With the handle still selected, move the handle to the right and watch the curve bend toward and then over the point.

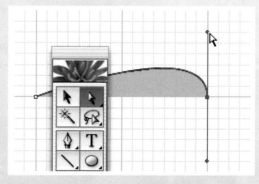

FIGURE 4.41   Use the Direct Selection tool to select the top handle.

FIGURE 4.42 Move the handle to the left and watch the preview line show the new curve. Move the handle to the right over the point and watch the preview line bend, creating a nice curve.

3. Delete the path, using the Selection tool (V), by selecting the path and pressing the Delete key.
4. Using the Ellipse tool (L), draw a circle that is 1" by 1" (Figure 4.43).

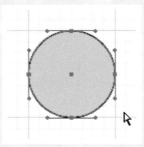

FIGURE 4.43 A circle contains four points and four curves.

As you can see, a circle is made up of four points and four curves. Using the Selection tool (V), you can scale the shape vertically, horizontally, and diagonally. By using the Direct Selection tool (A), you can modify its shape.

5. Using the Direct Selection tool (A), drag a marquee around the topmost point of the circle. Notice that the handles for that point appear, as do the top handles for the points at its middle edges. The other handles will not be affected by the next step.
6. Click on the top-right handle and drag it to the right about .5 (Figure 4.44).

The blue preview line shows the new curve. The curve looks strange because you are moving only one handle, straight across. If you move the handle up or down, the curve becomes more dynamic.

7. Select the same handle that you just moved and drag it up. While dragging the handle, hold down the Shift key. The handle is now constrained to 45° angles. Move the handle into the same position as the handle shown in the middle of Figure 4.45.

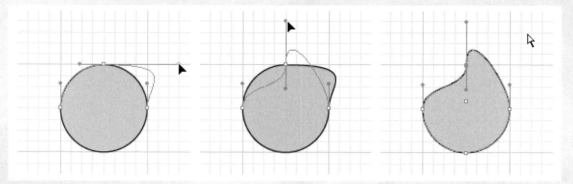

FIGURE 4.44   As you move the handles, the preview line shows you how the curve will change with the new placement of the handle.

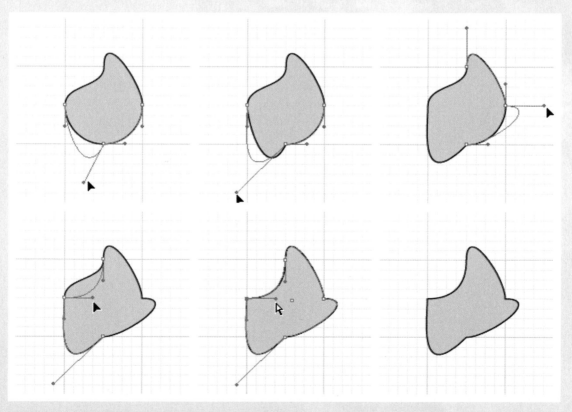

FIGURE 4.45   Holding down the appropriate key, click the desired handle to move only that handle. Notice that the handles do not move together anymore. Remember to select the point first and then the handle.

Notice that the handles move together or in tandem. This is done by default, but can be remedied by holding down the Alt key on a PC or the Option key on a Macintosh as you drag the handle. (Refer to Figure 4.45 for the next few steps.)

8. Using the Direct Selection tool (A), select the bottom point of the shape. (We can't call it a circle anymore.)

9. Press and hold the proper key on the keyboard (PC: Alt; Macintosh: Option). A plus sign (+) will appear near the right of the cursor. This sign is a visual clue that we are about to modify the handle. Select the handle on the left, and while holding down the mouse button and the proper key, drag the handle down $1/2$". These handles do not move together, and will not from this point on. Once you have moved one handle independently from the other, they will not work in tandem anymore.

Hold down the correct key on the keyboard before clicking the handle! If you hold down the key after you have selected the handle, the path will be duplicated. If this happens, undo the last command (PC: control + Z; Macintosh: command + Z) and try again. By nature, the Alt and Option keys are used to drag duplicates of selected shapes from the original.

10. Select the point on the right and, while holding down the proper key, select the bottom handle and pull it up and to the right as shown in the third panel of Figure 4.45.

11. Select the point on the left side of the shape, and move its top handle down and inside the shape toward the right. Also hold down the Shift key to constrain the handle to 45° increments, resulting in the shape in the sixth panel of Figure 4.45.

By "pulling" these handles we can create and modify curves and begin to venture into more complicated drawing techniques.

The Direct Selection tool can also be used to move points, lines, and objects that reside within groups. Whereas the Selection tool allows us to move groups an entire objects, the Direct Selection tool lets us select things (points, lines, handles, etc.) within objects and groups.

CREATING THE FOURTH SHAPE

With the basics of the Pen tool defined, creating this fourth shape will be easier. It will take some patience on your part, and a combination of straight and curved lines to complete this intricate shape (Figure 4.46).

1. With the fourth grid centered in you work area; select the Pen tool (P) from the toolbar.

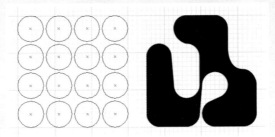

FIGURE 4.46   The fourth grid and the resulting shape.

 You might want to turn off the Snap To Grid option (PC: control + shift + "; Macintosh: command + shift + ") while you do this exercise. The circles are .7" wide and high and do not fit well within a grid that is divisible by quartered fractions (1", .75", .5", .25", .125", etc.). You might also want to hide the grid (PC: control + "; Macintosh: command + "). Both options can also be turned on/off by selecting them again from the View menu.

2. Click to place a point above the first circle in the second row of the grid.
3. Position your Pen tool over the point on the left side of that same circle and click and drag to create a point and a curve. Keep "pulling" the curve until it matches the quarter circle. Release the mouse button.
4. Skip down to the fourth row and place a point on the left side of that circle as well. Continue to place points and pull curves until the shape in Figure 4.47 is completed. After you have completed the shape, go back and select and modify handles as needed.

These shapes will be saved and used in the next chapter. Additional tutorials illustrating more advanced tools and techniques will be used to distort and manipulate these shapes into other shapes.

SUMMARY

This first project is probably the most difficult in terms of both the content and production process. It presents new ideas and involves procedures that could be very difficult if you have no previous experience in design theory or digital production. This is why it is divided into two parts. All the basic concepts and procedures needed to create the next six projects are introduced here. The next projects will build from this and there will be less production material to consider as the book progresses.

As you have experienced from the first part of this project, design is based on structure. There are many rules to learn before you can create intuitive designs without the underlying organization of the basic elements

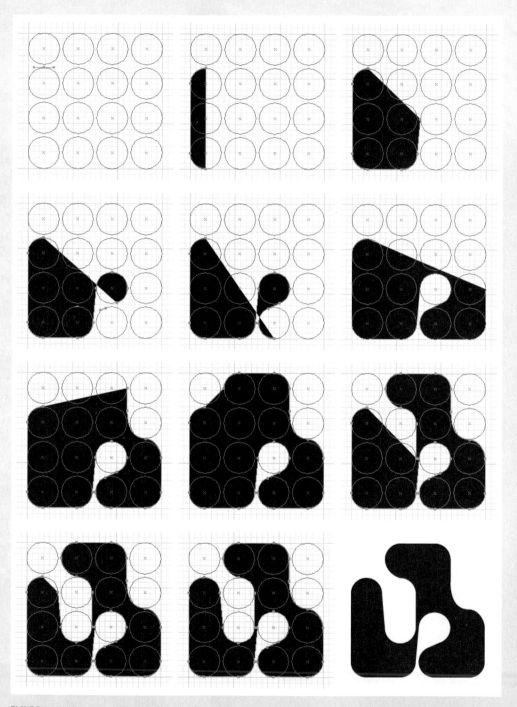

FIGURE 4.47   Steps in creating the final shape.

and principles of design. Think about the times you have succeeded in improvising in an activity that required a basic foundation before you really felt like you knew what you were doing. A comparison may be drawn to other arts that require structure, such as music, or a sport that requires finesse that could only be acquired from a solid understanding of the basics. Too often our only experience with visual creativity has come from purely intuitive processes. However, if you want to use visual expression as design, understanding the fundamentals of how we see and what we are all looking for becomes a necessity. You must understand the beats per measure and the key you are composing or playing in if you are going to improvise through music. You have to know the rules and the physical requirements if you are going to compete or perform in a sport. In the same way the fundamentals of design, and how to create it, must be understood before you can improvise and perform successfully.

5

DESIGN PROJECT ONE: MODULAR DESIGN PROJECT PART TWO

INTRODUCTION

Part two of the Modular Design Project will use the final shapes created from the grids in part one from the previous chapter (Chapter 4). Reviewing part one, the basic structure and resulting shapes should demonstrate unity with some variety, and asymmetrical balance using non-objective shapes. This next part of the project will concentrate on variety and how to create interesting shapes using distortion and manipulation. The final designs may be very different from the shapes created in part one. They will show contrast through the dynamic use of line direction, types of shapes, weights of shapes, and inventive use of negative space. As in part one, solutions will be created digitally, giving the reader more foundation in the basics of the computers and graphics software.

CONTENT

The Basic Problem Defined

Using the four shapes you designed in part one, distort and redesign each shape using the design principles of unity and variety. Each of the four designs should be asymmetrically balanced.

An interesting shape is a balance of variety and harmony. It is up to the individual designer to decide where and to what degree these principles will apply, as will be discussed in the conceptual process portion of this chapter.

As you change the picture frame you are also designing and defining the negative space and positive shapes. To make this point clear, a second design focusing on the negative shape or space converted to a positive shape should be created.

Background

Creating Variety and Harmony

Part one of the Modular Design Project was mostly concerned with establishing structure through unity. Part two also uses unity but concentrates more on variety. Consider the following suggestions that emphasize variety, balanced with unity.

To achieve variety, intensify contrast by designing a large shape next to a small shape, curves next to angles, short shapes next to long shapes, thin shapes next to thick shapes, and so on. There should be good visual hierarchy. If every part of the design is made up of a variety of shape, weight, and size, visual hierarchy can be achieved.

To preserve unity, make sure there are similar angle directions; parallel, vertical, and horizontal sides to shapes; curves; and different types of shapes. If your design begins to look too confusing, go back and take a look at the underlying structure. Exaggerate and distort shapes if they feel too boring (see Figure 5.1).

Communicating with Non-Objective Shapes

"Can non-objective shapes communicate an emotion or visual message?" In Figure 5.2, the first simple design on the left uses a shape that communicates very little; however, when another shape is added in the right place, it can result in an idea or an emotion. The middle design on the top row illustrates the idea of height; the third design, a feeling of heaviness.

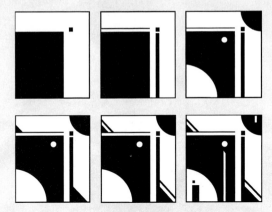

FIGURE 5.1   The upper-left design illustrates variety through the use of varied weights. The upper-middle design makes use of long thin shapes in contrast to thick and short shapes, creating variety. The design on the upper right is an example of contrasting types of shapes. The lower-left design adds variety by introducing two diagonals. To create variety, thinner diagonals are added in the lower middle design. To unify and create more variety, the lower-right design adds a variety of vertical shapes to help unify all the other shapes into a harmonious design made up of an assortment of different shapes, line directions, and visual weights.

The design on the left bottom suggests a dynamic movement downhill; the second design on the bottom, the feeling of tension; and the right design on the bottom, a feeling of tranquility or emptiness.

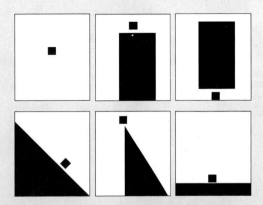

FIGURE 5.2   Examples of visual messages communicated through the use of non-objective shapes.

Depending on the relationship to other shapes, non-objective shapes can either deliver a visual message or elicit a particular emotion. Visual weight, placement, line direction, and contrast are just a few principles of design that may be used for non-objective shapes to give them meaning. The next chapter deals with letterforms, which do not represent anything other than a shape that has been assigned a meaning. Throughout this book we will examine the emotional quality of shapes and how to create specific visual messages using simple, non-objective shapes.

Other Applications of Non-Objective Shapes

The specific application of designing shapes with unity and variety can be seen in the asymmetrically balanced painting at the left in Figure 5.3. Notice how the black shapes describing the background of the painting on the right are similar to the shapes created in this chapter. These black shapes illustrate why we must be aware of the design of space or negative shapes but, more important, how non-objective shapes can be used to analyze and create interesting compositions.

 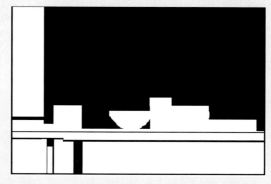

FIGURE 5.3   Example of how the lessons concerning the modular project can be incorporated into the creation and understanding of works of art such as painting. *Still Life with Violet Cup* © 2003. Reprinted with permission from Chris Terry.

CONCEPTUAL PROCESS

Now that you have the problem defined and all the background for this project, you can begin the conceptual process outlined in Chapter 3. The following are a few rules to keep in mind while you are focusing on your design solution.

- Don't let the base shapes from part one restrict you too much. These shapes were only meant to give some direction in beginning this process.
- Keep shapes simple. It will make designing easier.

- Design within an established "picture frame." Experiment with different proportions.
- More intuitive options may be explored in less time by using traditional tools such as a pen or pencil to create approximations of a design. The indirectness of the computer can inhibit spontaneous design options. Many roughs should be explored to ensure that all alternatives have been considered. Narrow the choices down to the ones that best meet the criteria, and then begin the process of producing an accurate representation of your sketches.

Figure 5.4 shows examples of the conceptual process based on the four shapes created in the Modular Project, part one. In each of the four sections, the preliminary rough sketches are located on the left. A very

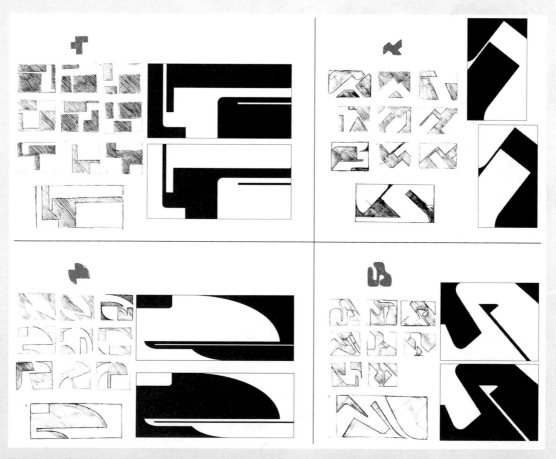

FIGURE 5.4   Sketches based on the basic shapes from Chapter 4 are on the left of each of the four sections. The final designs and reversed final designs, created using Adobe Illustrator, are on the right. *Modular Design* © 2003. Reprinted with permission from Mark Hyatt.

small darker shape located at the top of the rough sketches is a thumbnail of the shape created in Chapter 4. The middle sketches are thumbnails of alternative solutions using distortion and manipulation to create an exaggeration of the original design. The bottom larger sketch is the final rough that will be used to approximate the final designs. This final rough sketch will be traced using the computer to create the finished design. The "Production Process" part of this chapter explains scanning and the steps required to create the finished design. Computer hardware and software can help with multiple options and alternatives once the initial design is realized. Digital methods will also ensure the accuracy and well-crafted production of your designs. The final design and a reverse of the positive shapes to negative shapes and vice versa are located on the right of the rough sketches in each of the four sections in Figure 5.4. The reversed design is used to help visualize the principle of figure/ground.

Figure 5.5 is an alternative example of the beginning grid, primary shape, and composite design that is one step from being finished. The preliminary images are still rough but communicate accurately what the final design will look like. They will be traced and cleaned up using Illustrator. Figure 5.6 is an example of an alternative final design created using Illustrator.

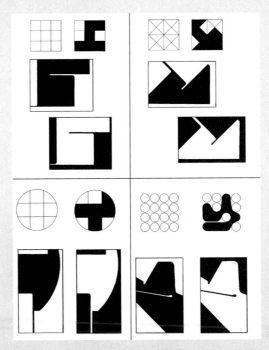

FIGURE 5.5 Example of the rough grid, base shape, composite final shape, and reverse negative final shape. The final shapes will be cleaned up using Illustrator.

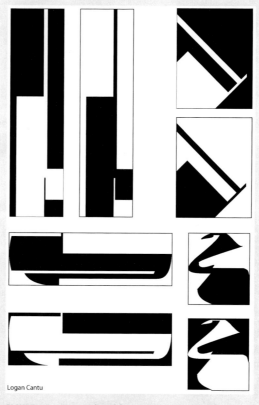

Logan Cantu

FIGURE 5.6   Example of four alternative designs created using Illustrator. *Modular Design* © 2003. Reprinted with permission from Logan Cantu.

PRODUCTION PROCESS

After the conceptual process of creating the final or primary shape is complete, scan the rough or comp into the computer. Using the object-oriented program, Adobe Illustrator, trace the rough design and complete the production process. The final form will be a digital file either for print or to be viewed on a computer monitor. The following sections deal with all the digital tools and techniques you will need to complete this project. The basics of scanning and more involved drawing tools will be outlined step-by-step in tutorials designed to create the final four forms.

Scanning Basics

After you have finished creating the distortions based on your primary imagery created from the grids, you are ready to go to the next step, which is to scan your final drawings for each design into the computer and bring them into Illustrator for tracing.

Scanning

Have you ever used a copy machine? It is a lot like using a scanner. A scanner is a device that is connected to your computer that helps you make a copy of your photograph or drawing, which you can then edit using software on your computer (Figure 5.7).

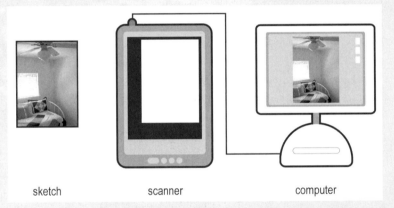

sketch   scanner   computer

FIGURE 5.7   To scan you need three things: an image, a scanner, and a computer.

There are many different kinds of scanners. The most popular kind of scanner is the desktop scanner. A few years ago, scanners were really expensive. Today they can be found for less than $50 and are available everywhere. Scanners are so inexpensive they are often bundled for free with computer purchases. Any desktop scanner will do for this exercise, as will any software.

1. While seated at the computer, power on both the computer and the scanner.
2. Open the top lid of the scanner and place your sketches face down on the scanning bed. Most scanners scan from top to bottom; so place your page in the top-right corner of the glass.
3. Close the lid on the scanner.

Most scanners come with software that you can install on your computer. However, the best software comes with drivers for Photoshop, so that you can directly import/scan your image into Photoshop.

You may want to refer to the manual that came with your scanner or the Help section of the software that was packaged with it if you have any installation questions.

4. Launch the software you will use to scan your image. For Photoshop users with the necessary drivers installed, launch Photoshop, choose `File >` `Import` from the top menu, and select the appropriate application/ scanner.

The default setting for each scanner and software might be different. What follows are general things to look for.

5. Preview the image. This might require pressing a button named "Preview" or some scanners may automatically begin by previewing the image.

A "preview" is a quick scan of your image. Most software allows you to pre-set different qualities and settings before doing a final scan. A scanner "reads" every line of an image as the scanning head passes down along the scanning bed. It imports that information line by line into the computer (Figure 5.8). Some scanners scan in multiple passes so patience may be necessary.

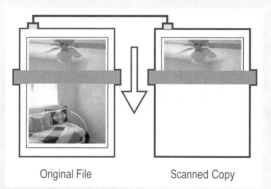

Original File   Scanned Copy

FIGURE 5.8   A scanner reads the images line by line and sends that information to the computer.

6. Crop the area that you wish to scan.

The software should allow you to crop the area of an image, so that you don't waste time scanning empty areas of the document. The selection box can be moved by mousing over the edges of the box until arrows appear, allowing you to adjust the selection in or out, up or down (Figure 5.9).

7. Set the resolution of your image to 72 ppi (pixels per inch).

The resolution of the image is important. Without going into too much technical jargon, the higher the ppi, the better the quality of the image (Figure

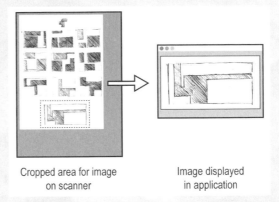

Cropped area for image   Image displayed
on scanner   in application

FIGURE 5.9   Use the scanning software's built-in cropping tools to select the area that you wish to scan.

5.10). When the resolution is set to 300 ppi, the scanner scans 300 pixels (the basic unit of measurement in computer graphics) of information per inch. For high-quality archiving scans or scanning for printed publications, a higher quality is necessary. When a scanner scans at 300 ppi, it is often much slower.

FIGURE 5.10   This image has been scanned at a size of 1" by 1" at three different resolutions: 300 ppi (left), 150 ppi (middle), and 72 ppi (right). The images have been scaled 200%. The 300 ppi image has more dots, giving it a finer print quality.

Because we need only to use these images on the screen it is a waste to scan more information that we need. Your monitor's resolution is 72 pixels per inch, so by scanning at that resolution you will easily be able to get the information that you need.

If you wish to find a common ground, then scan at 150 ppi. While the scan will be better than a 72 ppi image, it will not have the excess of information a 300 ppi scan would have.

8. Click Scan or Save. Now sit back and let the scanner do the work.

If you are scanning into Photoshop, you will have to save the image. Do so by selecting `File > Save`. In the Save dialog box, select a location to save your image to, name the file, and save it as a TIFF file. A TIFF file is a multi-purpose file that can handle multiple color depths with equal ease.

If you scanned the image using some other software, save the file onto the desktop or in a specific location.

9. Repeat this process until all of your sketches have been scanned.

Scanning is simple. Having the power to bring images from outside the computer into the computer is a wonderful thing. Follow the simple steps and you can scan in anything you want to: photographs, paper, fabric, lace, soft textures, and so on. Further on in the text are other exercises that will require scanning. Refer back to this section as you need to.

TUTORIAL

IMPORTING THE FILE INTO ILLUSTRATOR FOR TRACING

Now you are ready to bring the images into Illustrator.

By placing the images in Illustrator, you can use the tools and techniques discussed previously to trace the images and complete the project of distortion covered in the next section.

1. Launch Illustrator and create a new document by selecting `File > New`. Set the page size to Letter, the units to Inches, and the orientation to Portrait. Name the file accordingly (Figure 5.11).

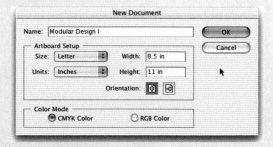

FIGURE 5.11   Create a new document with these specifications.

2. Choose `File > Place` to open the Place dialog box. Find the file that you wish to place, select it, and click Place.

If you choose to uncheck the Link box, the image file will be embedded in the document, increasing the file size. If it remains checked, then you must keep the image that you have placed in the same location at all times. Illustrator will look for it each time the file is opened. If you have moved the file, the program will prompt you to find it. The file is now placed within the page (Figure 5.12).

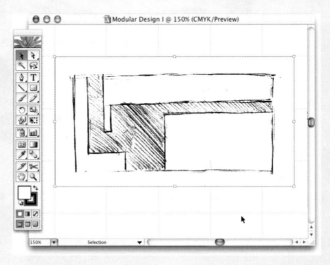

FIGURE 5.12   The image of the thumbnails is now placed in the page. You may position it wherever you want in the document area.

3. Open your Layers palette by selecting `Window > Layers`. (Your Layers palette may already be visible.)

In your Layers palette there should only be one layer named "Layer 1."

4. To change the name of this layer, double-click the name of the layer to open the Layer Options dialog box or from the Options menu of the Layer palette, choose "Options for "Layer 1" (Figure 5.13).

FIGURE 5.13   Open the Layer Options dialog box by selecting Options for "Layer 1" from the Layer Options menu.

5. In the Layer Options dialog box, name the layer "Thumbnails" (Figure 5.14).

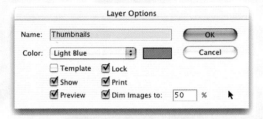

FIGURE 5.14 The Layer Option dialog box.

6. While in the Layer Options dialog box, check the Dim Images to: box. This setting reduces the brightness of the image according to the setting on the field to the right. Enter 50 into that field. Click OK.

You will notice that the image is less bright and easier to look at.

7. Create a new layer by clicking on the New Layer icon in the Layers palette (Figure 5.15).

FIGURE 5.15 The Create New Layer button.

8. Name the layer "Tracings." Follow Step 4, previously mentioned, to name the new layer.
9. Lock the "Thumbnails" layer by clicking in the Lock box (Figure 5.16).

This setting will keep you from inadvertently moving or working on the layer with the image.

10. Open the Layer Options for the "Thumbnails" layer, by double-clicking on the "Thumbnails" layer or select the layer and select the appropriate option from the Layer Option menu. Uncheck the Print box. Click OK.

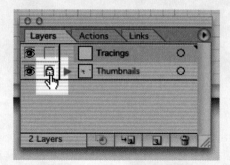

FIGURE 5.16   Click in the Toggle Lock area of the layer.

The layer will not print with this box unchecked. As you trace your thumb-nails, you may periodically want to print them out to see how they look. If you do so, the information on that layer will not print, making it easier to see your tracings (Figure 5.17).

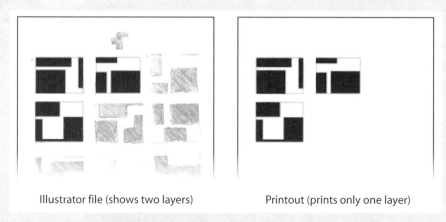

Illustrator file (shows two layers)   Printout (prints only one layer)

FIGURE 5.17   With the Print box unchecked in the "Thumbnails" layer, only the "Tracings" layer will print.

Repeat this process for every set of thumbnails and for other similar pro-jects. You are now ready to trace over your sketches.

TUTORIAL   **TRACING YOUR ROUGHS**

Now that you have scanned your final sketches into the computer and have placed them into an Illustrator document you are ready to trace the images into their final form.

From what has been discussed so far, you have several options for completing this task. Whether to use the Shape tools, the Pen tool, the Pathfinder, or a combination of tools to finish these images is up to you.

USING GUIDES

Using a combination of guides and the Pen tool you can create the shapes necessary to trace your roughs.

Turn on the grid by selecting `View > Show Grid` (PC: control + "; Mac: command + "). You'll notice the grid is behind the image. This cancels out our using the grid to keep our lines and points straight. We have to come up with another option. That option is using *guides*.

Turn the grid off by selecting the appropriate option from the menu or with the key command.

By default the grid is set to appear "in back." That can be changed in the Preferences. Accessing the Preferences is different for PCs and Macs. On the PC, choose `Edit > Preferences > Guides & Grid...` *(control + K). For the Mac in OS X, choose* `Illustrator > Preferences > Guides & Grid...` *(command + K). In the resulting dialogue box, uncheck the "Guides in Back" checkbox to bring the guides to the front.*

Earlier in the text, you created shapes and changed them into guides so that it would be easier to use the Pen tool to create your primary designs. The points drawn were "snapped" to the grid as a means used to keep control.

Whereas changing the shapes to guides was useful then, it is not very useful to us now. Another alternative has to be thought of. That alternative is guides.

Guides are horizontal and vertical lines that allow us to line up objects visually on the page and they also act as helpers in drawing shapes.

To create a guide, you simply have to drag a guide from the rulers and place it within the document area. Follow these steps in aiding you in the explanation and use of the guides.

1. Show your rulers by selecting `View > Show Rulers` (PC: control + R; Mac: command + R).

Horizontal and vertical rules should now be seen at the top and left sides of the document window. The unit of measurement reflects the one set in the creation of the new document, in this case, inches.

You may change the unit of measurement after the creation of a new document by selecting `File > Document Setup` *and choosing another option under Units.*

2. Create a horizontal guide by placing your cursor in the area of the ruler (as shown at the top of Figure 5.18). The cursor will change to an arrow regardless of what tool is selected. As you click the mouse, notice that a dotted line appears attached to the tip of the arrow. Drag that line down into the window and line it up where you would like it to go and then release the mouse button to place the guide.

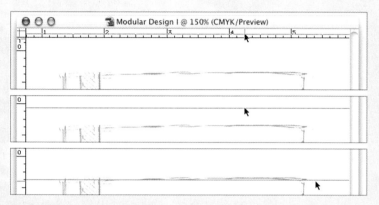

FIGURE 5.18   To create a horizontal guide, click and drag a guide from the horizontal ruler.

A guide is now visible at the point where you dropped the dotted line. On most computers the color of the guide is defaulted to blue.

3. Create a vertical guide by placing your cursor in the area of the ruler on the left (as shown at the left of Figure 5.19). Click and drag the line out into the window and line it up where you would like it to go and then release the mouse button to place the guide.

FIGURE 5.19   To create a vertical guide, click and drag a guide from the vertical ruler.

4. Continue to create guides along every vertical and horizontal edge you need (Figure 5.20).

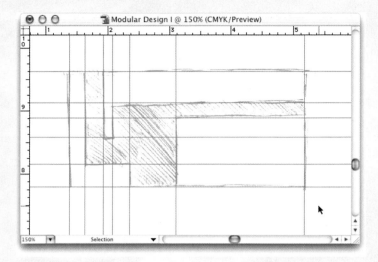

FIGURE 5.20   Create a guide for every edge that you will need in order to draw the shapes successfully.

TRACE YOUR ROUGHS: PRIMARY DESIGN I

Now that the guides have been set, you are ready to trace the first sketch.

1. With the Pen tool (P) selected, make sure that the fill is set to none and the stroke to black (Figure 5.21). By leaving the fill color blank, the auto-fill property of the Pen tool is null, making it easier to trace the image.

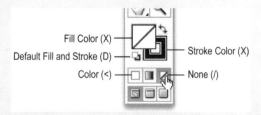

FIGURE 5.21   The color selection section of the Tools palette is used to set the stroke and fill of various tools.

2. Draw the interior shape of the sketch by clicking—only on the vertices of the guides. Your last point placed should overlap the first one to complete the path (Figure 5.22).
3. With the new shape selected, fill the shape with black by activating the Fill color by clicking on it, bringing it to the front. Then from the Swatches palette (View > Swatches), select the black swatch. The shape is then filled (Figure 5.23).

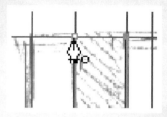

FIGURE 5.22 Use the Pen tool to draw the interior shape of the design. Close the path by placing the last point over the first.

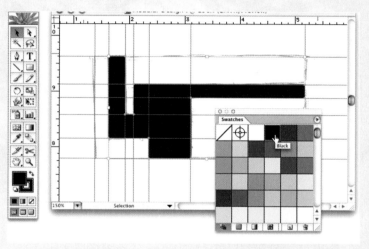

FIGURE 5.23 Fill the shape with black by clicking on the black swatch in the Swatches palette.

4. Choose `Select > Deselect` to deselect the shape (PC: control + shift + A; Mac: command + shift + A).
5. Select the Rectangle tool (M). Set the fill to white.
6. Draw a large rectangle over the shape, according to the drawing and the guides (Figure 5.24).

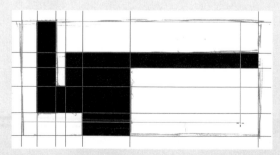

FIGURE 5.24 Use the Rectangle tool to draw a white rectangle over the first shape.

7. Right-click on the shape and choose `Arrange > Send to Back` from the pop-up menu. This command sends the shape behind the one below.

 Note: This option is also available by selecting `Object > Arrange > Send to Back` *(PC: control + shift + [; Mac: command + shift + [).*

Shapes are drawn on each layer with a certain placement order or hierarchy. The newest shape is drawn on top of the others. The order of these shapes can be rearranged in several ways.

The Arrange option (`Object > Arrange`) allows you to shuffle the order of an object or group of objects by the following:

Bring to Front: Brings the current selection to the top of the stack of the current layer.

Bring Forward: Brings the current selection up one level in the hierarchy of the current layer. If you want to bring an object up two levels, perform the operation twice.

Send Backward: Sends the current selection back one level in the hierarchy of the current layer. If you want to send an object back two levels, perform the operation twice.

Send to Back: Sends the current selection all the way to the back or bottom of the hierarchy of the current layer.

The white box acts as a border for the shape, completing it.

8. Select both shapes by using the Selection tool coupled with the Shift key.
9. Copy and paste the shapes. Move the new shapes below the first.
10. With the Selection tool, click on the black shape of the ones you just pasted.
11. From the Swatches palette, select white for the fill. The shape that was black is now white.
12. Select the white rectangle and change its fill to black.

You have now simply inverted the colors of the shape to create a negative version of the image (Figure 5.25). This contrast of images shows the balance of the image, whether black on white or white on black.

This is not the final step. You can still further modify the shapes by adding other subtle shapes or lines to the design to enhance the unity and aesthetics of the design. In Figure 5.26, the shape that has been used for this example has been further constructed to attain that feeling of balance.

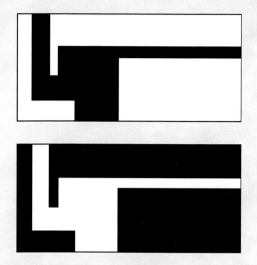

FIGURE 5.25 Invert the colors of the shapes by changing white fills to black, and black fills to white.

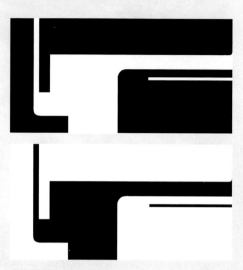

FIGURE 5.26 The final image from this primary design.

TRACE YOUR ROUGHS: PRIMARY DESIGN III

Using what you have learned in the previous section is adequate for completing the assignment of finishing the final designs for the second primary design. Now switch your attention to the third design, the sketches developed from the grid of squares and the circle.

1. Open the document that you created for tracing the sketch of the third design. (This was done on your own, using the steps from the Placing Images in Illustrator exercise.) Using the Zoom tool (Z), zoom in 150% on the image that you are going to trace (Figure 5.27).
2. If they are not visible, show the rulers and select `View > Snap to Point`. You do not need the grid visible for this exercise.
3. Use guides to create the rectangle shape to the first thumbnail.
4. Using the Pen tool (P), begin to build the straight portions of the design by clicking and placing points. Start in the bottom left-hand corner and draw up the line, moving right and so on. Stop when you come to the first curved line. To make things easier, you might want to make the fill "none" so that the auto-fill feature is disabled.
5. The fifth line segment curves in. To draw that curve, place a point at the end of the would-be curved segment and, with the button still pressed, "pull" the handles out from the point and down to the right. Watch the preview line and stop (release the mouse) when they line up.

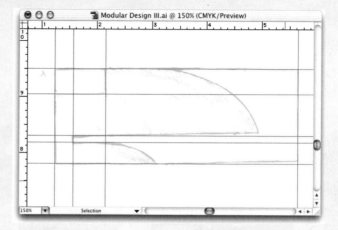

FIGURE 5.27   Starting the design.

Continue to draw the rest of the lines and the last curve as shown in Figure 5.28. You will go back and clean up the curves in the next few steps.

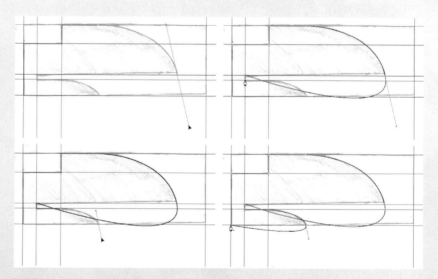

FIGURE 5.28   Create the shape by tracing the image that you placed.

6. With the Direct Selection tool (A), draw a marquee around the first curve point to select it.

This will reveal the two handles. You will need to move the bottom handle independently from the top one to fix this curve (Figure 5.29).

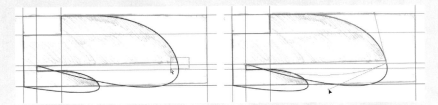

FIGURE 5.29   Cleaning up the curves requires use of the Direct Selection tool and its modifier key, to move the handle independently.

7. Hold down the appropriate key on the keyboard to make the handles move independently (PC: alt; Mac: option), and click on the bottom handle. Drag it to the left. Watch how the curve begins to disappear.
8. While dragging the handle, hold down the Shift key.

Pressing the Shift key constrains the handle's movement to 45° angles. Notice how the handle snaps to the horizontal guide, immediately fixing the curve and making the line straight.

9. Use the same techniques to "fix" the second curve.
10. Fill the shape with black.
11. Select the Rectangle tool (M) and set the fill to white. Draw a rectangle over the top of the shapes, using the guides.
12. With the rectangle selected, choose `Object > Arrange > Send to Back` to send the white box to the back.
13. Copy and paste the two shapes (as in the last exercise) and reverse the fills to achieve a negative shape (Figure 5.30).

FIGURE 5.30   Make a copy of the shape and reverse the fills.

Again, using this shape as a jumping point, further modify it in order to en-hance its design (Figure 5.31).

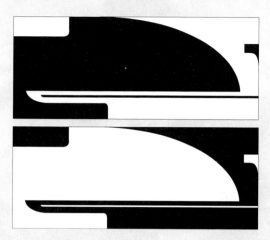

FIGURE 5.31   The modified shape based on the traced primary design.

QUESTIONS YOU SHOULD ASK YOURSELF

The finished shapes should consist of four designs and their negatives for a total of eight designs. Review the suggestions and criteria for giving a design unity and variety. Is your design unified? Do all the parts feel like they fit? Is there enough variety or is there too much variety? Is there a specific line direction? Are there multiple line directions? If so, which one dominates? Which one is less dominant?

When multiple line directions and weights of shapes feel equal, the viewer cannot focus on them one at a time. Visual hierarchy is needed in this case.

Are the angled shapes located on one side of the composition and the curved or rounded shapes on the other? Is chaos being created because there are too many different kinds of shapes of similar size located in the same area? Chaos is a result of the lack of hierarchy so the eye cannot focus on one shape at a time.

If the shapes were similar in size and similar kinds of shapes, the re-sult might be boring. This portion of the composition would seem very uninteresting unless the shapes were exact and created a pattern.

Because of the similarity of shapes, patterns act more like applied tex-ture and they form relationships that are seen as one shape. Pattern and texture will be discussed in detail in a later chapter.

Each of the four final designs should have unique characteristics but you may notice a similarity between each of them. By examining all four at once you can begin to see consistency between shapes. These similarities can be analyzed and observed as general strengths and weaknesses in your designs.

SUMMARY

This project is a fundamental exercise in finding the relationship between elements of design using the principles of design. Each shape should be balanced between unity and variety. The principles of unity and variety are so universal they can be seen in a variety of ways other than via two-dimensional visual design. Look at the shape of your favorite car and notice the contrast and harmony of every angle of the body and even the dashboard. Is there a favorite building near you? Is it a well-balanced mixture of unity and variety? Can you think of a movie that is so unified it became boring? How about a movie that has so much variety it was a mass of chaos? Have you had a week that went on day after day with nothing new happening or changing and suddenly it was Monday again? Can you remember a Saturday that you had planned perfectly only to find out that nothing you had planned was going to work out because of an emergency or unexpected event? These are examples of imbalanced design and you can certainly feel uncomfortable if you are experiencing it.

6

DESIGN PROJECT TWO: LETTERFORMS AND SHAPE

INTRODUCTION

Letterforms are the most commonly used element graphic designers use to communicate a message. They are used individually or in conjunction with graphic shapes or objects as pictographs, trademarks, and other information symbols. Grouped as words they become wordmarks, titles, and headlines. Organized into blocks of text the shapes created by lines of type can communicate more that just the meaning of the words. Close observation of letterforms and the ability to see type as shapes is one of the most important concepts graphic designers must understand. Letterforms are shapes that communicate beyond their written message. All the design principles that relate to any shape can also be applied to letterforms.

Chapter 10 will discuss more specific information about type and how to use type in design. Value and color as it relates to type will also be introduced in Chapter 10. The project detailed in this chapter deals more specifically with letterforms.

Content

Defining the Basic Problem

Using the inherent structure and expressive quality of letterforms, two to five letters from the same or different fonts will be combined and positioned to create one composition. This design will be done only in black and white to emphasize shape, space, and line. If a more harmonious design is the objective, then type from the same or similar fonts should be used. Multiple contrasting fonts can be used if the emphasis is on variety. Be careful to retain unity in this type of design. It is very easy to overuse fonts, which can result in chaos.

Follow the same conceptual and production procedures as you did for the Modular Design Project. Design each of the shapes with as much variety as possible to create interest, but avoid too much variety. Use related shapes, angles, and placement to ensure the design is unified and harmonious. An interesting shape is a balance of variety and harmony. It is up to the individual designer to decide where and to what degree these principles will apply.

As with all designs dealing with shape, follow the suggestions listed below.

- To achieve unity make sure there are similar angle directions; parallel, vertical, and horizontal sides to shapes; curves; and different types of shapes.
- To achieve variety intensify contrast.
- There should be good visual hierarchy balanced with unity.
- Keep shapes simple.
- Design within an established "picture frame." Experiment with different proportions.

The relationship between letters as positive and negative shapes (figure/ground) should be explored and the end result should be two asymmetrical designs, one the negative of the other, making the positive shapes black and the space or negative shapes white and visa versa. The second shape or negative is created to illustrate the following design principle: As you design a positive shape or figure you are also designing the space around the positive shape, called a negative shape or ground. Figure 6.1 is a rough example of this project. Notice the variety of shapes and how the letterforms are cropped. Many are not even recognizable as letters. You may want to forget these are letterforms and concentrate on creating an interesting design that is a balance between unity and variety.

FIGURE 6.1   Rough example of the Letterform Project.

Background

Letterforms as Shapes

The Modular Design Project in the previous two chapters used an underlying structure of grids to organize and give harmony to a design. This project will use the structure of letterforms to do the same. Letters have a specific structure because they are developed as a system more commonly called an alphabet. These systems are made up of similar and related shapes to give continuity from letter to letter, making reading much easier. There are many different styles of type systems called fonts. This difference in fonts may depend on the time period in history in which they were created, the technology that created them, and/or the current media and communication demands. Fonts are made up of harmonious shapes that relate to one another in a system with just enough variation of shape to define the individual letters of the alphabet (see Figure 6.2). More details about fonts and their history will be outlined in Chapter 10.

FIGURE 6.2 A contemporary alphabet designed with an emphasis on harmony and rectilinear shapes recalling the design of Constructivism. This font was selected as an example because of its obvious adherence to a simple system and clarity of relationships between letters. *Van Doesburg Typeface* © 2003. Reprinted with permission from Mike Clayton.

Letters do not represent anything figurative or realistic. They are shapes that have been given a specific symbolic meaning. Basically letterforms are non-objective shapes that can be designed using the same principles that would apply to the Modular Design Project or any other shape. Figures 6.3 and 6.4 are examples of how the principles of unity and variety can apply to letterform compositions.

Letterforms as Communication Design

For communication purposes, type can be directly related to objects or figures. They can reflect the same characteristics as real or stylized shapes, thus forming a direct relationship between type and image (see Figure 6.5).

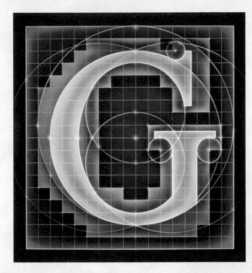

FIGURE 6.3 Example of a letterform design used as a poster. The emphasis is on unity even though there are a variety of shapes and lines. Look at the grid and unifying circular shapes reminiscent of the Modular Design Project. You should also notice how variety is achieved through the contrast of curvilinear and rectilinear shapes. *G* © 2003. Reprinted with permission from Alan Hashimoto.

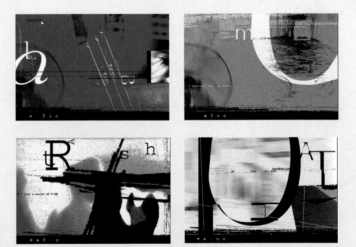

FIGURE 6.4 Example of letterform design using four screen shots from a Web site. The emphasis is on variety. There is very little unity except for the black button area on the bottom demonstrating continuity from page to page. All the organization of these designs is coming from the sophisticated use of visual hierarchy and the minimal use of color. *Self Promotion* © 2003. Reprinted with permission from Jiong Li.

FIGURE 6.5   Examples of forming a relationship between type and images using harmony found in both the letterforms and lines and shapes of the stylized figures and objects. *Word and Image* © 2003. Reprinted with permission from Patrick Wilkey. *www.visiocommunications.com*.

The project outlined in this chapter is directly related to the design of trademarks, wordmarks, posters, and other graphics that rely heavily on type as a design element. Figure 6.6 and Figure 6.7 are examples of using letterforms and figure/ground to create corporate identities, posters, and other graphics. In Figure 6.6, the top two designs use letterforms as design elements, thus establishing a visual connection with the stylized objects and figures. Compare these two designs with the three in Figure 6.5. The designs in Figure 6.5 use the stylized images as the dominant visual. The top two designs in Figure 6.6 do the opposite. The type is the dominant element. Both have good hierarchy but communicate in different ways. The bottom two designs in Figure 6.6 are examples of figure/ground and use stylized shapes that reflect similarity of type, object, and shape.

Look at Figure 6.7. Notice how variety is used to contrast the thin organic and flowing shapes with the more structured letterform in the upper-left design. The upper-right design also uses the contrasting thin cursive letter and a heavy geometric shape to create variety and interest. There is a diagonal line direction prominent in both designs, which suggests movement and dynamics. The bottom corporate identity contrasts rectilinear and curvilinear shapes as well as visual weights to produce a solid corporate feel. The vertical line direction in the center and the heavy base of the letters suggests power and stability. Notice how differ-

FIGURE 6.6   Example of the relationships that exists between objects, letters, and figure/ground. *Slake Logo, Boise Zoo, Tee-Shirt Logo, Boise Zoo Logo, Dino Park Logo* © 2003. Reprinted with permission from Bob Winward.

ent these two companies must be. One corporate identity communicates the feeling of movement and lightness and the other communicates something solid and well established.

FIGURE 6.7   Examples of corporate identities that use letterforms and figure/ground as design elements to communicate the image of a company. Top: *Signature Logo* © 2003. Reprinted with permission from David Cahoon. Bottom: *Trademark* © 2003. Reprinted with permission from Alan Hashimoto.

Anatomy of a Letterform

Designers must be able to recognize and identify the parts of a letterform before they can use them properly. Some of the terminology used to identify these parts is straightforward and other terminology is abstract. Refer to the diagram in Figure 6.8 for the following terms.

FIGURE 6.8 The anatomy of a letterform.

Ascender: The vertical part of a lowercase letterform that rises above the x-height (b, d, f, h, k, l, t).

Baseline: The imaginary horizontal line on which all the bases of all letterforms seem to rest.

Bowl: The curved part of the letterform that encloses the counter.

Cap Height: The height of a capital letterform measured from the baseline to the cap line.

Cap Line: The imaginary horizontal line to which all capital letters arise.

Counter: The enclosed or partially enclosed area of a letterform. For example, the center of the "e" or "o," or the vertical space between the vertical strokes of the "u" or "n."

Cross Bar: The horizontal line connects the two vertical strokes.

Descender: The vertical part of a lowercase letterform that falls beneath the baseline (p, g, q).

Serif: The small decorative strokes at the ends of the main strokes.

X-Height: The height of a lowercase letter that contains no ascenders or descenders.

Discerning the Interesting Parts of Letterforms and the Conceptual Design Process

Now that the basic parts of the letter have been identified, you can begin to learn the differences between typefaces. Typefaces are groups of letters that share a commonality in stroke, measurement, and style.

Figure 6.9 is a selection of four examples of typefaces. Each typeface is sized uniquely. Some typefaces have strokes that are the same throughout the font (VAG Rounded) whereas others have variation in the stroke (Parisian). Some have serifs (Goudy Old Style), others do not (Avante Garde).

abcdefghijklmnopqrstuvwxyz
VAG Rounded Bold

abcdefghijklmnopqrstuvwxyz
Goudy Old Style

abcdefghijklmnopqrstuvwxyz
Avante Garde Bold

abcdefghijklmnopqrstuvwxyz
Parisian Medium

FIGURE 6.9   Four examples of typefaces.

The objective of this assignment is to combine letterforms or parts of letterforms to produce one interesting asymmetrical design. Taking two of the fonts (VAG Rounded and Avante Garde), single out some of the more interesting letters based on the aforementioned characteristics.

With the letters selected, sketch on paper a couple dozen ideas of how these shapes can be combined to fulfill the requirements of the assignment. Pick two to five letters and arrange them into shapes. Rotate them, make them different sizes, and reflect (or flip) them as seen in Figure 6.10.

FIGURE 6.10   A final sketch of a type combination design.

Once you have finished these thumbnails, use them as a reference for how you will place the characters in the design on the computer.

| TUTORIAL | **PRODUCTION PROCESS** |

USING THE TYPE TOOL IN ILLUSTRATOR

The Type tool (T) is one of the most straightforward tools in the program. It allows you to type into the document.

1. Launch Illustrator and create a new document. Name the document Type Combo. Click OK.
2. Select the Type tool (T) from the toolbar as seen in Figure 6.11.

FIGURE 6.11   The Type tool's location in the toolbar.

3. Click anywhere in the document to set the insertion point for beginning your type. Then type a few characters.
4. With the Type tool, you can select the text as a whole or as individual characters. Simply place the insertion point before the character or characters you would like to select and then click and drag to select them.

At this time, you can change several attributes of the letters. These options are in the Character palette.

5. Open the Character palette by selecting View > Type > Characters.

With the Character palette in view, the attributes of font choice, point size, and other options are available.

6. You can change the typeface or font using the Font pop-up menu (Figure 6.12).

FIGURE 6.12   Select from the fonts you have installed on computer through this pop-up menu.

7. Change the size of the text by clicking on the Font Size pop-up menu in the Character palette (Figure 6.13).

FIGURE 6.13   The Font Size pop-up menu with the size set to 12 pt and 36 pt.

Other options in this palette will be explained further in another chapter.

CONVERTING TYPE TO PATHS: CREATING OUTLINES

When the text is printed or displayed on the screen, the computer reads its font file so that it understands how to shape, place, and space each character. Have you ever used a particular font in your document in a computer lab and then returned home, only to open the file and see the characters are all wrong? It means that you used a font that is not installed on your computer at home.

The text that you type in any software depends on the font. A font is a little file used by your operating system. This file holds the character information for all the letters, numbers, punctuation, special characters, and other symbols. Each font is a different file. This file must be located in its proper place to be used.

Basic text can only have very few modifications made to it. You can change its size, color, and spacing, but as it is, it cannot be modified structurally.

The font file that the typeface is dependent on is a collection of vector paths that the computer uses to accurately display and print the font. In

Illustrator you can change the font from being dependent on the font file into compound paths based on that information. These paths can be modified in much the same way that you have modified points in previous projects.

1. Use the Type tool (T) to place the characters of your design.
2. Open the Character palette by selecting `Window > Type > Character` (PC: control + T; Mac: command + T).
3. With the text selected, set the typeface that you wish to use. Also set the size of the font to 72 pt.
4. Select the text box using the Selection tool and covert the font to paths by selecting `Type > Create Outlines` (PC: control + shift + O; Mac: command + shift + O).

The letters are now converted into compound paths of points and lines. By default, the letters are grouped together. To move them independently they must be ungrouped (Figure 6.14).

FIGURE 6.14   By default, letters that are converted to paths are grouped.

5. With the letters still selected, choose `Object > Ungroup` (PC: control + shift + G; Mac: command + shift + G).

These letters/shapes can now be moved independently with the Selection tool (V).

For the example (as shown in the sketch in Figure 6.10), the letters "i" and "k" from the typeface VAG Rounded and an "i" from Avante Garde were selected. All three letters have been converted to outlines.

USING THE TRANSFORM TOOLS: REFLECT AND SCALE

The Transform tools allow you to modify the appearance of shapes in a variety of ways. To make the shape larger or smaller, you would use Scale. To flip the shape vertically or horizontally, you would use Reflect. To change the angle, use Rotate. If you look closely at the sketch you can see how each of these commands are used to create the final design. Let's start by working with the 'k."

1. Drag the "k" to the middle of the page so that it will be easy to work with. Leave the two "i" shapes off to the side.
2. With the "k" selected, chose the Reflect tool (O) from the toolbar. It is nested under the Rotate tool (Figure 6.15).

FIGURE 6.15   The Reflect tool is nested under the Rotate tool. When a nested tool is selected, it replaces the tool that was there first. To access that tool again, click and hold on the button and select it again.

The Reflect tool flips the object across an invisible axis called the *point of origin*. The point of origin is a target-like symbol that appears on the object when a Transform tool is activated. You can move the point of origin by placing the cursor over it and clicking and dragging.

3. Move the point of origin of the "k" shape to the left (Figure 6.16).

FIGURE 6.16   The Reflect tool flips the shape according to an imaginary axis. The point of origin is a target-like symbol.

4. Place the cursor over the "k" shape and click and drag the cursor to the left, while holding the Shift key.

The "k" will begin to rotate around the point of origin, with the shape always pointing toward the point of origin. Holding the Shift key will constrain the reflection to 45° angles and the Alt or Option keys will allow you to drag a copy.

Shapes can be flipped along a specified axis from the Reflect dialog box. To open the dialog box, choose `Object > Transform > Reflect` (or double-click the Reflect tool).

5. With the "k" shape flipped and still selected, choose the Scale tool (S) from the toolbar (Figure 6.17).

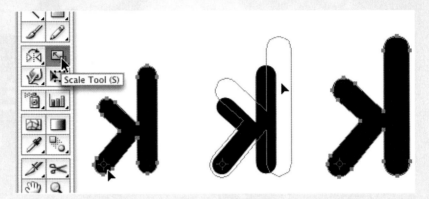

FIGURE 6.17   Here is the location of the Scale tool in the toolbar. Set the point of origin and, using the Shift key, proportionally scale the "k."

6. Set the point of origin to the lower left-hand corner and click on the shape and drag up and to the left, holding the Shift key.

This tool, coupled with the Shift key, scales the shape proportionally. This tool also has a dialog box that can be accessed by double-clicking the tool in the toolbar or selecting `Object > Transform > Scale`.

THE DIRECT SELECTION TOOL: "PULLING" POINTS

With the "k" shape as a path, we can distort the letter by moving some of the points within the image. To elongate the bottom of the stem of the "k" as well as the leg, do the following:

1. Select the Direct Selection tool (A) from the toolbar. Click and drag a marquee around the points in the bottom of the stroke to select them (Figure 6.18).

FIGURE 6.18   Drag a marquee around the bottom of the "k" to select the points on the path. Use the preview lines as a guide for moving the points.

Notice that the points selected are now white and the rest of the points in the path are solid. This is a visual clue that you have points selected.

2. With the Direct Selection Tool, click and drag the points down about .5".

The preview lines show you how the path is going to be changed. Do not release the mouse yet.

3. While dragging down, hold the Shift key to constrain the points' movement horizontally (Figure 6.18). Release the mouse button to place the points.

4. Drag a marquee around the points in the leg of the "k" shape to select them (Figure 6.19). Drag them over to the left and down until they match the new baseline set by the other points.

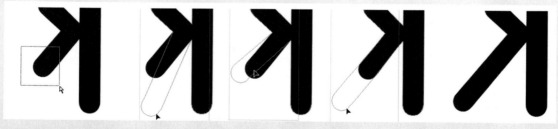

FIGURE 6.19   Drag a marquee around the bottom of the left leg to select the points on the path. Do not use the Shift key when moving these points; trust the preview lines to guide you in keeping the thickness of the stroke the same.

Points can also be moved independently from each other. Using the Shift key, you can select either a single point or multiple points.

CHANGING FILLS AND STROKES USING THE TOOLBAR

The "k" shape has a fill of "black" and a stroke of "none." Fonts, by nature, are filled but contain no stroke. To help you in this exercise, you might want to switch that around and make the fill "none" and the stroke "black."

1. With the "k" shape selected, click on the Swap Fill and Stroke (Shift + X) button in the toolbar (Figure 6.20).

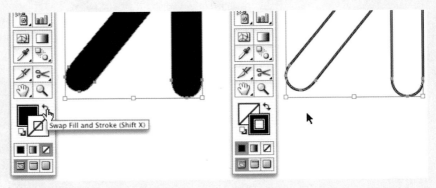

FIGURE 6.20   Use the Swap Fill and Stroke to quickly change the basic attributes of the shapes.

USING THE TRANSFORM TOOLS: ROTATE AND SCALE

In the drawing for the design, the "i" shape is angled to match the top leg of the "k." Using the Rotate tool and its point of origin will be rather helpful.

1. Move the Avante Garde "i" to the left top of the "k." Swap its fill and stroke.
2. With the selected "i" shape at the top of the "k," as pictured in Figure 6.21, select the Rotate tool (R) from the toolbar. It might be nested under the Reflect tool, because they share the same space in the toolbar. Do not move the point of origin.

The Rotate tool acts the same way as the Scale and Reflect tools. It also has its own dialog box that can be accessed by either double-clicking on the tool or selecting `Object > Transform > Rotate`.

3. With the Shift key pressed, rotate the "i" shape 45° counter-clockwise.
4. Select the Scale tool (S) and scale the "i" shape so that it appears to almost touch the top leg of the "k" shape.

Use the Shift key to keep the proportion of the shape during scaling. Watch the preview lines and use them as a guide for placement.

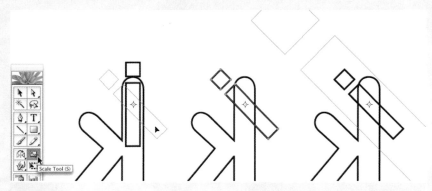

FIGURE 6.21   Move the block shaped "i" over the top of the "k" as shown. Use the Rotate tool with the Shift key to rotate the "i" 45°. Use this image as a guide for scaling the "i."

In the Scale dialog box, there is a setting that affects the shapes that are scaled (Figure 6.22). If this box is checked, a 1-pt line scaled to 400% will become a 4-pt line. If unchecked, the stroke will scale normally. To reset the point size of the line, do so in the Stroke palette.

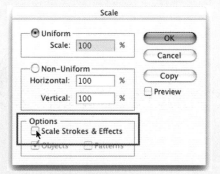

FIGURE 6.22   The Scale Strokes and Effects box determines whether they will transform with the objects. If left unchecked, a shape with a stroke of 3 points is scaled down 50%, the stroke will still be at 3 points. If checked, the stroke would change to 1.5 points.

5. Upon successful scaling, use the Selection tool (V) to move the "i" shape so that it appears in a place similar to that in Figure 6.23.
6. Use the Direct Selection tool (A) to select the square shape that rests above the "i." Delete it by pressing the Delete key.

The dot from the VAG Rounded "i" will be used to replace the dot from the Avante Garde "i."

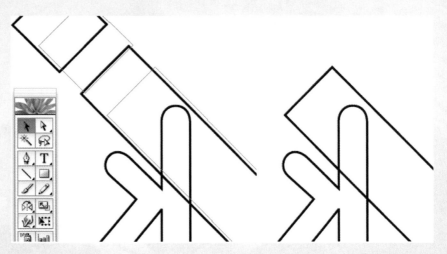

FIGURE 6.23   Position the shape so that it is similar to the image shown. The Direct Selection tool allows you to select objects with groups.

7. Move the second "i" shape next to the other shapes.
8. Use the Direct Selection tool (A) to select and delete the stem of the "i" shape, leaving the round dot.
9. Move the dot so that it is just up and left from the first "i" shape. Scale it so that it appears to be similar to that shown in Figure 6.24.

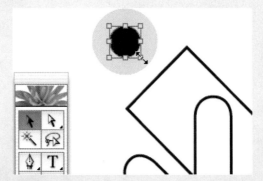

FIGURE 6.24   Scale the dot about 200% and move it to its proper place above the "i."

USING THE PATHFINDER TO DIVIDE SHAPES

To achieve the effect of negative space in the area where the "k" and "i" overlap, use the Pathfinder to divide the two shapes into three.

1. Using the Selection tool (V), select the overlapping "i" and "k" shapes.
2. Open the Pathfinder by selecting `View > Pathfinder`.

3. With the two shapes selected, click on the Divide button of the Pathfinder (Figure 6.25).

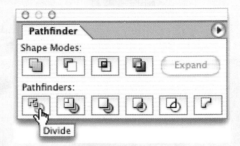

FIGURE 6.25 With the shapes selected, click the Divide button on the Pathfinder.

There are now three shapes that can be filled separately to achieve the desired effect. Because objects that are altered using the Pathfinder are grouped together by default, the Direct Selection tool (A) must be used to select the shapes within the group.

4. Using the Direct Selection tool (A), select the larger part of the "k" shape. Change its fill to "black" and stroke to "none" by clicking on the Swap Fill and Stroke button on the toolbar (Figure 6.26).

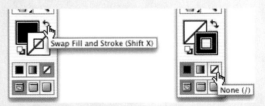

FIGURE 6.26 The Swap Fill and Stroke button switches the attributes of the stroke and fill with each other (left). To remove the stroke from a shape, bring the stroke to the front and click the "None" button (right).

5. Repeat this process for the larger part of the "i" shape.
6. Carefully select the overlapped area. Set the fill and stroke to Default Fill and Stroke (D), by clicking on its button in the lower left of the toolbar. Then select the stroke and set it to "none."

Three letters have been successfully combined into an interesting design.

USING CLIPPING MASKS

To add a better sense of asymmetry and balance, cropping shapes can help to tighten the design. Right now the shapes look like an overlapping "i" and "k." By focusing on a part of the design, we can add a better sense of unity and variety to the design.

Clipping Masks allow us to use shapes to act as a mask, only revealing the area of the image that overlaps.

1. Using guides as a means of visualizing lines, crop the design on the top, left, bottom, and right (Figure 6.27).

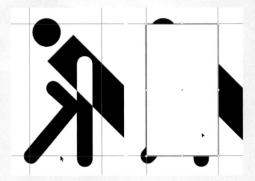

FIGURE 6.27   Use the guides to frame the design (left). Draw a shape to size according to the guides made to frame the image (right).

2. Select the Rectangle tool (M) and draw a shape within the guides. This shape will be the mask.
3. Using the Selection tool (V) select the white shapes, the dot, and the overlapped shape group (Figure 6.28).
4. Right-click on the white shape and choose Make Clipping Mask (Figure 6.28). As an alternative to right-clicking, choose `Object > Clipping Mask > Make` (PC: control + 7; Mac: command + 7).

The white box disappears and only allows the areas that overlap the shape to come through. The integrity of each shape is intact.

5. To polish off the image, draw a box with a fill of "none" and a stroke of "black" to act as a border around the image.

Copy and paste the design to another part of the document and invert the fills to get another perspective on the design (Figure 6.29). Also rotate and reflect the image and see the design changed for the better.

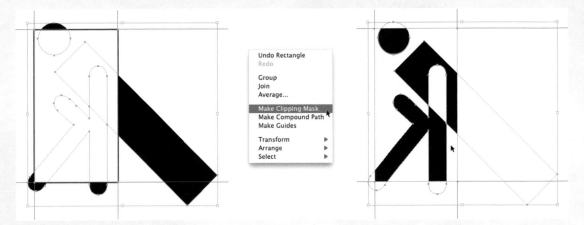

FIGURE 6.28 Select all the shapes that will be affected by the mask (left). Select Make Clipping Mask from the pop-up menu (middle) or from the Object menu at the top. The top shape creates a "window" or mask for the other shapes to show through (right).

FIGURE 6.29 Create an inverted copy of the image to get another perspective on the design.

SUMMARY

Letterforms are the most common visual element used to communicate a message. Unfortunately, to most of the public, they are not associated with design. The written word is everywhere and the visual quality of words usually ignored. Designers should make a special effort to see the design potential of letterforms. When you watch television or go to the movies notice the type used for the titles or credits. Do the shapes and spacing fit the mood of the show? If you go shopping take a closer look at labels and packaging. Notice the type and the way it is used with other design elements. Is the type appropriate to the contents or cost of the product? Study the type selected for publications. Is it functional and does it visually represent the editorial content or information? This assignment was designed to introduce you to letterforms as design elements and to expand the principles of design to include other non-objective shapes. There is another project later in this book that deals with letterforms as design elements. It will expand the element of type to include value and color.

DESIGN PROJECT THREE: FIGURE ABSTRACTION AND NON-OBJECTIVE SHAPE

INTRODUCTION AND THE BASIC PROBLEM DEFINED

Design Project Three consists of five separate sequential designs beginning with a symmetrical, closed form abstraction of a human figure and ending with an open form, asymmetrically balanced non-objective shape. Details of this project will be discussed in the "Conceptual Process" portion of this chapter. Figures 7.1 to 7.3 are a few examples of this project.

This project incorporates all the design concepts and digital skills acquired in the previous projects. It will introduce and expand on four design principles and explore new digital drawing techniques and procedures. The four principles that will be the focus of this chapter are: (1) abstraction, (2) sequence and continuity, (3) discovering the relationship between abstract and non-objective shapes, and (4) open and closed form.

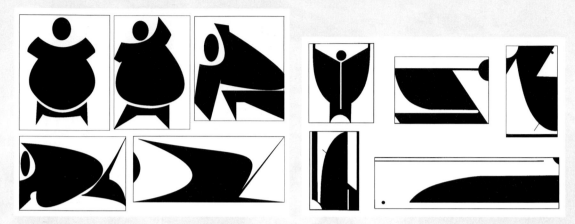

FIGURES 7.1

FIGURES 7.2

FIGURES 7.1–7.3   Examples of Design Project Three: Figure Abstraction and Non-Objective Shape. *Figure Abstraction 1* © 2003. Reprinted with permission from Tiffany Galbaldon. *Figure Abstraction 2* © 2003. Reprinted with permission from Michael W. Smith. *Figure Abstraction 3* © 2003. Reprinted with permission from Meliza Aaron.

FIGURES 7.3

CONTENT

Background

Abstraction

Abstraction is the process of reducing natural shapes down to their simplest form. As mentioned in Chapter 2, it is part of the design process directly related to trademarks and other communication visuals such as

FIGURE 7.4 Examples of abstraction. *Genesis* © 2003. Reprinted with permission from Jim Godfrey. *Red Hawk, Ed-Net, Two Dogs* © 2003. Reprinted with permission from Patrick Wilkey, *www.visiocommunications.com.*

posters, packages, and illustrations, to name a few. Figure 7.4 shows a few examples of abstraction used as trademarks and symbols.

Sequence and Continuity

A sequence as it relates to visual design is a series of images organized in a specific order. Continuity, also detailed in Chapter 2, is the idea that something is carried over or connected to another element. The project in this chapter consists of a sequence of five images designed with continuity. Sequence and continuity are a necessary part of understanding animation, motion graphics, corporate identities, layout design, and the integration of the many parts associated with architecture and interior design. Figure 7.5 is an example of an animation sequence that combines still photography and computer-generated animation. Figure 7.6 is an example of abstract symbols for a university Web site and an animated sequence of two of these symbols.

The Relationship Between Abstract and Non-Objective Shapes

Because each of the five images created for this project are designed in sequence with continuity, they naturally establish a relationship between the first abstract figure design and the non-objective last design. Refer

FIGURE 7.5 Example of a series of stills taken from an animation that combined still photography and computer-generated graphics. *Selected frames from "American Sansei" animation* © 2003. Reprinted with permission from Alan Hashimoto.

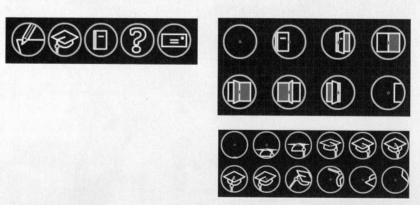

FIGURE 7.6 Example of five abstracted symbols located on the left. These pictographs were for a university Web site. Two of the five symbols use animation for communicating and entertainment. *Pictographs* © 2003. Reprinted with permission from Mike Clayton.

again to Figures 7.1 through 7.3. This process should point out that non-objective shapes can communicate emotions and information without using a recognizable object.

Closed and Open Form

Closed form refers to a composition or design that feels as if an entire scene is in view within a picture frame. There is a feeling of enclosure with a distinct focal point that all the other elements are centered around. Closed form usually suggests a more classic or formal balance. The first of five images that begins this chapter's project should be closed form.

Open form is a composition or design that feels as if a scene were cropped and one is able to view only a portion of it. Contrary to closed form, there is a feeling of expansiveness with elements that seem to extend beyond the picture frame. Open form feels less formal and is usually asymmetrically balanced. The last of the five images should be an open form composition. Figure 7.7 is an example of two scenes from an animation that exemplifies closed form on the left and open form on the right.

 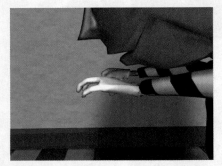

FIGURE 7.7   These images are stills taken from an animated sequence. Selected frames from the animation *"The Mime"* © 2003. Reprinted with permission from Nathan Tufts.

Conceptual Process

The following will help you to create five separate sequential designs: from a symmetrical, closed form abstraction of a human figure to an open form, asymmetrically balanced non-objective shape.

Design One: Figure Abstraction

This is the most important design because it is the foundation for the other four. More attention will be given to this part of the conceptual process.

Study the characteristics of a human figure. Divide the figure into 3 to 5 simple symmetrical shapes and stylize these shapes through the use of unity and variety. Unity may be achieved by making sure the shapes are related in some way. Placing a variety of contrasting shapes and weights next to each other will give the figure interest. The negative space is also being designed so be sure to indicate a picture frame. In Figure 7.8, using three abstract figure designs, three diagrams of each design will detail what gives these shapes harmony, variety, and contrast. The three designs as they appear in the sequence are located on the top line. The second three images as you look down the series indicate what kinds of shapes give the entire design harmony. The first design on the second line illustrates harmony by using vertical shapes, the second design horizontal shapes, and the third design similar diagonals. The third row down also illustrates harmony through the use of curves, half circles, and circles. When used in conjunction with the second row's vertical, horizontal, and diagonal shapes, contrast and variety are the result. Notice how each rounded shape is a different size, which adds to the variety of the designs. The last row of designs indicates other contrasting shapes that will give variety and contrast to the designs.

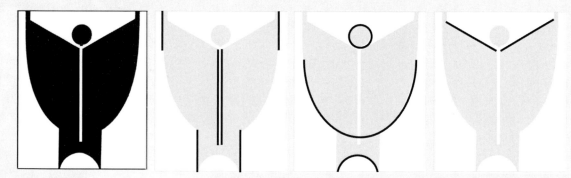

FIGURE 7.8   Using three abstract figure designs, three diagrams of each design will detail what gives these shapes harmony, variety, and contrast.

Notice how all the shapes are different weights. They also use alternating round shapes contrasted by flat or sharp shapes. Both of these ideas give variety to the entire design.

This next series of images details one way you could begin your first design and points out how variety and unity are achieved throughout the design. These shapes could be drawn traditionally but have been presented here digitally so the shapes are very clear and easy to understand (see Figure 7.9). Beginning with the design at the upper left, harmonious shapes are balanced throughout this first design by a variety of weights and distances (space) between them. Next, the middle top design shows how thin vertical shapes that are different lengths and widths unify these shapes. Unity is maintained by the line direction of the new shapes with different lengths and weights, establishing variety. The upper-right shape contrasts the flatness of the previous shapes by alternating round sides of each shape for variety. The lengths are slightly adjusted to ensure that all the shapes relate to one another. The lower-left shape adds some diagonals. Each diagonal is different but they all create shapes that show a firm base to help relieve the tension of the previous round shapes. The lower-middle design re-introduces new vertical shapes to create arms and legs. These verticals are evenly distributed throughout the design; the shape that creates the legs repeats the flat horizontal and vertical sides to create a relationship with the other horizontal and vertical shapes. The last design adds a few accents that are smaller, repeated shapes which maintain harmony throughout the design. Notice how adjustments to the neck shape help it become more related to the other shapes.

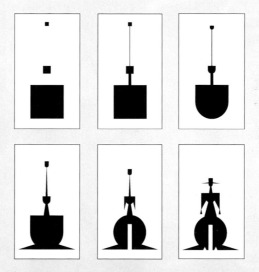

FIGURE 7.9   This series of images details one way you could begin your first design and points out how variety and unity are achieved throughout the design.

The concept of abstracted and stylized figures can be seen in many forms of design. Two examples are illustrated in Figures 7.10 and 7.11. These images are a series of stills taken from computer-generated animations.

FIGURE 7.10   Notice the variety of weights of shapes that give the figure a feeling of power. The sharpness of all the shapes gives the feeling of protection and aggression and also helps harmonize all the parts of the figure creating unity. *Character Animation Study* © 2003. Reprinted with permission from Nathan Tufts.

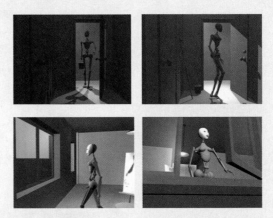

FIGURE 7.11   Notice the variety of lengths and weights of shapes that give interest and expression and how they are unified by the similarity of the round shapes found in the head and joints of the robot. These shapes are in contrast to the long, sharp shapes of the limbs. *Selected frames from the animation "The Painter"* © 2003. Reprinted with permission from Chad Griffiths.

Designs Two, Three, and Four: Sequential Designs

Each shape in this sequence should have the same amount of change or manipulation from design to design. Starting with a change from Design One, the abstract figure, Design Two would show the same degree of change leading to Design Three, and Design Three the same amount of change to Design Four, leading to the final design. Each of these designs does not have to resemble a figure; they are merely steps toward the fifth and final design. Each composition should be well thought-out and should follow the principles of any good design, some of which are unity, variety, and balance.

If the degree of change is similar, the entire project will have continuity and harmony. Through a calculated series of changes, a natural progression of shapes will illustrate an evolution and a relationship between an abstract recognizable figure and non-objective shapes. Review Figures 7.1 to 7.3 and notice the subtle changes between each design. Look again at just the beginning and ending designs. The first design, which is closed form, is significantly different than the final open form design. This exercise demonstrates how two apparently opposite types of compositions can still be related.

Design Five: Asymmetrical Non-Objective Design

This final design ends the sequence. It should be the result of a logical and well-paced series of designs leading from an abstract human figure to an interesting, unified, and asymmetrically balanced non-objective composition. They are similar to Projects One and Two in this book. This last design and possibly Designs Two, Three, and Four should follow most of the suggestions in the "Conceptual Process" sections located in Chapters 5 and 6.

All Five Designs: Conceptual Process

For most design solutions, the best way to begin the visualization process is by using traditional tools such as a pen or pencil to create approximations of design solutions. Many roughs should be explored to make sure all the alternatives have been explored. Narrow the choices down to the ones that best meet the criteria, and begin the process of producing an accurate representation of your sketches (Figures 7.12, 7.13, and 7.14).

FIGURE 7.12   Begin this project with several thumbnail sketches of Design One (five-shape figure). Next, narrow down these thumbnails to just one sketch that will be the starting point for the next four designs.

FIGURE 7.13   Create thumbnails for the sequence from abstract figure to non-objective shape. Narrow these down to the best ones and combine all the designs into one composition.

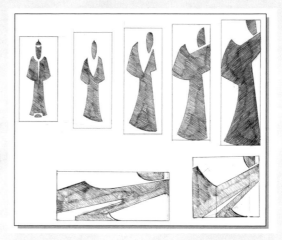

FIGURE 7.14   After all the alternatives have been tested, settle on the best designs and begin the digital production process.

TUTORIAL   DIGITAL PRODUCTION PROCESS

PREPARING YOUR PROJECT

As in past projects, begin by scanning the sequence of designs. These scans need to be only 72 ppi and grayscale. If all the drawings are on one sheet (as in Figure 7.14), scan the entire sheet. If not, scan the images one at a time, cropping them as needed.

After the images are scanned, create a new document and save it as "Figure Abstraction." If the scan you are using is wider than it is tall, you may want to change the orientation of the page in the Layout View. If so, then in the New Document dialog box set the Orientation of the page to Landscape (Figure 7.15). Changing the orientation to landscape rotates the page 90°, making the page display so that the width is longer than the height.

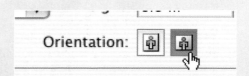

FIGURE 7.15   Because the scan in the example is wider than it is tall, it would be ideal to change the Orientation of the page to Landscape.

The new document is displayed in Landscape mode in the work area. Also displayed is a faint dotted line, with a $^1/_2$" inset all the way around the page. This is the area of the page that the printer will print. Anything not contained within that boundary will not be printed.

You can "hide" the lines by selecting View > Hide Page Tiling. To show the page tiling if it is hidden, choose View > Show Page Tiling.

Place the scan on the work area by selecting File > Place as you have done in previous exercises. This image will automatically center in the document area. If you need to scale the image to fit, or import more than one image, do so now and arrange them on the page.

With the Layers palette visible, double-click "Layer 1" to set its **options** (Figure 7.16). Name the layer "Drawings" and check the Lock and the Dim Images to boxes. The layer will be locked and the images dimmed to the specified percentage. Uncheck the Print box so that the images will not display when printed.

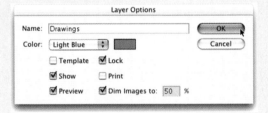

FIGURE 7.16   Set the layer's properties in the Layer Option dialog box.

Create a new layer by either clicking on the Create New Layer icon in the Layers palette or choose New Layer from the pop-up menu.

Double-click the new layer and, in the Layer Option dialog box, name the layer "Tracings."

View the entire page in the screen by choosing View > Fit in Window (PC: control + 1; Mac: command + 1). You can also view the page at actual size by selecting View > Actual Size (PC: control + 2; Mac: command + 2).

With the Zoom tool (Z), click and drag a marquee around the first step of the figure abstraction drawings as shown in Figure 7.17. Then release the mouse. The area selected zooms in to fill the screen. If you have gone too far, with the Zoom tool (Z) selected, hold down the Alt key (PC) or Option key (Mac) and the "+" sign in the cursor will turn into a "-" sign allowing you to zoom out. Use the aforementioned shortcuts for fitting the page to the window if you need to start over.

FIGURE 7.17   Use the Zoom tool to zoom in on a specific area.

TRACE AND CREATE THE FIRST FIGURE

Using tools and techniques that have been covered previously, trace the drawings to create the designs.

There are two different methods of completing this project.

In the description of the project you were told to create a figure and then draw three intermediary designs before you reach the final non-objective design. Drawing each step on paper helps to keep a balance and order to what you are doing from start to finish. Visualizing each step helps you to work out the kinks that may occur as you make the transitions from one shape to the next. Then, in Illustrator, all you would have to do is trace each of the drawings, the real work having already been completed on paper.

However, while it is ideal to work out your designs on paper, you can create the first figure and then use that design to create the variations or steps toward that final design. This allows you to use the computer to create the intermediary steps in the design.

For this first section, we will focus on tracing the drawn images.

Part of the description of the project stated to create a *symmetrically balanced figure*. Because the figure is symmetrical, it is the same on both sides. Using the tools you have already learned, this will be simple. With a little forethought, you might realize that all you have to do to the initial figure is draw one side and then flip and join it. The following steps will help you in this process.

USING THE PEN AND CONVERT ANCHOR POINT TOOLS

With the Pen tool (P) selected in the Tool palette, set the fill to "none" and the
stroke to "black."

View your rulers by selecting `View > Show Rulers` (PC: control + R; Mac: command + R). Drag a vertical guide from the left and place it right in the center of your scan, bisecting the symmetrical figure.

In Figure 7.18, for example, the Pen tool (P) was used to draw from the inside of
the robe and then points were placed, and handles were pulled as needed
to create the left side of the main shape of the figure. The path should not
be closed.

Using the Zoom tool (Z), focus on the lower-left corner of the robe.

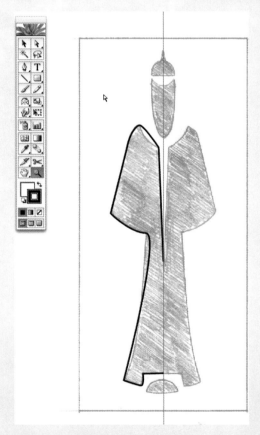

FIGURE 7.18   Using the Pen tool to draw the left
side of the robe.

The corner of the robe is a right angle with no handles to pull. It is called a *corner point*. Using a tool called the Convert Anchor Point tool (Shift + C), you can change a "handle-less" corner point to a point with handles, which is called a *smooth point*.

The polygon shape in Figure 7.19 has four corner points. With the Convert Anchor Point tool, click on a *corner point* and pull out handles to make it a *smooth point*.

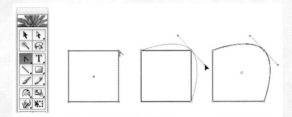

FIGURE 7.19   Using the Convert Anchor Point tool, you can change a corner point to a smooth point.

Likewise, the shape in Figure 7.20 has four smooth points with handles. The Convert Anchor Point tool helps you to remove the handles and make it a corner point.

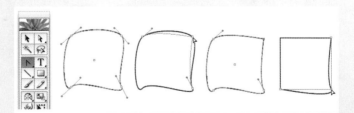

FIGURE 7.20   Using the Convert Anchor Point tool, you can change a smooth point to a corner point.

Select the Covert Anchor Point tool (Shift + C). This tool is part of the Pen tool set. To select the tool, click and hold on the Pen tool until the subset opens. Then select the fourth tool that looks like an open right angle (Figure 7.21). This is the Convert Anchor Point tool.
With the Covert Anchor Point tool selected, click and drag on the corner point to change it to a smooth point with handles (Figure 7.22).

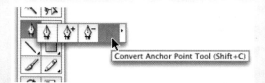

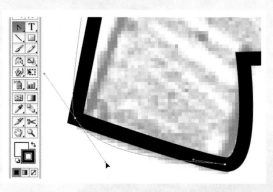

FIGURE 7.21 The Convert Anchor Point tool is hidden in the Pen tool subset.

FIGURE 7.22 Use the Convert Anchor Point tool to change the corner point to a smooth point.

Using the Direct Select tool (A) in cooperation with its proper modifier key (PC: Alt; Mac: Option), move each of the handles independently to create the correct curve for each line (Figure 7.23).

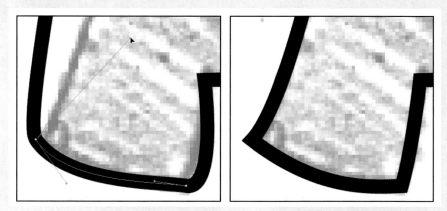

FIGURE 7.23 Fix the corner of the robe by using the Direct Selection tool to modify the handles independently.

View the page at actual size by selecting `View > Actual Size` (PC: control + 2; Mac: command + 2).

USING THE REFLECT TOOL AND "JOINING" POINTS

Now that the first line segment has been created, we can use the Reflect tool (O) to copy and flip the line. Then we will make the two line segments become one closed path.

With the Selection tool (V), select the line that was just created.
Select the Reflect tool (O) from the first transform subset under the Rotate tool
(Figure 7.24).

FIGURE 7.24   The location
of the Reflect tool.

Move the Point of Origin (the target icon) to the center guide by mousing over
the target-like symbol and click-and-dragging it (Figure 7.25). This will be
the axis at which the line will reflect.

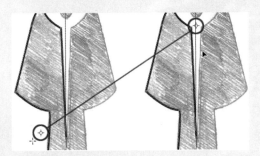

FIGURE 7.25   Move the point of origin to the center
guide. This is the axis at which the line will reflect.

After the point of origin is placed, move the mouse over to the left of the guide
and press and hold the Shift and Alt key (PC) or Shift and Option key (Mac).
A double arrow icon will appear. Drag the cursor to the right and the line
will copy and reflect over the point of origin. Release the mouse, then the
modifier keys. The reflected line appears.
As shown in Figure 7.26, use the Direct Selection tool (A) to drag a marquee
around the top end points at the base of the robe (or any two points that
are near each other). The Direct Selection tool allows you to select points
within a line. This allows you to select two points even though they are on
two different paths.
With the two points selected, choose Object > Path > Join (PC: control + J;
Mac: command + J) from the top.

FIGURE 7.26 Select both of the points as shown using the Direct Selection tool.

If the Join dialog box appears, there are two options to choose from (Figure 7.27). If you want the new point to be a corner point, click the Corner box. If you want the new point to be a smooth point, check Smooth. In this case, check Corner. Click OK.

 If the dialog box does not appear, then the two points selected were not right on top of each other. A straight line is created to join the paths and you must manually fix the curves.

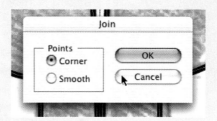

FIGURE 7.27 Select "Corner" from the Join dialog box.

Using the same steps, select and join the two points at the bottom of the robe as well. This action closes the path.

With the Selection tool (V), choose the robe shape and fill it with black.

USING THE PATHFINDER

The last three shapes that make up this figure are the face, hat, and feet. Using the Pathfinder palette will make quick work of this.

If the Pathfinder is not visible choose `Window > Pathfinder`.

Center the area of the head and hat on the screen using the Zoom tool (Z) or the scroll bars.

Select the Ellipse tool (L) from the Tools palette. It may be hidden under the Rectangle tool. Set the fill to "none."

For a bit of quick review, if you hold down the Shift key while drawing a shape, it will be constrained proportionally to a 1:1 ratio. A rectangle will become a square and an ellipse, a circle.

If you hold down the Alt key (PC) or the Option key (Mac), the shape will draw from the center out.

If you hold down both modifier keys, the shape will draw from the center out proportionally.

With the Ellipse tool, draw an ellipse for the head. Use the Alt key (PC) or the Option key (Mac) to draw from the center out from the guide to center the shape (Figure 7.28). Draw a second shape as shown in Figure 7.28 as the "subtraction" area from the first shape.

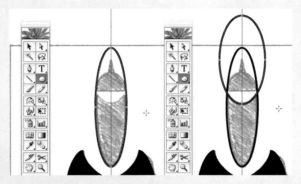

FIGURE 7.28   Draw an ellipse from the center out as shown. Then draw the second shape as shown on the right.

Select both shapes and click on the Subtract from Shape Area button (top row, second button) to subtract the area of the second shape from the first (Figure 7.29). Click on the Expand button to convert it to one shape. Fill the shape with black.

Use an ellipse and a rectangle to create the primary shape for the hat. Use the Subtract from Shape Area and the Expand buttons to create the semicircle (Figure 7.30).

Select the Polygon tool from the Rectangle tool subset.

Click once near the hat shape to open the Polygon dialog box (Figure 7.31). In the dialog box you can set two options: 1) the radius of the shape and 2) the number of sides. To create a triangle, enter 0.25 in the Radius field and 3 in the Sides field. Click OK.

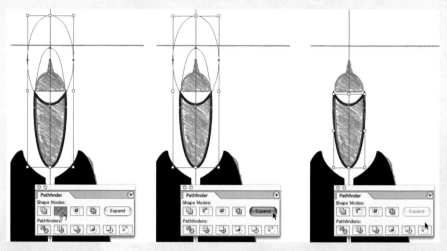

FIGURE 7.29 Use the shape on top to subtract from the area underneath, use the Expand button to make one shape and then fill it with black.

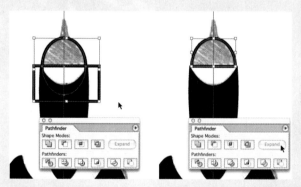

FIGURE 7.30 Draw a circle and then a rectangle as shown to create the basic form of the hat.

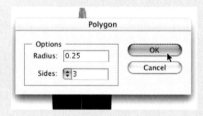

FIGURE 7.31 The Polygon dialog box.

Simply resize the triangle to the proper shape. There is no need to hold down the Shift key to keep it proportional because we need it to be a spike for the hat. Once resized, position it over the top of hat so that it overlaps (Figure 7.32).

Select both the hat shape and the triangle. Click on the Add to Shape Area button (top row; first button) to add the areas of the shapes together (Figure 7.33). Then fill with black.

Select the Hand tool (H) from the Tools palette or hold down the spacebar to temporarily activate it. Click and drag up in the document area to scroll the page down to the feet area.

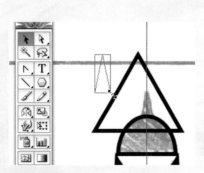 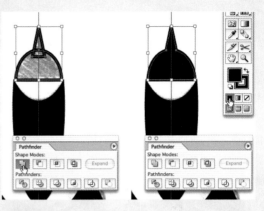

FIGURE 7.32 Scale the triangle accordingly and overlap the shape at the top of the hat.

FIGURE 7.33   Add the areas of the two shapes together using the Pathfinder and fill the resulting shape with black.

Draw two ellipses similar to the ones in Figure 7.34. With both shapes selected, click on the Intersect Shape Areas button (top row; third button) to intersect the shape and leave behind the foot shape. Click the Expand button and fill the shape with black.

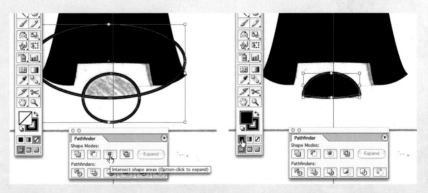

FIGURE 7.34   Use two ellipses and the Intersect Shape Areas button in the Pathfinder to create the feet shape (left) and fill with black (right).

Select `View > Actual Size` to see the completed first figure.

Select all four shapes and set their strokes to "none" for the best effect.

From the top menu choose `File > Print`. The result is the figure minus the scanned image and guide (Figure 7.35).

Select `File > Save` to save the current document.

FIGURE 7.35 Print the document to see the completed shapes sans drawing and guides.

USING GROUP/UNGROUP

To finalize our first figure, let's group the four shapes together.

Select all the shapes with the Selection tool (V).
Choose `Object > Group` (PC: control + G; Mac: command + G) from the top menu to group the shapes together.
Now that the shapes are grouped into one item, use the Select tool (V) to move the group around or the Direct Selection tool (A) to select a shape within the group.

MODIFY THE FIGURE: MOVING POINTS AND HANDLES

If you wish to continue with the project by simply tracing each drawing, please continue to the "Using the Clipping Mask" section following this one.

If you wish to use the tools within Illustrator to help you experiment with new shapes and steps to your final design continue with this section.

By duplicating the first tracing you can keep the original intact while experimenting with the copy.

With the group selected, choose `Edit > Copy` (PC: control + C; Mac: command + C) to temporarily store the group into the clipboard's memory.
Select `Edit > Paste` (PC: control + V; Mac: command + V) to paste a copy of the group into the document. Paste as many copies of the figure as you would like to experiment with.

Select the second group and choose `Object > Ungroup` (PC: control + shift + G; Mac: command + shift + G) to ungroup the shapes.

Using the tools that we have already discussed, modify the points and curves of the shapes so that they create other interesting shapes. Add points, subtract points, or delete unnecessary shapes. In Figure 7.36 there are a few examples of simple variations from the first figure.

FIGURE 7.36   Variations of the first figure created by simply modifying curves and points.

When you have achieved an acceptable second step in the figure, group the shapes, copy and paste, and then ungroup them and start on the third step. Then the fourth. Then the fifth. And so on until you have created the five figures (Figure 7.37).

FIGURE 7.37   The final five figures created from experimenting with the tools.

USING THE CLIPPING MASK

Whether you traced all five drawings (Figure 7.37) or created them within the software (Figure 7.38), use clipping masks (as seen in the previous chapter) to crop the shapes.

FIGURE 7.38   The final five figures traced from the drawings.

In Chapter 6, clipping masks were used to give the design a better sense of asymmetry and balance. Using them here will also add to the design. In Figure 7.39, the rectangle is used to "crop" the area of the organic shape. Another rectangle is placed over the top of the resulting shape to help enclose or *trap* the design. The same process will be done with each of the five shapes you created.

FIGURE 7.39   An example of using the Clipping Mask in Illustrator.

Draw a rectangle over the desired shape (Figure 7.40) with the Rectangle tool (M).

Copy that rectangle to the clipboard (PC: control + C; Mac: command + C) so that it can be applied later as a border to the image.

Select the group of shapes and the rectangle.

Choose `Object > Clipping Mask > Make` (PC: control + 7; Mac: command + 7) to make the mask.

FIGURE 7.40 Draw a rectangle to act as the border and clipped area.

From the Edit menu choose `Edit > Paste in Front` (PC: control + F; Mac: command + F) to paste a copy of the rectangle directly on top of the clipped area. Set the fill to "none" and the stroke to black.

Group the clipped area and the rectangle border by selecting them and choosing `Object > Group` (PC: control + G; Mac: command + G). By grouping them together now, they can be moved easily in later steps. Figure 7.41 shows the final result.

FIGURE 7.41 The final figure abstraction with the clipping mask and the border.

Repeat this process for all the other shapes. If the shape does not require a clipping mask, outlining it with a rectangle will do just fine.

Save your progress.

PRINTING THE FINAL FILE

In order to give the best possible presentation, you will need to arrange the five designs on the page before printing them out.

Remember the dotted line border at the beginning of the tutorial? It showed us where the printable area of the document was. We will use it as a guide for placing the figures.

Turn the Page Tiling Preview back on by choosing `View > Show Page Tiling`. Arrange the figure abstractions within the dotted line area. Scale them down if necessary to make room for all of them (Figure 7.42).

Choose `File > Print` to print the page. Because the Print box on the "Drawings" layer is unchecked, only the contents of the "Tracings" layer will print.

 If you would like to print one design at a time, simply move the other designs out onto the pasteboard area outside of the Page Tiling Preview and print the one design.

Save your file and close it.

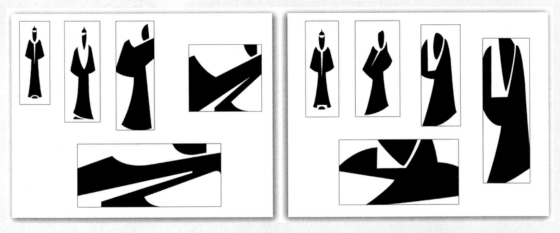

FIGURE 7.42   The final result for each option on the first figure tracing. Left: *Figure Abstraction* © 2003. Reprinted with permission from Mark Hyatt. Right: *Figure Abstraction* © 2003. Reprinted with permission from Mike Clayton.

SUMMARY

The fierce competition for audience attention is accelerating every day. The huge amount of visual and textual material being thrown at the population is being delivered through a never-ending supply of new media and formats for electronic communications. Everyone's attention span and tolerance for viewing images and deciphering messages is getting shorter.

Designers must be aware of and incorporate abstraction as a big part of the communication process. Abstraction is the idea of reducing something down to its simplest form. It makes information easier and quicker to read and understand. Trademarks, symbols, posters, packaging, media introduction motion graphics, movie previews, television commercials, Web graphics, music, headlines, titles, and advertising of any kind are just a few examples.

The next time you go to the store notice how many labels, trademarks, packages, posters, and signs that flash by you in a single short trip. If you are very perceptive and a quick counter, you will see that it could be in the hundreds or thousands.

Other important points of this chapter are the relationships of non-objective shapes to expressive abstract shapes, continuity and sequence, and open and closed form.

Understanding how to make non-objective shapes relate to one another in interesting ways is vital to any designer. The remaining projects in this book deal with shapes that do not necessarily represent anything in particular but are designed to create recognizable objects and non-objective designs that communicate a concept or idea.

Successful use of continuity and sequence can also be easily noticed in music, narrative storytelling, and in motion pictures. Can you think of a movie, novel, or concert you have recently attended where the continuity or sequence was improperly handled? When any work of art is void of continuity it will seem disjointed and disconnected. If a sequence is not properly put in the correct order, confusion is usually the result. This is the same for visual design.

Open and closed form compositions have very different results, even when the subject matter, values, colors, textures, and shapes are the same. Try to use a closed form composition as an option for each of the following four projects in this book. Try to use an open form solution for each project. Notice how differently you have to think when you change from designing closed to open form compositions and visa versa. This may be why most artists and designers have chosen one or the other to create their masterpieces. Which way do you prefer to design? Why?

Design Project Four: Value

Introduction and the Basic Problem Defined

As defined in Chapter 1, value describes light and dark. It is dependent on light, without which value does not exist. Light permits us to see the contrast of values that make up shape and form.

Value and its relationship to shape and design principles are the main topics of this chapter. Project Four is a design exercise that uses the shapes of value found in a photograph. Through the processes of distortion, stylization, and abstraction the result will be an interesting, harmonious, and unique design. By closely studying the lights and darks of a photograph, it is possible to see the differences in these values and create shapes.

Similar to previous assignments, an object-oriented program will be used to complete this project. New ideas concerning value, masking, layers, swatches, and other imaging techniques and tools will be introduced. Figure 8.1 shows several examples of this project.

FIGURE 8.1   Examples of the value project. Top left: *Value Design* © 2003. Reprinted with permission from Charlotte Pages. Top center: *Value Design* © 2003. Reprinted with permission from Cantu Logan. Top Left: *Value Design* © 2003. Reprinted with permission from Audrey Gould. Bottom left: *Value Design* © 2003. Reprinted with permission from Jonathan Harrison. Bottom center: *Value Design* © 2003. Reprinted with permission from Fon Ulrich. Bottom right: *Value Design* © 2003. Reprinted with permission from David Cahoon.

CONTENT

Background

Characteristics of Value

Looking back at Chapter 1, value is defined. The basic characteristics of value and how it is used in visual design is discussed in Chapter 2. The following is a brief review of the characteristics of value as a design element.

Extreme contrast of values in a design gives a sense of clarity and depth. Similar values may give a sense of subtlety and shallowness.

When values are very light the term *high key* is used. Lighter values suggest a brighter, happier mood. Conversely, values that are dark are called *low key*. They usually feel somber and serious.

Value is also used to describe volume two-dimensionally by imitating the way light reveals a form or object. The lightest values are in the direct line of light whereas the darker values are in shadow.

Figure 8.2 is a good example of the variety of characteristics and principles associated with value. It is very rare that you will find such a wide range of value examples in one composition. This painting/drawing is successful in creating a design that unifies these very different uses of value. The skull on the left contains values that are highly contrasted. There is a sense of depth and clarity. An arm located just below the skull feels somber because the values are very close. The profile at the right of the skull is a good example of values that are primarily dark and low key. The value of the area around the hands near the bottom of this composition uses very light values, or high key values.

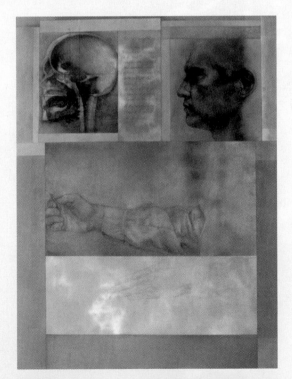

FIGURE 8.2 Example of a work of art that incorporates almost every characteristic of value. *Vanitas: Sensus Communis* © 2003. Reprinted with permission from Adrian Van Suchtelen.

Asymmetrical Balance Using Value

Achieving asymmetrical balance using shape is very literal; the larger the shape, the heavier it will seem. By using an invisible fulcrum or center point a large shape may be balanced by a smaller shape. This is accomplished by moving the fulcrum and shifting the smaller shape closer to the edge and the larger shape closer to the fulcrum on middle of the composition. (Refer back to Figure 2.41 in Chapter 2).

Value can asymmetrically balance compositions through the use of contrast. The more contrast of value between a shape and the background, the more visual weight it will have, relative to the size of the shape. This means both the size and value of a shape should be considered when asymmetrically balancing a design. Figure 8.3 is a simple diagram that details this concept. The example on the left shows two shapes that are the same value and same weight. The same shapes are found in the example directly to the right, but the shape at the left is a lighter value. Notice how much heavier the shape at the right feels. The two examples at the right deal with balance and the value of colors. The two red shapes in the example in the middle right are evenly balanced. The example on the right shows how a color that is light in value (yellow) seems to visually weigh less than the red shape of the same size on the right.

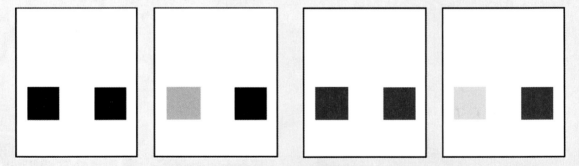

FIGURE 8.3   Both the size and value of a shape should be considered when asymmetrically balancing a design.

Designing with Value

Value becomes visual only when it is used in conjunction with a shape or form. When designing with value it is obvious you are also designing with shape. All the principles related to shape apply to compositions that use value. The one principle that requires special attention is that each individual value must be evenly balanced throughout a design; these values must be designed in regard to visual hierarchy. This means that if you basically have three values that make up your design, one value must visually weigh more than the other two, and one of the remaining two must visually weigh more than the other. This is an example of visual hierarchy using value. In addition to this idea of hierarchy, each value must be visually balanced throughout the composition. If a value or many values are used only in one area of a composition and not distributed throughout the design, it is similar to using only square shapes on one side of a design and only round shapes on the opposite side. The result is a lack of unity.

To summarize this concept in terms of the universal principles of harmony and variety, values must be used with regard to visual hierarchy for variety and must be evenly balanced throughout the composition, for unity. Figures 8.4 and 8.5 are examples of this concept. Notice how each value is evenly distributed throughout the compositions and each value is used in different visual weights.

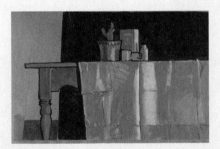 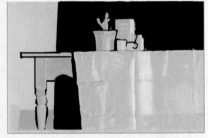

FIGURE 8.4   Example of a painting where the basic values have been separated out and illustrated by darker values to clearly show the distribution. The top-left image is the original painting. The image to the right isolates the darkest values. The bottom-left image has isolated the lightest values and shows them against darker shapes. The bottom-right image shows the middle values. *Cactus* © 2003. Reprinted with permission from Chris Terry.

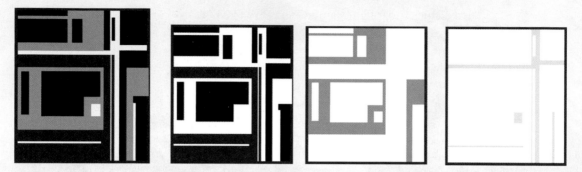

FIGURE 8.5   Example of a non-objective design that, similar to Figure 8.6, isolates each value to illustrate the concept that successful designs using value should be evenly balanced and that each value distributed with regard to visual hierarchy. The larger design on the left is the complete design. The three designs on the right show the distribution of isolated values. *Intersection* © 2003. Reprinted with permission from Alan Hashimoto.

Value and Design Using Photography

The following photographic examples (Figures 8.6 through 8.8) emphasize shape and value as the main focus. Visual hierarchy, unity of shapes, dynamic line direction, and well-defined values are all part of this gallery of well-designed photographs.

FIGURE 8.6   Example of a photograph using high contrast, vertical line direction, and isolated well-designed shapes for drama and dynamics. *Line Men, Colorado* © 2003. Reprinted with permission from PatrickConePhotography.com.

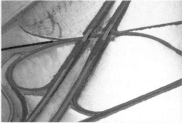

FIGURE 8.7   Example of a photograph that uses the shape of roads as a design element. Notice how you can analyze the unity and variety of the shapes using the lesson of past chapters dealing with non-objective shapes. *Great Salt Lake - Aerial, Utah* © 2003. Reprinted with permission from PatrickConePhotography.com.

FIGURE 8.8   Example of a photograph that shows well-designed shapes revealed by a single light source. *Centenarian's Hands* © 2003. Reprinted with permission from PatrickConePhotography.com.

Value and Depth

Another property of value is its use in creating the illusion of depth or distance. The simple designs in Figure 8.9 illustrate several interesting points related to this idea. The simple design on the left is made up of shapes that are the same value. The second design on the right shows how contrasting values creates the illusion that things are closer. The shapes on the right of the black shape are closer in value to the white background so they seem to recede. The black background of the next design to the right shows that the white shape seems closer because it has more contrast than the other two shapes. The right design is an example of value and color. Notice how the darker value color seems closer.

Figure 8.10 is a photograph illustrating depth. Notice how the horizontal line direction gives a sense of openness. Take a close look at the dark figure delicately balanced by a small dark shape on the far right.

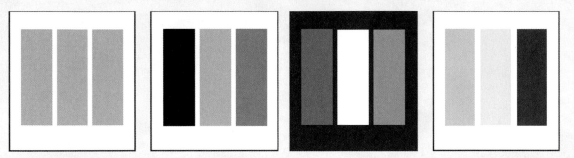

FIGURE 8.9 Value is useful in creating the illusion of depth or distance.

FIGURE 8.10 Photograph showing depth. *Woman on Salt Flats, Utah* © 2003. Reprinted with permission from PatrickConePhotography.com.

Conceptual Process

Now that you are more familiar with the digital tools and techniques of the production process, and because the general conceptual process is not such a mystery, there will be more overlapping of these two ideas. Your familiarity with the basics of the computer and related software should help you find more alternative and efficient ways of creating the finished form. Digital techniques will become a natural part of solving visual problems but be aware that what is easier isn't always the best. Try to follow the steps involved in the conceptual process outlined in Chapter 3, and allow for intuitive problem solving for the most creative results (see Figures 8.11 and 8.12).

The project requirements associated with this chapter are not too involved. You will need to either find an appropriate photograph or take one yourself, and create your own asymmetrically balanced composition using designed shapes and three to five values. The subject matter is up to you, and you can use any or all of the tools you've learned up to this

FIGURE 8.11   Example of a preliminary line drawing and final value project. *Value Design* © 2003. Reprinted with permission from Patrick Wilkey. *www.visiocommunications.com*.

FIGURE 8.12   Example of a thumbnail, preliminary line drawing and final value project. *Lighthouse* © 2003. Reprinted with permission from Mike Clayton.

point. Remember to balance unity with variety, and to use appropriate types of line directions and types of shapes to result in proper hierarchy. The shapes themselves could be non-objective and combined to create stylized, abstract, or a non-objective design. Review Figure 8.1 for examples of the final compositions and Figures 8.6 to 8.8 and 8.10 to help you select a photograph. The following section on the production process will give you more details concerning the selection and production of the proper images for the successful completion of this project.

TUTORIAL

TRADITIONAL AND DIGITAL PRODUCTION PROCESS

PREPARING YOUR PROJECT

In previous chapters and exercises, step-by-step examples were given to guide you through the process of learning the tools in. From this point on, concepts become the emphasis of the examples, so that you might continue with your own work. Take what is being shown here and apply it to your own designs. The steps are the same, but the results might vary.

As has been mentioned previously in this text, a great deal of the actual design can be done on paper before ever touching the mouse. This project is a prime example of that notion.

Figure 8.13 shows an example of the entire process from start to finish. In this case, the designer took a photograph of a lady in a black dress (top left), created a series of simple line drawings (top middle and right), outlined different areas of value, and discarded unnecessary details in the process. After the line drawing was complete it was scanned into the computer, where the image was cropped (bottom left), taken into, and filled with various shades of gray to show value (bottom right).

Selecting the Source Material

When choosing the image for this assignment, concentrate on simple images that have high levels of contrast (lights and darks). Flat images will be a little difficult to translate into a portfolio-quality piece.

Here is a quick test that you can do to determine if an image has enough contrast to be successful . . . squint at it. When you squint, all detail is abandoned and your eyes search the lights and the darks of the image for recognizable shapes. Figure 8.14 shows two examples of blurred images. Can you make out what they are? The one on the left is a lighthouse, and the one on the right is a close-up of a small boy. The first image is easily recognized due to the even

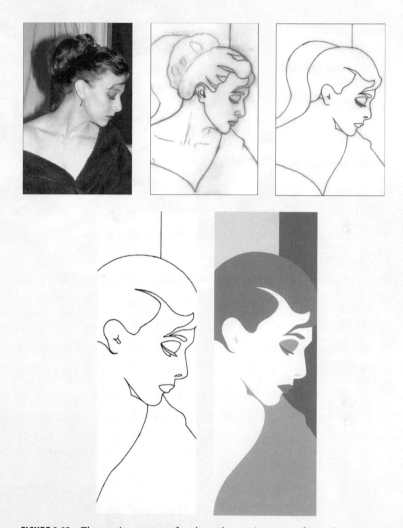

FIGURE 8.13   The entire process for the value assignment, from the original photograph to the final value study. Reprinted with permission from Chad Griffiths.

balance of lights and darks. The second, however, has too many dark values and too few light values to make the image really "pop" at you.

Changing the Levels of an Image

There are methods of "evening the tones" of images digitally. Using your scanner or any imaging software you can adjust the levels of gray in an image.

FIGURE 8.14 Example of two blurred images.

Naturally balanced images work the best, but with some tweaking any image could work.

Some scanners may allow you to change the brightness and contrast as you scan the image into your computer. This is not the best result. It is better to scan the image first and then take the image into a program to modify it.

Figure 8.15 is the original scan of the image of the little boy. Below the image is the histogram of the image, a visual representation of the levels of gray in the image. There are 256 levels of gray in a grayscale image as discussed in Chapter 9. On the left is 0 (black) and on the right is 255 (white). The height of the lines in between is the number of pixels in the image at that particular level of gray. Notice that a majority of the pixels are concentrated on the left of the graph, which means that the image is too dark. For optimum results, there should be an even number of light and dark pixels.

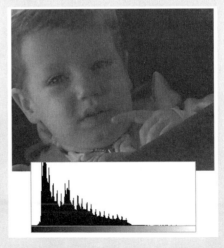

FIGURE 8.15 The original image and its histogram.

There is a quick fix in Photoshop that automatically evens out the levels. With the image opened in Photoshop, choose `Image > Adjust > Auto Levels` (PC: control + shift + L; Mac: command + shift + L). The process of using Auto Levels is quite simple. The software determines two points in the image: the lightest area and the darkest area. The lightest area becomes 255 (white) and the darkest area becomes 0 (black). The software then automatically redistributes the amount of pixels evenly throughout the value of the image.

In Figure 8.16, on the left is the original image and on the right is the corrected image with its histogram. Notice how every level of gray is represented in its histogram; this gives the image a good tonal range.

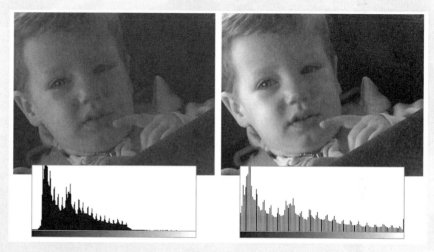

FIGURE 8.16   The before and after images with their respective histograms.

CREATING THE FIRST DRAWING

The first drawing that you create from the source material should be a contour line drawing or a simple shaded drawing. Try to divide the image up by light and dark shapes (Figure 8.17).

Drawing on paper gives you the freedom to express the shapes and gives more leniencies in the design.

If you are not confident in your drawing abilities, use tracing paper to create the line drawings. Continually tracing over the image can help when simplifying the drawing. A light table may also be of use.

CREATING THE SIMPLIFIED DRAWING

With the first drawing done, redraw the image, reducing the number of shapes. Do several drawings until you have broken the image down into its

FIGURE 8.17 Examples of simple line and shaded drawings.

shapes. Once completed, begin to experiment by shading in the drawings with various shades of gray with dye markers or pencils. If necessary, reduce the number of shapes and values further by repeating this process as many times as necessary. This is the "rough."

Once the "rough" is complete, tighten up the design into a "comp" by defining the final shapes and filling them with the shades of gray that will closely resemble the finished values (Figure 8.18).

When you are pleased with the final value drawing, scan the drawing into the computer at 150–200 ppi in order to see the detail in the curves or corners.

FIGURE 8.18 Examples of the final value drawing.

TRACING THE IMAGE: USING LAYERS AND SUBLAYERS

Begin by creating a new document in Illustrator. Follow the same steps as you have done previously to place the image into the document.

Place the tracing image in the new document.

Remember to name the layer you are placing the image on, and to turn off its Print option, Lock the layer and set its Dim Images to between 30–50%. Open the Layer Options dialog box, by either selecting it from the Layers palette option menu or by double-clicking the layer itself.

With the tools that you have learned in previous exercises, trace the image to create the various shapes.

Layers have been discussed, but Sub-layers have yet to be explained. In this example, the window to the lighthouse will be drawn to illustrate the point.

Create a new layer created named "Window." Zoom in on the window at the base of the lighthouse tower. Draw a rectangle around the casing of the window. Set the fill to "none" and the stroke to black.

Click on the gray arrow in front of the layer named "Window" to expand the sublayer. Sub-layers are visible when you expand the layer by clicking on the arrow before the layer name, as shown in Figure 8.19.

The rectangle that has been drawn now appears under the "Window" layer and is identified by the name "Path."

Rename the sublayer by either selecting Options for <Path> from the Layer option menu or by double-clicking on the name <Path>. Change the name to Outer Window. Then click OK.

Draw the other rectangles to create the rest of the window.

Notice that as you draw a rectangle, a new sublayer named <Path> is created for each instance. The finished window is made up of six individual rectangles. It is confusing to tell which is which without naming them.

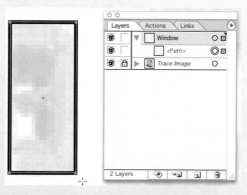

FIGURE 8.19 Layers contain sublayers that hold the individual paths. The more shapes you draw the more sub-levels are created within that layer.

Naming each individual path is unnecessary in most cases, but it is a good practice to get into if you find yourself having trouble identifying parts of the drawing.

Name each <Path> that was created. Identify the shape by clicking on the circle shape to the right of the <Path> name. This highlights the shape in the document (Figure 8.20).

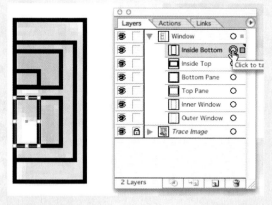

FIGURE 8.20   Clicking on the circle to the right of the sublayer name selects the shape in the document.

Grouping Sublayers

Using the Selection tool (A), drag around all the shapes to select them.

Select Object > Group (PC: control + G; Mac: command + G) to group the objects together.

When shapes are grouped together, they are placed into a sublayer called <Group> that can be expanded and collapsed by the arrow in front of the name (Figure 8.21). This <Group> can be renamed.

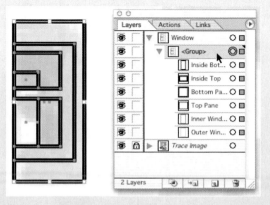

FIGURE 8.21   Grouping objects places the paths into a <Group> sublayer. It is expandable so that the contents may be displayed and selected.

Rename the `<Group>` by double-clicking the name (or selecting Options for `<Group>` from the Layers Option menu). Name the group "Middle Lighthouse Window."

When `<Group>`s are ungrouped, the `<Path>`s are still placed under the layer, with their names and attributes intact.

With the group still selected, set the fill color to white.

Changing the Stacking Order of Layers

Now that the shapes have fills, the next step is easier. As you go through and draw the various shapes for the design you will, at some point, get the order of the shapes mixed up. The hierarchy of the sublayers is the same as layers. The stacking order goes from top to bottom: whatever is on top is on the top and whatever is on the bottom is on the bottom. Sublayers can be moved within the sublayers or from one layer to another.

To move a layer in , follow these steps:

Select the layer that you want to move. (To highlight the object, click on the circle to the right of the name.)

Drag the layer up or down to the new location within the list. A horizontal black line will show where the layer will be placed. Release the mouse to set the new location. The image will change to reflect the modification.

In the example of the group "Middle Lighthouse Window," the "Outer Window" sublayer was moved from the bottom of the stack to the top within the group. The large white rectangle covers all the other shapes, blocking them from view.

Organization is key when dealing with overlapping shapes. Because the windows were created before the rest of the main lighthouse body, when filled with white, the shapes overlap the window. This is because the "Windows" layer is underneath the "Main Lighthouse." By moving the "Windows" layer above the "Main Lighthouse" layer in the stacking order, the windows now appear on the house (Figure 8.22).

THE SWATCHES PALETTE

In the prior exercises, color usage has been limited to black and white. Because this is an exercise in value, shades (percentages) of gray can be used to give depth and variety to the image. In this section you will learn how to create, delete, and apply color swatches to the shapes.

The Swatches palette holds three types of "fills." These three types of colors, color, gradient, and pattern, can either be viewed all at once or by category. In this exercise, color swatches will be used.

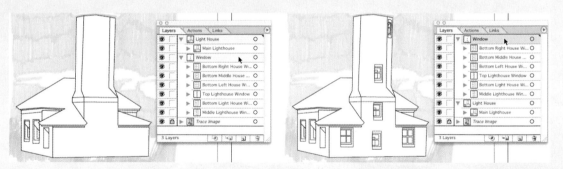

FIGURE 8.22 Layers can be restacked so that imagery that may have been lost or that may have fallen underneath a new part of the drawing can be moved to the top, where it may be seen again.

There are two views for the Swatches palette, the Thumbnail view and the List view. For the purposes of this exercise, the List view is necessary.

Open the Swatches palette by selecting `Windows > Swatches`.
Click on the second button at the bottom of the palette to view only the Color Swatches.
Change the view from Thumbnail to List by selecting List view from the palette options menu in the upper-right corner of the palette.

When viewing the colors in the List view, not only is a color swatch visible but the name of the swatch is also given. This can work to your advantage. The icon to the right of the name indicates that a color is either a process color (four-color triangle) or a spot color (square with a circle).

A *process color* is a color that can only be created by mixing cyan, magenta, yellow, and black (CMYK), such as on a printing press or a four-color printer. A wide variety of colors can be made from combining different percentages of each color on the press. Magazines, posters, and brochures are some examples of items that are printed using process colors.

A *spot color* is a premixed color that is printed separately from process colors. Mixing the process colors together cannot make all colors. Spot color is used when a precise color is needed, such as when printing a corporate logo. The *Pantone Matching System* (PMS) is often used as a guide for selecting these colors. Examples of the colors are available in printed form, for you to preview and select the correct colors. For this exercise, process colors will be used.

Creating Swatches

Because we are only working in a grayscale mode, and there are only four shades of gray set in the default swatches, you might need to add some swatches of your own. To create a new color swatch, follow these steps.

While holding down the Alt (PC) or Option (Mac) key, click on the Create New
Swatch button, which is the second button from the right at the bottom of
the Swatches palette (Figure 8.23).

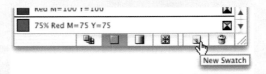

FIGURE 8.23   The location of the New Swatch
button on the Swatches palette. Holding down
the Alt or Option key will automatically open the
dialog box. If you just click the button, you have
to manually open the dialog box.

The New Swatch dialog box opens (Figure 8.24). In this dialog box you can set
the following attributes.

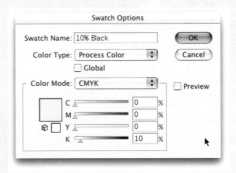

FIGURE 8.24   The New Swatch dialog box.

Name the new swatch 10% black.
Set the Color Type to Process Color.
Check the Global box

By checking the Global box, if you come back at any time and change
the attributes of the color of this swatch, all the objects that use this swatch
will be updated to reflect the changes. If you had the swatch set to 10%
black, but wanted to change it to 15%, all objects that were 10% black would
appear as 15% black.

From the Color Mode, select CYMK (or Grayscale). Set the slider on K (black) to
10, or type "10" into the field to the right. Set the three other sliders to "0."

Click OK. With the other three colors set to "0," only black will appear in the swatch.

You have now created a new swatch. Repeat the process, as many times as necessary, to create the many other shades of gray you might need.

Deleting Swatches

There are many other swatches in this document that are not needed. You may choose to delete the unnecessary swatches by selecting the swatch and clicking on the Trash Can icon at the lower-right side of the palette. Be warned that if you deleted a swatch it is gone. There is no "Swatch Reset" in the document. Swatches deleted will only affect the current document, not the system. You may delete multiple swatches using the Shift and Control/Command keys to select the swatches before pressing the button.

It is wise to take the time to delete all the swatches that you aren't going to use and to create ones that you will need. Create a new swatch for every 10% of black (i.e., 10%, 20%, 30%, etc.). You may restack the swatches like you did with the layers and sublayers earlier in this text.

Applying Swatches

To apply a color swatch to a shape, follow these steps:

With the Selection Tool, select the "Outer Window" shape.
In the toolbar, make sure that the Fill Swatch is active (in front of the Stroke).
Select the 20% black color swatch.
Fill the other shapes according to Figure 8.25.

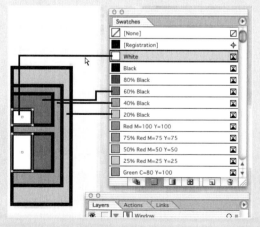

FIGURE 8.25 Using the image, fill in the rest of the shapes appropriately.

Select all the shapes in the window and remove the stroke (Figure 8.26).

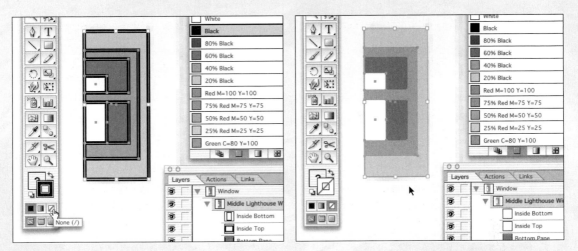

FIGURE 8.26   Set the stroke on all the shapes to "none" and watch as the values give the design a sense of depth.

Without the stroke, the values in the image become very apparent. You can see the window receding into the building. There's a slight problem: the interior of the window does not seem dark enough.

Change the two shapes with 60% black to 80% black ("Top Pane" and "Bottom Pane").

With the darker shade inside the windows, they recede more. This is due to a better contrast of the lights (the outsides of the window) and the darks (the inside). The highlights in the windows help to bring the value back out from the room.

Redefining Swatches

To redefine a color swatch, simply double-click the swatch or select Options For in the Swatch palette options menu. Choose the new color attributes and click OK. Unless the Global box is selected for each color and applied beforehand (signified by a small red square next to the process color icon) the color that was changed would not affect the current shapes of that color. When you create a new color swatch, click the Global button. Here's an example:

Prior to assigning colors to your design, set all swatches to Global by double-clicking on them and checking the correct box.

Assign colors to the shapes, by first selecting the shape and then applying the color.

On the lighthouse, the 20% black color looks too dark. Because Global colors were applied to the colors, if the attributes of the 20% black color are changed, all the shapes with 20% black as their color will change.

Double-click the 20% black swatch to open the Swatch Options (Figure 8.27).

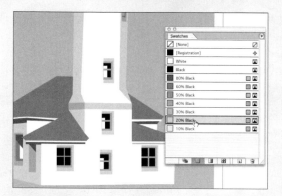
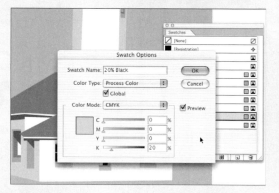

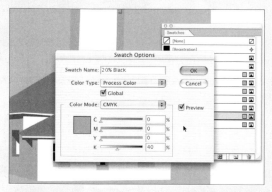
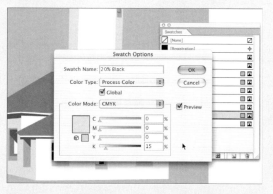

FIGURE 8.27 Using Global colors can help you save time when making large color changes in your design. The 20% black that is being used on the sides of the lighthouse looks a little too close to that of the sky. By going darker (bottom left), the tower stands out too much. At 15% black, there is enough of a change that it is noticeable.

Check the Preview button. By checking this button, the changes that you make will be previewed in the document.

Set the K slider to 40 and press the Tab key. Pressing the Tab key selects the next field, thus invoking the preview. The sides of the lighthouse get too dark.

Set the slider to 15 and press the Tab key. The sides of the lighthouse lighten enough that their color no longer interferes with the sky.

Rename the Swatch Name to 15% black. Click OK. The new color is activated and the color is changed throughout all the shapes that were once 20% black.

By using Global colors, color changing becomes less tedious.

FINISHING THE DESIGN

To polish this design, here are a few pointers:

Refer to the previous exercises for details on resizing and cropping. Even though your design might be spread across several layers, create a new layer at the top for the shape that will be the cropping mask. But be warned, when the mask is made, all the contents from all the layers jump to the top layer and become bound by the clipping mask. An alternative to using a clipping mask is using stroke-free white rectangles on the four sides of your design.

SUMMARY

This is the first of four projects that deal with individual research and expression in terms of subject matter and style of designing. Now that you understand the basic principles of design using line, shape, and value, you can begin to experiment with many options and alternatives. As you make your design decisions, a personal style will begin to emerge. A preference for certain subject matter is only a superficial beginning. What types of compositions do you prefer, asymmetrical or symmetrical, closed form or open form? Did you use mostly curvilinear or rectilinear shapes for this project? What is the dominant line direction? Do you have a preference for designs that emphasize unity or variety? Will you be experimenting with low key or high key values for future designs? Given that the next three assignments are fairly individualized, will you be using realistic, stylized, abstract, or non-objective shapes? It may be a little early to know exactly what your personal preferences are in terms of design. However, the more images you create, the chances of a similarity between designs will be evident. As you experiment with design options and become more familiar with the tools, you will discover an individual style. At the end of the last project in this book, look back and see if there are any similarities to your project solutions. Retain what you think is successful and begin to change those things that are not working. In many ways, if you are experimenting with original solutions, your design projects will be a reflection of you.

9

DESIGN PROJECT FIVE: COLOR THEORY

INTRODUCTION

Color is the most complex of the elements of design. It requires an in-depth look and a more detailed discussion than the other elements. This chapter will be an extended discussion on the background and content of color theory, followed by a comprehensive design project that incorporates color theory and its relationship to all the elements and principles of design.

The general characteristics and properties that are universal in the study of color will be the focus of this chapter. The principles and concepts presented will help you make informed color choices. These design decisions will be balanced with the knowledge of the subjective nature of color. Color in terms of emotional communication requires a vast understanding of the habits and background of the audience. Defining color design problems usually requires a large amount of objective thinking because there can be so many options and exceptions involved in the solution. The information contained in this chapter and the color project should give you the background and basic training necessary to define and create successful visual designs using color.

Content

Background in Color Theory

Defining Color

There are two basic systems of color, *additive* and *subtractive*. These two systems differ based on the source of the light. If the source is direct, such as light from a spotlight, computer monitor, or television, the system of color mixing is called *additive*. Light is added to create various colors. The three primary colors of an additive system are red, green, and blue. When all three colors overlap they will produce white. When two complimentary or opposite colors in an additive system of color overlap they will produce a colorless gray or white.

If the source of the light is reflected or absorbed by the surface of an object, the system of color mixing is called *subtractive*. Objects have no color of their own, only the ability to reflect certain rays of light and absorb others. You can see these different rays of light by putting white light through a prism. A prism breaks white light into the various colors of light we see in a rainbow. A red object absorbs all the rays except for the red ones. Black objects absorb all the rays. White objects reflect all rays of light. Paintings are a good example of the subtractive system of color mixing. The primary colors of a subtractive system of color are blue, red, and yellow. When all three colors are mixed in equal amount they produce a dark or muddy gray. When two opposite or complementary colors are mixed in the subtractive system the result is a muddy gray

Most of this section will deal with subtractive color. It is the color we are most likely to observe in natural settings. Additive color, as it relates to digitally created color and computer monitor displays, will be discussed later in this chapter. Figure 9.1 diagrams the basics of the subtractive and additive color-mixing systems. The diagram at the left illustrates how the sun's rays or white light contains a full spectrum of colored rays we cannot see without the use of a device such as a prism. In the subtractive color mixing system only the red rays are being reflected from the tomato and the other rays will be absorbed. If this tomato were green, only the green rays would be reflected. The diagram on the right shows an example of the additive color-mixing process. Red, green, and blue colored spotlights are mixing together to produce white. Red and green lights are mixing to produce yellow; green and blue are mixing to produce cyan; and red and blue are mixing to produce magenta.

As a product of light, color will change depending on its environment. During the day, direct sunlight brings out the brightness in the color of outdoor objects. At dawn, with less light coming from the low-

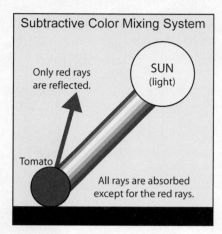
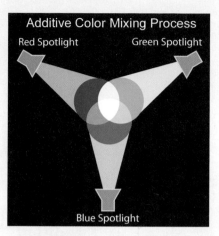

FIGURE 9.1 The basics of the subtractive and additive color-mixing systems.

setting sun, objects will be lit less directly and from one side. The same objects at this time of day will display contrasting light and dark colors. At night, these objects will have little light and color will be muted and may not even be present. A white chicken may appear pale yellow in the early morning light and muted cool gray at night (see Figure 9.2).

FIGURE 9.2 Computer-generated model that is using ambient and atmospheric lighting to duplicate day and night light. There are a few spotlights illuminating some of the areas. Notice how the color changes from warm tones during the day and cool tones at night. Even the spotlights that are a source of the consistent lighting are affected. *Venetian Design* © 2003, *Night Venetian Design* © 2003. Reprinted with permission from Anson Call.

Even when the light is the same, color perception changes depending on surrounding colors. A dull color may seem brighter when placed against its opposite or complementary color (see Figure 9.3).

 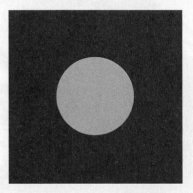

FIGURE 9.3 Example on the left shows two similar colors placed one on top of the other. The example on the right shows one of these colors placed on top of its complement.

An intense color may appear dull when placed against a color that is the same value or intensity (see Figure 9.4).

FIGURE 9.4 Example of a color shape placed on a white background is on the left. An example of the same color placed on a color shape that is the same value and intensity is on the right.

A light color will seem brighter when placed against a color that is dark (see Figure 9.5).

 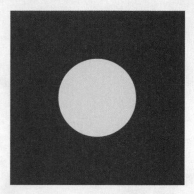

FIGURE 9.5   Example of a light color shape placed on a white background and an example of the same color shape placed on a darker color background.

The terms hue and color are often confused with one another. *Hue* describes the different parts of the color spectrum commonly found in a rainbow or reflected through a prism (see Figure 9.1). Red, orange, yellow, green, blue, and purple are hues. *Color* also describes these parts of the spectrum but includes the different colors that may be made from these hues. Chartreuse, lime, and forest, are names of colors that are related to a green hue. Orange is the hue in the colors brown, beige, or tan.

The most common organization displaying and illustrating the relationships between hues is the 12-hue color wheel. It is divided into three categories (Figure 9.6).

1. The *primary* colors: red, yellow, and blue are the three colors that make up all other colors.
2. *Secondary* colors are mixtures of two primary colors. Yellow and red make orange, red and blue make purple, and blue and yellow make green.
3. The six *tertiary* colors are made from the mixture of a primary and a secondary color located next to it on the color wheel. Blue-green, yellow-green, yellow-orange, orange-red, red-purple, and blue-purple are the six tertiary colors.

Every color has a *value*. It is based on the lightness and darkness of its hue. The value of a color can be made lighter by adding white. This is called a *tint*. By adding black a color is made darker. This is called a *shade* (Figure 9.7).

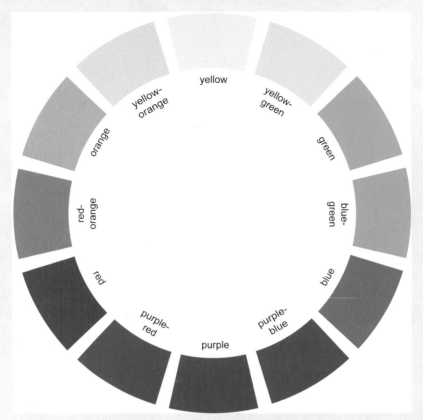

FIGURE 9.6 Twelve-hue color wheel indicating primary, secondary, and tertiary colors.

FIGURE 9.7 The shape to the left is a red hue. White is added to this hue to make the shape in the middle a tint. Black is added to the original red hue, creating the shape on the right that is a shade.

On a color wheel, colors are not shown at the same value. Each color is shown unmixed and pure. At this pure level, yellow is very light in value and blue is much darker in value (see Figure 9.8).

FIGURE 9.8   The hues, yellow and blue, in their pure state. The same hues, yellow and blue, with the color removed, leaving only the value of both colors.

Value, like color, is influenced by the values that surround it. Most light values will seem brighter on a dark surface and much darker on a light surface (Figure 9.9).

FIGURE 9.9   Example of a light value shape on a white background and an example of the same light value shape on a much darker surface.

Surrounding a color with a black or very dark line will make the color seem richer or clearer. It keeps the color from spreading out and gives the shape a sharp, crisp feeling. By surrounding a color with white or a lighter color the opposite will happen. The color will seem to spread and seem less crisp (Figure 9.10).

Intensity or brightness is another property of color. In a pure and unmixed state, a color's brightness is at its full intensity. Intensity is different from the value of a color. If white is added to a color it will become lighter in value but lower in intensity. If black is added to a color it will also become lower in intensity but darker in value. Another way to lower a color's intensity is to add its complement. The complement of a color is the color that is positioned directly across from it on a color wheel. For example, yellow is the complement of purple, and red is the complement

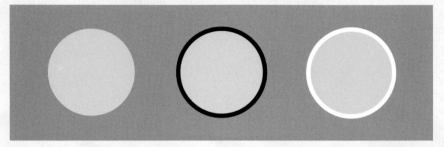

FIGURE 9.10   Example of a color on a neutral background. Example of the same color with a black outline. Example of the same color with a white outline.

of green. If the two complementary colors are added together in equal amounts the result will be muddy gray. Placing a color next to its complement may heighten the illusion of intensity. This gives the effect that is exactly opposite of mixing two complementary colors. By positioning complementary colors in close proximity to each other, contrast is heightened and the result is a visual sensation that seems to make each color brighter (Figure 9.11).

FIGURE 9.11   Yellow shape on a white background. The same yellow shape on a purple or complementary color background.

Color and Unity

A color scheme is a system of colors that creates a visual relationship to add harmony or interest to a design or work of art. Using a traditional color wheel, four basic color schemes may be described.

   Monochromatic. One hue and all of its tones and shades make up this color scheme. A very harmonious and unified feeling is usually achieved through the use of this color scheme, depending on the range of values. The wider the range of values, the more contrast and activity is created. A close range of values usually suggests a more calm feeling (Figure 9.12).

FIGURE 9.12   Example of art using a monochromatic color scheme. The values in this design are closely related, creating a very calm, classical feeling. The variation in the sizes of the objects gives variety to this otherwise extremely harmonious composition. *Vanitas: Violin, El Camino Seeds* © 2003. Reprinted with permission from Adrian Van Suchtelen.

Analogous. A combination of hues located next to each other on the color wheel create an analogous color scheme. Similar to other color schemes, tones and shades are also included. The feeling expressed by most analogous color schemes is one of harmonious tranquility (Figure 9.13).

Complementary. The hues located directly across a color wheel give a lively and active feeling to this color scheme. This feeling of excitement is amplified when these colors are used at full intensity (see Figure 9.14).

Triadic. This color scheme consists of three hues located equal distance from each other on the color wheel. The color scheme of blue, red, and yellow is the most common example of a triadic color

FIGURE 9.13   Example of art using an analogous color scheme. The color in this composition is somber because most of the values of the colors are darker and subdued. There is a dynamic diagonal line direction and extreme asymmetrical balance that is making this painting feel dramatic, and at the same time quiet. The analogous colors are unifying this design and the strong contrast in values is creating variety. *Searching* © 2003. Reprinted with permission from Greg Schulte.

FIGURE 9.14   Example of a photograph that uses a complementary color scheme. Notice there is no identifiable focal point but by effectively using value and color contrast, this composition becomes very interesting. *Cattails* © 2003. Reprinted with permission from PatrickConePhotography.com.

scheme. Triadic color schemes generally give the feeling of dynamic activity. As with a complementary color scheme, a more active feeling is achieved through the use of full-intensity hues (see Figure 9.15).

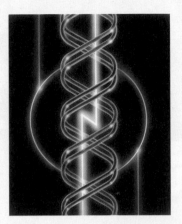 

FIGURE 9.15   The example on the left is a design that illustrates biology and electronics using a triadic color scheme to create dynamic contrast. *DNA* © 2003. Reprinted with permission from Alan Hashimoto. The example on the right is a photograph that uses a triadic color scheme to create drama. Notice how hierarchy and color are used together effectively. The dark shadow shape is given the most weight, followed by the contrasting yellow, and then the dark red background with a few accents of blue to complete the color scheme. *Yellowstone Firefighter, 1988* © 2003. Reprinted with permission from PatrickConePhotography.com.

Color in a composition may feel unified through the use of tonality. Tonality is the presence of a dominant hue or color. A variety of colors may make up a composition but there is a general overall feeling of a particular hue (see Figure 9.16).

Color and Variety

Similar to the other elements of design, color can give a composition variety as well as unity. As with all elements of design, variety is accom-

FIGURE 9.16 The example on the left is a painting that emphasizes an earthy warm tone. There is a wide range of colors that can be identified, but the overall warm tone dominates. Notice how visual hierarchy is achieved through the formal organization of the various shapes and sizes. *Vanitas: Sun Maid, Hanging Man* © 2003. Reprinted with permission from Adrian Van Suchtelen. The example on the right is an illustration that emphasizes a cool, dark tone. Notice how there are two focal points. One is the large reddish purple planet shape contrasting with all the dark blue shapes and the other is created by an extreme contrast in value of the silhouetted figure in front of the automobile headlights. *Alien Jaywalker* © 2003. Reprinted with permission from Alan Hashimoto.

plished by using contrast. One method that has already been discussed is using complementary or triadic color schemes. Colors that are located farther away from each other on the color wheel will have more contrast.

As previously discussed, tonality is the presence of a dominant color or hue. The presence of this dominant element can be contrasted by using other areas of differing hues and colors. This will add interest through variety and establish focal points. These contrasting colors should be used in varying weights and should implement the concept of visual hierarchy. As previously discussed, hierarchy is used to organize each area of emphasis so that it does not conflict or take away attention from another area of emphasis. Focal points must be viewed one at a time in stages. One focal point will get the most attention. The viewer's eye will then move to another subtler focal point and from there to another. The careful staging of focal points and areas of emphasis will lead the viewer from one part of a design to the next until the entire design has been viewed in detail (see Figure 9.17).

Warm and Cool Colors

A common way that colors may be used to contrast or unify each other is through the use of warm and cool colors. The feeling of warmth is associ-

FIGURE 9.17   Example of a variety of colors organized using visual hierarchy. Note that the dominant color or tone is a brownish yellow-orange, followed by areas of red, then green, with smaller areas of blue, and purple accents. Later, in Figure 9.24, the primary colors related to this illustration are isolated to emphasize the distribution of color. *Garden Heroics* © 2003. Reprinted with permission from Alan Hashimoto.

ated with past experiences, with images and objects that emit heat, or objects that are hot to the touch. The sun and fire are two examples of how we associate colors such as yellow, orange, and red with the feeling of warmth (see Figure 9.18).

On the other side of the color wheel, colors such as blue-green, blue, and blue-violet tend to give us the feeling of coolness. These colors are associated with blue water or other cool objects and images (see Figure 9.19).

We generally think of the colors yellow through red-violet as warm colors on the color wheel and yellow-green through violet as cool colors. An interesting illusion created by warm and cool colors is that warm colors tend to come forward and cool colors recede. This idea may be used to create depth or emphasize one element of a composition over another. An example of this would be a warm figure placed against a cool background (see Figure 9.20).

Color Discord

Discordant colors are color combinations that have no identifiable relationship with each other. Color discord is the opposite of color harmony. These combinations make maximum use of contrasting and contradictory colors to intentionally catch the eye and surprise the viewer. Discordant colors are located far apart on a color wheel but do not combine to make

FIGURE 9.18 Example of a design that uses warm colors. This photograph was taken during a fire at Yellowstone National Park. *Old Faithful Fire, 1988* © 2003. Reprinted with permission from PatrickConePhotography.com.

FIGURE 9.19 Example of a design that uses cool colors. This photograph not only gives us a look at the coldness of winter but also the light tonality gives the snow a sense of lightness. Wasatch Mountains in Winter © 2003. Reprinted with permission from PatrickConePhotography.com.

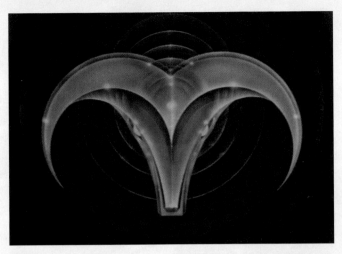

FIGURE 9.20   Example of a composition that uses warm colors to bring a shape forward, with cool colors in the background. *Aries* © 2003. Reprinted with permission from Alan Hashimoto.

a triadic or complimentary color scheme. Discord is best achieved when colors are close to the same value. This increases the chance that true colors will be observed and discord will be more obvious (see Figure 9.21).

FIGURE 9.21   Example of a design that demonstrates color discord. *Spring Romance* © 2003. Reprinted with permission from Alan Hashimoto.

Color and Design

Review Chapter 8. All the design principles that relate to value also relate to color. The following is a summary of the design principles that both color and value have in common.

The more contrast of value between a shape and the background, the more visual weight it will have, relative to the size of the shape. This rule also applies to contrast of color. The more visual contrast between colored shapes, the more visual weight the shapes will have (see Figure 9.22). The example on the left shows two shapes that are the same color and same weight. The same shapes are found in the example directly to the right, but the shape at the left is a lighter value. Notice how much heavier the shape at the right feels. The two examples at the right deal with balance and the contrast of colors. The second design from the right is an example of contrast of value and color, and will make the visual weight appear heavier. The complement of purple is yellow. Notice how the yellow shape has more visual weight than the red shape. In the example on the right, the color of the background is changed to a complement of red, making the yellow shape feel lighter and the red shape heavier.

FIGURE 9.22   The more contrast of value between a shape and a background, the more visual weight shape will have. The more visual contrast between colored shapes, the more visual weight the shapes will have.

You can also apply the idea of contrast to the sense of depth. Contrasting or complementary colors will seem closer, and unified or analogous colors will seem farther away. Take another look at Figure 9.22. The more the contrast, the closer the shape will seem. Figure 9.23 is a photograph that uses color and value to create depth.

Colors should be balanced throughout the composition for unity, and designed with variation using visual hierarchy. Figures 9.24, 9.25, and 9.26 are examples.

FIGURE 9.23   Photograph creating depth through the use of value and color. Notice how the darker values in the clouds and island make them seem closer. They are also purple in contrast to the light yellow-orange colors of the far-away horizon and distant clouds. *Great Salt Lake, Utah* © 2003. Reprinted with permission from PatrickConePhotography.com.

FIGURE 9.24   Example of an illustration and isolated colors pointing out the balanced distribution of color as well as the variation in weights of colors to achieve good visual hierarchy. Notice the yellow is used more than the other colors, and red is the second most-used color. Without looking at the original illustration you can tell by the weights of these colors that the tone will be yellow-orange. *Garden Heroics* © 2003. Reprinted with permission from Alan Hashimoto.

FIGURE 9.25 Example of asymmetrical balance using color. The color red is weighted far to the right but is balanced by the light color of the dog. Red is the dominant color but the dog is a more dominant value. *Dalmatian, Montana* © 2003. Reprinted with permission from PatrickConePhotography.com.

FIGURE 9.26 Example of a painting that uses value and color to create a dynamic composition. On first inspection, the diagonal line direction of the contrasting light and shadow seem to create most of the dramatic action in this painting. Looking closer you will notice that contrasting orange shapes located near the lit center and at the top of design forces your eyes back to top of the painting for another look. These complementary-colored shapes prevent your eye from being carried off the lower-left corner by the shadow. *Long Shadows* © 2003. Reprinted with permission from Glen Edwards.

DESIGN PROJECT FIVE: COLOR

Basic Problem Defined

Using the information from the section on color theory, create an interesting color design focusing on shape. Design Project Five combines at least three color elements from three different sources and, through the processes of stylization, distortion, and abstraction, a color object-oriented design will be created. This assignment has been designed this way for several reasons: (1) The three elements (figure, inanimate object, and environment) are distinct types of shapes. The figure is curvilinear, the inanimate object will most likely be more rectilinear, and the environment may consist of either type of shape or both; (2) Using different types of images for the original source material will be more of a visualization challenge and will help with the understanding of different types of printing, resolutions, and digital-input devices. The designer cannot rely on a single image which could be directly traced, owing all of the credit to the original designer; (3) Making this a stylization, distortion, or abstraction project gives the designer more freedom to explore beyond realism. The emotional quality of the shapes and colors will be more evident. The focus will be placed on the basic principles of design rather than subject matter; and (4) Arbitrary color allows the designer to explore a variety of color schemes and color combinations. Because the design can be non-representational, there should be more freedom in choosing colors.

These requirements should help you create an interesting and unique design.

Conceptual Process

The following is a specific series of steps and requirements for this color project.

- Select a theme or central idea that involves designing at least three of these elements into one composition. 1) human figure or animal, 2) inanimate object (machine, building, etc.), 3) environment or shapes and objects related to a particular place or setting.
- Research visual reference materials such as magazines, books, life drawings, or photographs.
- Select at least three reference materials that can be combined to create one composition. These original visual references will be called source material. They can be color or black and white.
- Visualize the source material together as one composition. Crop, distort, and manipulate any or all of these visuals into a harmonious

design with variety. Each source reference does not have to be in proportion or to scale in relationship to one another. For instance, the environment may be cropped to show a small portion of it or expanded and exaggerated to be more vertical or horizontal. Elements such as trees, mountains, or buildings may be deleted, multiplied, or exaggerated. The figure or animal may be larger or smaller in scale to the environment. You may combine several figures or animals into one organic form or crop into just the face or head. The inanimate object can be handled the same way.

- You can use as many figures or inanimate objects as you like. The object of this exercise is to explore a variety of shapes and to visualize and design separate elements into one composition.

- The best way to visualize these elements together is by viewing all the reference material at once and creating thumbnail sketches that combine the material. This is the quickest way to visualize a variety of options and to analyze the relationships between separate elements. Position, proportion, and scale of each visual can be studied in advance. Changes can be made early to save time and energy.

- A more restrictive and less imaginative way to visualize elements together would be to scan each source material and combine them in Photoshop. Because the source material is from a separate source it may look unrelated. Some manipulation is needed to ensure that the elements from source material fit together properly. Using the tools available in this paint program, each element should be manipulated and distorted to help create a more harmonious design. One drawback to visualizing this way is the tendency to stick too closely to the original source material, which may cause the design to lack cohesiveness and individuality.

- Once the source material can be visualized together either as a thumbnail sketch or a Photoshop collage, the shapes and values can be analyzed. If you are designing with color source material that does not feel harmonious, or the material is in black and white or gray scale, don't worry about it. Just concentrate on the shapes and values. The color can be added or fixed later. Trace the outline of all the shapes you can define and add other lines to help harmonize your design and give it variety.

- Simplify and organize the elements into interesting and harmonious shapes.

- Your design can be a stylization or an abstraction.

- Experiment with various picture frame proportions.

- Experiment with different values and color schemes. The color and values should reflect the mood and style of your theme.

Figures 9.27 and 9.28 are examples of this project.

FIGURE 9.27   The design on the left uses curvilinear non-objective shapes and analogous color scheme. *Color Design* © 2003. Reprinted with permission from Richard Hopper. The stylized design on the right also uses curvilinear shapes. The saturated complementary colors create a sense of intensity. *Color Design* © 2003. Reprinted with permission from Erica Herrerea.

FIGURE 9.28   The stylized design on the left uses curvilinear shapes. The variety of colors is harmonized by similar values. *Color Design* © 2003. Reprinted with permission from Rudy Anderson. The design on the right is an example of a more sophisticated design using complementary color schemes and curvilinear shapes. Gradients are used throughout this design to give it variety and the illusion of form. *Chronicles of Namia, Aslan* © 2003. Reprinted with permission from Phillip Kesler.

TUTORIAL

DIGITAL PRODUCTION PROCESS

PREPARING YOUR PROJECT

Following the steps as outlined in the previous project, gather your research and begin the process of sketching out thumbnail drawings. Create a tightened drawing of the lines to be traced and proceed to scan the drawings. Trace the designs in Illustrator and create a composite placement. Upon completion of the line work, make sure that you have only used closed paths. This will help you color the objects more efficiently.

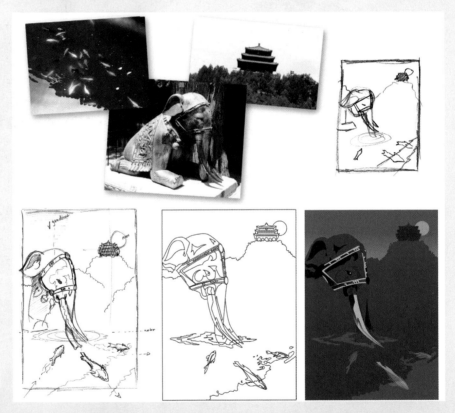

FIGURE 9.29 The process of using research, thumbnails, roughs, comps, and a finish can be applied to this project as well. *Photos, Sketches, and Final Design* © 2003. Reprinted with permission from Mike Clayton.

Mixing Colors

In the value exercise you worked exclusively with grayscale tones to add emphasis to the values of the design. The same method is used here for drawing, but you are allowed to use color in your design.

By limiting you to the K slider (in the value exercise), all you could use was a monochromatic color scheme of gray. The percentage number typed into the field was the percentage of black used in that shade.

There are several methods of "mixing" color based on the kind of computer system and software you use. These different methods of selecting colors are known as color modes.

The different color modes can be found in the Color palette Option menu (Figure 9.30). Two color modes we will discuss are CMYK (subtractive) and RGB (additive).

FIGURE 9.30   There are several color modes within Illustrator. They can be selected from the Option menu of the Color palette.

CMYK

Cyan, magenta, and yellow, along with Black (also known as the Key plate), are mixed to create colors for the image when printed on a press or with a four-color printer. By using different percentages of C, M, Y, and K, thousands of colors can be reproduced. Independently moving each slider or typing the number into the proper field can set these values.

For example, to create the color red you would mix 100% of M and100% of Y (Figure 9.31). C and K are not necessary, and therefore have values of 0%.

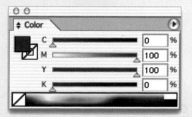

FIGURE 9.31   The CMYK values of the color red.

Mixing 30% of C and 15% of M, with Y and K set to 0%, would make a cool light blue.

To achieve the color white, all percentages would be set to 0, whereas black is created when K is set to 100%.

RGB

To create images for the Web and to be viewed primarily on monitors, RGB colors are used. Unlike CMYK, RGB uses different *levels* of the color (numbered between 0 and 255) to create the color.

With a level set to 0, the color is absent, and with 255 the color is at full strength. Because RGB is additive, all levels set to 0 would create black—the absence of light—and all levels set to 255 would create white—the full intensity of light (Figure 9.32).

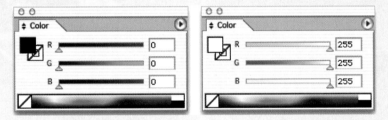

FIGURE 9.32   The RGB values of black (left) and white (right).

If the red were at a level of 255, with green and blue at 0, the red would be at full intensity, creating red. Likewise, with a red of 250, a green of 245, and a blue of 35, yellow is created.

MIXING AND ADDING COLORS TO THE SWATCHES PALETTE

ON THE CD

With a clean Swatches palette, you will create the colors that you will need for your design. For this example we have taken a detail of the koi from the China composition, found on the CD-ROM.

We would like to stick with a color scheme that is close to the colors in the photograph, murky green-black water, so that the orange and white fish will stand out. The fish in this particular detail is orange in color, so by balancing that color and mixing it with red, the analogous color scheme of the fish will sit wonderfully on the complimentary-colored background.

Because your project will ultimately be output to a color printer, the CMYK color mode will be used.

1. Open the file *9koi.ai* found on the CD-ROM.
2. If the Swatches palette is not visible, select it from the Windows menu.
3. Set the view of the Swatches palette to List View (Figure 9.33).

FIGURE 9.33   Change the view of the Swatches palette to List View.

4. If the Color palette is not visible, select it from the Windows menu.
5. Set the color mode to CMYK from the Color palette Options menu.
6. To create the murky green-black water, set the sliders in the Color palette to the following: C = 90; M = 0; Y = 90; K = 50.

The cyan and magenta mix together in even percentages to create a deep green. Black is added to darken the color.

7. Click on the New Swatch button in the Swatches palette to add the new color swatch. Double-click the new swatch to open the Swatch Option dialog box (Figure 9.34).

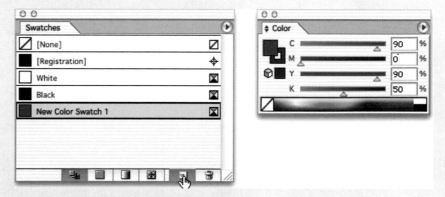

FIGURE 9.34   Click the New Swatch button to add a new swatch to the list.

8. In the dialog box that appears, name the swatch "Dark Green Water." Make sure that the Color Type is Process Color. Also make sure the Global property box is not checked. Click OK (Figure 9.35).

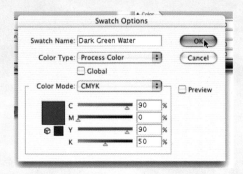

FIGURE 9.35 Name the swatch and set the proper items.

The newly named swatch now appears in the Swatches palette.

9. Using the Selection tool, select the large rectangle in the background.

Its fill color is white as are the fill colors of the other shapes in this file.

10. With the rectangle selected, make sure that the Fill swatch in the Tools palette is in the foreground.
11. Click on the "Dark Green Water" color in the Swatches palette to set the color of this rectangle (Figure 9.36).

The color of the water is not dark enough. Trying to get a sense of the color from the little swatch is very difficult. It's a good practice to apply the color to a larger shape to see if the color is the right one. In this case, the green is too light.

12. With the rectangle still selected, drag the color slider for K from 50% to 70% (Figure 9.37).

The color of the rectangle darkened slightly. If a shape is selected when you modify the color in the Color palette, that change is reflected in the selected object.

This might change the color of the shape, but it does not change the "Dark Green Water" swatch in the Swatches palette.

13. Double-click the "Dark Green Water" to open its Options dialog box.
14. Change the 50% to 70% in K. Click OK.

The swatch has now been updated to reflect the new color. Now attention will be turned to the orange color of the fish.

15. Deselect the rectangle by clicking anywhere outside of it or by selecting `Select > Deselect` from the top menu.

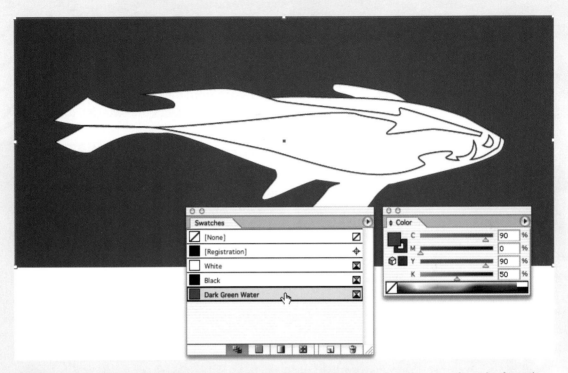

FIGURE 9.36   Set the color of the background rectangle by first selecting it, then choosing the color from the Swatches list.

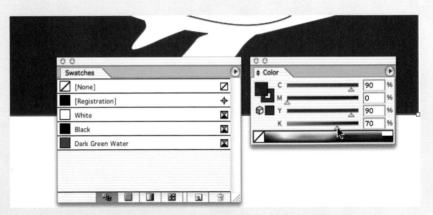

FIGURE 9.37   Change the level of black from 50% to 70% to darken the green color.

16. To create the orange color, set the sliders in the Color palette to the following: C = 0; M = 40; Y = 100; K = 0.

The magenta and yellow mix to create the orange color.

17. To test the color, drag the Fill swatch from the Color palette to the center shape of the fish. The shape takes on the color of the swatch (Figure 9.38).

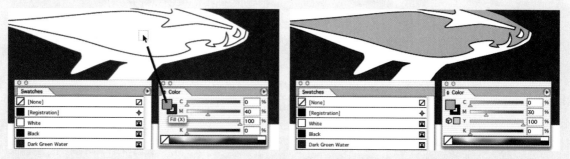

FIGURE 9.38   Test the color by dragging and dropping it onto the center fish shape (left). The shape takes on the color of the swatch (right).

18. Add the swatch to the Swatches palette by dragging the Fill swatch from the Color palette to the Swatches palette (Figure 9.39).

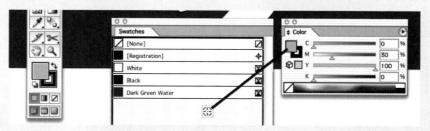

FIGURE 9.39   You can also add swatches to the Swatches palette by dragging and dropping them.

Dragging and dropping the Fill swatch is another way to add swatches to the Swatches palette.

19. Name the swatch "Medium Orange."
20. Create the following colors and add them to the Swatches palette:
    Light orange: C = 0; M = 30; Y = 100; K = 0
    Dark orange: C = 0; M = 60; Y = 100; K = 0
21. Add the "light orange" swatch to the top shape of the fish, and the "Dark Orange" swatch to the bottom shape, nose, and top-right fin, as shown in Figure 9.40.

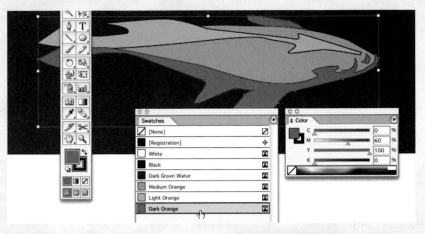

FIGURE 9.40   Use this image as a guide for coloring the rest of the shapes.

22. Remove the black stroke from all the shapes by selecting them all and setting their stroke to "none."

Looking at the orange shapes on the dark green background (with no strokes) makes the fish stand out a little too much. The colors do not seem to be very unified. To compensate for this, it is necessary to create a darker orange for the bottom of the fish. Because Global color is not being used, we have to do it manually for each shape.

23. Create a fourth orange color called "Darker Orange" with these settings: C = 0; M = 70; Y = 100; K = 10.

By adding black to the color, the darkness of the green begins to tie into the orange.

24. Change the colors of the bottom of the fish (plus its nose and top-right fin) to the new "Darker Orange" color. Likewise, set the middle shape to "Dark Orange" and the top shape to "Medium Orange."

The fish is now a little darker and fits in well with the dark water. The other koi in the design will have the same colors, though some may be lighter or darker to show their depth in the water (Figure 9.41).

USING GRADIENTS

Gradients can be used when you want one color to blend into another. The sky is not simply blue. It gets darker as you reach the horizon. Gradients can give emphasis to key parts of your design. They can bring attention to a concept, or simply add a twist of something different. There can be more than one color in

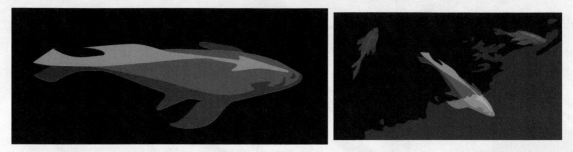

FIGURE 9.41   The final recolored fish (left). A variety of fish colored similarly (right).

a gradient; the basic gradient contains two colors. There are two kids of gradients: linear and radial.

A linear gradient contains two colors that blend into each other along a straight line. In Figure 9.42, the yellow blends into the red, creating an orange color in the middle. The yellow is known as the start color and the red as the end color. The diamond in the middle is the midpoint, where the colors meet. Each of the gradient sliders can be moved to modify the gradient.

FIGURE 9.42   A normal two-color gradient.

Figure 9.43 shows the end color moved in to the left, making the right side of the rectangle solid red and allowing the gradient to happen in only half the area. The midpoint is still halfway between the start color and end color.

FIGURE 9.43   By decreasing the distance between the ends, the transition of the gradient becomes tighter (left). The midpoint Gradient Slider can control the distance of the blend between two colors (right).

In Figure 9.44 (right), the midpoint has been moved to the right. This determines where the gradient will blend the two colors. The transition from yellow to the intermediate color is 80% of the total distance, giving the red only 20% of the distance to change.

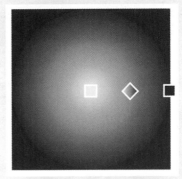

FIGURE 9.44   A basic radial gradient.

A radial gradient also contains at least two colors, but the start color is in the middle of the gradient and the end color on the edges (Figure 9.44). The midpoint works in much the same way, controlling the point as to when the blend occurs.

Creating a Gradient

ON THE CD

1. Open the file *9backplate.ai*, found on the CD-ROM.

   This file contains the line drawing for the background of the design. All the shapes have a black stroke and a white fill. All the objects are on the same layer for easy selection.

2. Open the following palettes from the Window menu: Swatches and Gradient.
3. Select tree area as shown in Figure 9.45 with the Selection tool.

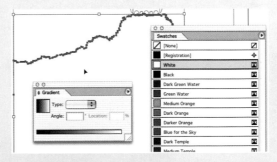

FIGURE 9.45   Select the large tree area.

4. From the Type pop-up menu in the Gradient palette, choose Linear (Figure 9.46).

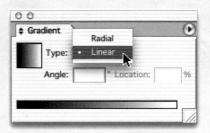

FIGURE 9.46   Choose Linear from the Gradient Type pop-up menu.

Automatically a black to white gradient fills the shape. Illustrator, by default, fills the shape with the last gradient created or selected.

5. From the Swatches palette, drag and drop the color "Green Water" onto the box below the start color in the Gradient palette (Figure 9.47).

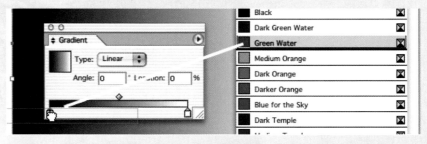

FIGURE 9.47   Drag the color swatch onto the box beneath the start point slider.

There is no other way to add a color to the gradient. You must predefine the color and place it in the Swatches palettes or drag it from the Fill swatch from the Color palette.

6. From the Swatches palette, drag and drop the color "Dark Green Water" onto the box below the end color in the Gradient palette.

By default the gradient has an angle of 0°, resulting in the gradient moving from left to right across the screen.

7. Type "-90" in the Angle field to rotate the gradient clockwise 90° so that the dark color is on the bottom.
8. Drag the Gradient Slider for the midpoint to the left until the Location reads 40% (Figure 9.48).

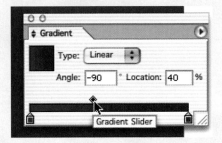

FIGURE 9.48   Move the midpoint slider to the left so that transition of the gradient contains more of the darker color.

This action extends the distance of the darker green on the bottom of the shape. Now the gradient swatch will be added to the Swatches palette for later use.

9.   While holding the Alt or Option key, click on the New Swatch button at the bottom of the Swatches palette to add the gradient. Name the swatch "Water to Trees." Click OK.

Notice that you cannot make any other changes to the swatch in the dialog box. Gradients are rather complicated, so the other options are disabled. If you do not see the swatch appear in the list, make sure the Show All Swatches is pressed.

Now we need to add the gradient to the sky.

10.   Select the rectangle above the trees. This will be the sky.
11.   Choose Linear from the Type menu.

The shape automatically fills with the last gradient. Changes to this gradient will not be reflected in the swatch or anything using the swatch.

12.   Set the start color to "Medium Orange" and the end color to "Blue for the Sky."
13.   Set the Angle to 90°, the End Color Gradient Slider to 75%, and the Midpoint Gradient Slider to 50% (Figure 9.49).

This helps to make the orange color just peek over the ridge, which gives it a cool glow above the trees.

14.   To add this gradient to the Swatches palette, simply drag the Fill swatch from the Gradient palette to the Swatches palette. Name the swatch "Sky Gradient."

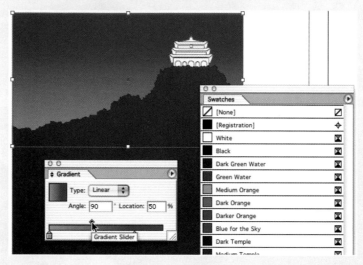

FIGURE 9.49   By modifying the Gradient Sliders a new dimension can be brought to ordinary gradients.

Although no radial gradients were used in this design, the process is still the same, except you would select Radial from the Type pop-up menu in the Gradient palette.

SUMMARY

Observe color in your daily routine and pay special attention to the conditions of the day or night, whether the light is natural or artificial, and the direction from which the light is coming from. Notice how this light affects the objects and textures around you. How do the changes in kinds of light, light source, and light direction affect how you feel?

Look at the color of designed environments such as sports arenas, theaters, parks, lobbies, shopping malls, and even your classroom. How does each affect your mood? Do you think the lighting is appropriate for the activity that is taking place?

Take a look at your clothing choices. Is there a particular color or color scheme that seems to suit you? What kind of image does your choice of color give? How do the colors you wear affect your mood?

The next two chapters will deal with projects using color concepts presented in this chapter. You should be able to make color choices appropriate to the visual feeling you want to communicate. Studying the characteristics and properties of color should help you to formulate plans for color schemes that will heighten the impact of your original art and designs.

10

DESIGN PROJECT SIX: TYPEFACE DESIGN

INTRODUCTION

Letterforms were introduced as an important design element in Chapter 6. This concept will be taken a step further in this chapter and include a brief historic classification of type as well as a section on hierarchy of visual information. A poster exploring a typeface of your choice will be designed incorporating these new ideas. This poster will be created in color using letterforms and lines of type as shapes. The emotional and communicative quality of a typeface will be researched and captured using the digital techniques and concepts you have learned up to this point. There will be other digital tools and procedures introduced, but the exact process of creating the final design will be up to you. Figures 10.16 to 10.18, located later on in this chapter, are a few examples to introduce you to this project.

CONTENT

Background

The following four ideas will be discussed in this section to give you the necessary information to begin the Typeface Design Project: 1) historic classification of typography, 2) type styles, 3) visual and information hierarchy, and 4) type as an element of design.

Historic Classification of Type

The project associated with this chapter deals with the research and selection of a typeface that will be used as the main design element in the creation of a poster communicating the essence of that typeface. A typeface is the name given to the specific letterform design system of an alphabet. To begin the process of selecting a typeface, this section will examine the basic characteristics of typefaces and explore the main categories under which they are grouped. There are literally hundreds of books dedicated to type and type design. Each book contains many different classification methods. The intent of this book is not to give you an in-depth look at typography, but to explore type as an example of shape and an element of design. Type is one of the most universal abstract systems of design that visually communicates on a regular basis. The shapes of type reflect the structure and forms of history and culture and it is for these reasons that type is one of the many topics included in this book. The following information will be an introduction to the basics of type classification. There will be enough material covered to complete the project but more information and research would be necessary for a thorough understanding of typography and its many uses.

There are a number of ways to group typefaces. The most logical way is to group type according to their function and the period in history in which they were created. By looking at history we can see how technical advancements and printed mass communications have influenced the design of typefaces. The reading habits of a particular culture at a certain period of time also influenced the way type was organized and distributed. These and many other factors associated with technology and communications can help us understand the similarities and differences that make up the various historic classifications of type. This section will cover only the basic categories in a brief manner.

Of the many typeface categories, the most general classification of typefaces are serif and sans serif. If you were to go one step further, the following five classifications might be enough to narrow down type choices to a more manageable number. Old Style, Transitional, Modern, Slab Serif, and Sans Serif are the five most familiar historic classifications of typefaces. There are many more, but these five will fill the basic requirements for selecting type for this chapter's project. Figures 10.1 to 10. 4 compare and contrast characteristics of five selected typefaces, serving as examples of each of the five historic classifications of typefaces.

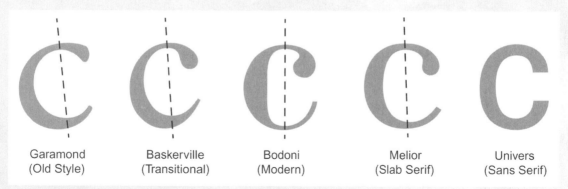

Garamond (Old Style) Baskerville (Transitional) Bodoni (Modern) Melior (Slab Serif) Univers (Sans Serif)

FIGURE 10.1   Examples of the differing x-heights in each classification. The dotted line indicates the x-height. The line at the bottom of each letter is the baseline. Notice how much smaller the Old Style typeface x-height is in comparison to the other typefaces, especially the Sans Serif typeface.

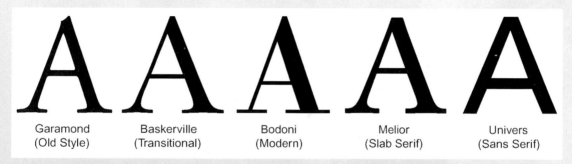

Garamond (Old Style) Baskerville (Transitional) Bodoni (Modern) Melior (Slab Serif) Univers (Sans Serif)

FIGURE10.2   Examples of differing stress. Stress is the diagonal slant of the typeface, illustrated by the dashed line going through the middle of each "c."

Garamond (Old Style) Baskerville (Transitional) Bodoni (Modern) Melior (Slab Serif) Univers (Sans Serif)

FIGURE 10.3   Examples showing the contrast in stroke between the two diagonal parts of the letter "A." Stroke is the degree of difference between thick and thin parts of a typeface. Notice how the transitional typeface, Bodoni, has an extreme contrast of stroke whereas the stroke of the sans serif typeface Univers shows no contrast.

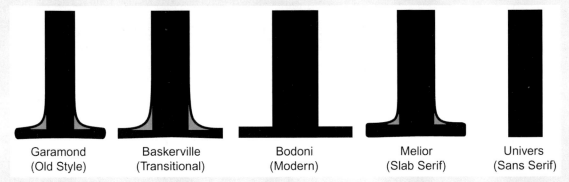

| Garamond (Old Style) | Baskerville (Transitional) | Bodoni (Modern) | Melior (Slab Serif) | Univers (Sans Serif) |

FIGURE 10.4 Examples of how typestyles compare and differ in relationship to serifs or lack of serifs. Notice the area that joins the serif to the stroke in Garamond, Baskerville, and Melior. This area, described with dark gray shading, and the idea of how the serif is joined to the stroke is called bracket. Notice how Bodoni is not bracketed and Univers has no serifs at all.

Old Style Typefaces

Understanding that printing techniques and paper were very crude in the early 1600s, this first type style had very little contrast between the strokes of letters and the brackets were very heavy. The stress or diagonal slant to Old Style letter is extreme (see Figure 10.5) Old Style typefaces generally feel more "human" and less "machined." Figure 10.5 shows four examples of Old Style typefaces.

Old Style Typefaces

Garamond
ABCDEFGHIJKLMNOPQRSTUVWXYZ
abcdefghijklmnopqrstuvwxyz

Palatino
ABCDEFGHIJKLMNOPQRSTUVWXYZ
abcdefghijklmnopqrstuvwxyz

Caslon 224
ABCDEFGHIJKLMNOPQRSTUVWXYZ
abcdefghijklmnopqrstuvwxyz

Weiss
ABCDEFGHIJKLMNOPQRSTUVWXYZ
abcdefghijklmnopqrstuvwxyz

FIGURE 10.5 Four examples of Old Style typefaces.

Transitional Typefaces

As the name implies, Transitional typefaces bridge the gap between Old Style and Modern typefaces. They have more refined serifs and more contrast in stroke than Old Style, but retain and sometimes accentuate heavy bracketing. When compared to Modern typefaces, Transitional typefaces do not have as much contrast in stroke. Transitional typefaces also have more stress. The changes observed from Old Style to Transitional can be attributed to the advancement in technology from the 1600s to the 1750s. The contrast in stroke, less diagonal stress, and more refined serifs and other features make Transitional typefaces feel a bit more "machined" but they still retain some humanist qualities. Figure 10.6 shows four examples of Transitional typefaces.

Tansitional Typefaces

Baskerville
ABCDEFGHIJKLMNOPQRSTUVWXYZ
abcdefghijklmnopqrstuvwxyz

Times Roman
ABCDEFGHIJKLMNOPQRSTUVWXYZ
abcdefghijklmnopqrstuvwxyz

Stone Serif
ABCDEFGHIJKLMNOPQRSTUVWXYZ
abcdefghijklmnopqrstuvwxyz

Perpetua
ABCDEFGHIJKLMNOPQRSTUVWXYZ
abcdefghijklmnopqrstuvwxyz

FIGURE 10.6   Four examples of Transitional typefaces.

Modern Typefaces

Contrary to what this name implies, Modern typefaces are not modern by our timetable. At the end of the eighteenth century these typefaces were modern and a very radical change from previous letterforms. Modern dimensions and characteristics are very exact and mechanical. They have little if any bracketing with an extreme contrast in the stroke, and no noticeable stress. Giambattista Bodoni was the most influential designer at this time. Many contemporary typefaces are reinterpretations of his original work. Figure 10.7 shows four examples of Modern typefaces.

Modern Typefaces

Bodoni

ABCDEFGHIJKLMNOPQRSTUVWXYZ
abcdefghijklmnopqrstuvwxyz

Modern

ABCDEFGHIJKLMNOPQRSTUVWXYZ
abcdefghijklmnopqrstuvwxyz

Fenice

ABCDEFGHIJKLMNOPQRSTUVWXYZ
abcdefghijklmnopqrstuvwxyz

Bernard Modern

ABCDEFGHIJKLMNOPQRSTUVWXYZ
abcdefghijklmnopqrstuvwxyz

FIGURE 10.7 Four examples of Modern typefaces.

Slab Serif Typefaces

Also referred to as Egyptian and Square Serif, Slab Serif typefaces are characterized by their blocky serifs and consistent stroke. They were first used sometime around the late nineteenth century and early twentieth century for their clarity of shape, which came in handy for crudely printed advertising and newspapers. These early Slab Serif typefaces used no bracketing and had no contrast in stroke. Later, a more sophisticated group of typefaces called Clarendons were introduced. They were a return to more contrast in stroke and minimal use of brackets but still incorporated the flat rectangle serif. Slab Serif typefaces used today consist of both the Clarendons and the designs of the non-bracketed, consistent stroke of the early Slab Serif typefaces, many of which resemble Sans Serif typefaces with simple rectangle serifs added on. Figure 10.8 shows four examples of Slab Serif typefaces.

Sans Serif Typefaces

Sans Serif typefaces have been around since the early nineteenth century, but were not popular until the Bauhaus and Art Deco movements made widespread use of them a hundred years later. Because of the lack of serifs, Sans Serif typefaces have the tendency to read vertically, not the traditional horizontal reading direction. They were not used extensively for text until the middle of the twentieth century. Adding more leading or space between shorter lines of type helped with the readability of Sans

Slab Serif Typefaces

Lubalin Graph
ABCDEFGHIJKLMNOPQRSTUVWXYZ
abcdefghijklmnopqrstuvwxyz

Rockwell
ABCDEFGHIJKLMNOPQRSTUVWXYZ
abcdefghijklmnopqrstuvwxyz

New Century Schoolbook
ABCDEFGHIJKLMNOPQRSTUVWXYZ
abcdefghijklmnopqrstuvwxyz

Melior
ABCDEFGHIJKLMNOPQRSTUVWXYZ
abcdefghijklmnopqrstuvwxyz

FIGURE 10.8   Four examples of Slab Serif typefaces. Notice the differences in serifs of the top two typefaces without brackets and the lower two Clarendons.

Serif typefaces. This new trend and the contemporary look of these streamlined typefaces have aided in their popularity. Sans Serif typefaces consist of simple machined shapes that have no extra flourishes. They appear uniform in almost every way. These design features make them suitable for the contemporary look of today's society and attitudes toward digital design. Figure 10.9 shows four examples of Sans Serif typefaces.

San Serif Typefaces

Univers
ABCDEFGHIJKLMNOPQRSTUVWXYZ
abcdefghijklmnopqrstuvwxyz

Helvetica
ABCDEFGHIJKLMNOPQRSTUVWXYZ
abcdefghijklmnopqrstuvwxyz

Gill Sans
ABCDEFGHIJKLMNOPQRSTUVWXYZ
abcdefghijklmnopqrstuvwxyz

Franklin Gothic
ABCDEFGHIJKLMNOPQRSTUVWXYZ
abcdefghijklmnopqrstuvwxyz

FIGURE 10.9   Four examples of Sans Serif typefaces.

Type Styles

Type styles usually refer to the variety of weights or widths of the letters in a specific typeface. There are many different names given to the same weight or width of a letterform. For this chapter we will be concerned with the most basic or common terms. The most important point is that typefaces are created in many different variations that emphasize a particular feeling but do not destroy the continuity or original integrity of the letterforms. The following is a description of the most common type styles (see Figure 10.10).

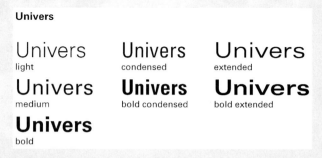

FIGURE 10.10 Examples of common typestyles or variations of the typeface Univers.

Medium

Medium is sometimes referred to as regular, book, or normal. It can sometimes be relatively heavier than these other variation depending on how many different weights are included with a particular typeface. The most basic or standard weight of a typeface can usually be described as medium.

Light

Light may sometimes be called thin. It is the lighter, thinner version of the medium typeface.

Bold

Bold is a general term for a heavier variation of the medium typeface. Depending on the degree of the heaviness of weight other terms such as demi-bold, semi-bold, heavy, extra-bold, ultra, or black may be used.

Condensed

Also referred to as compressed or narrow, condensed is the narrow version of a typeface that gives letterforms the appearance of a vertical line direction.

Extended

Extended or expanded version of a typeface is wider than the standard medium typeface. Because of the emphasis on width, a horizontal line direction is created by each letterform.

Visual and Information Hierarchy

Visual hierarchy was discussed in Chapter 2. It is the concept of organizing elements in a way so they do not conflict or take away attention from another element. Individual lines, shapes, values, and colors must be viewed one at a time in stages from the most important to the least important. The careful staging of elements based on visual hierarchy will lead the viewer from one part of a design to the next until the entire design has been viewed in detail.

This same concept may apply to visual information. Using hierarchy, the most important information should be observed and read first. The less important information should follow.

Figure 10.11 is an example of alternative title designs for a book cover. Beginning with the design on the upper left, the basic information is designed in a way that divides the words logically and lines them up to create a harmonious relationship. The second design on the upper row does the same using a different typeface, giving the title a lighter feeling. The next design to the right combines both typefaces to add contrast and variety, while keeping the two lines of type vertically lined up to create harmony. The visual hierarchy in these three titles is achieved because, as a predominantly English-speaking and English-reading culture, we tend to read from the top to the bottom and from left to right. Hierarchy is achieved because we read the top first. If the primary objective is to make sure viewers know this is a book on design, and the fact that it is "visual" or "fundamental" is the second objective, the design on the top row right would be one way to emphasize this. The design to the left on the second row is an example of how to emphasize the idea of "visual design" over "fundamentals." The design just right of it would do the same only in another typeface. The third design from the left is an example of how the type could be designed to emphasize "design," make "visual" secondary, and show "fundamentals" last. This design also creates contrast between all the words, and unifies the entire title by repeating the same typeface on the top and bottom. The design on the lower right introduces contrast in the typefaces and builds a firm base of heavier type, forcing the viewer to read down an angled slope. The larger "V" in "visual" creates a focal point, bringing the viewer's eye back to the top to repeat this process.

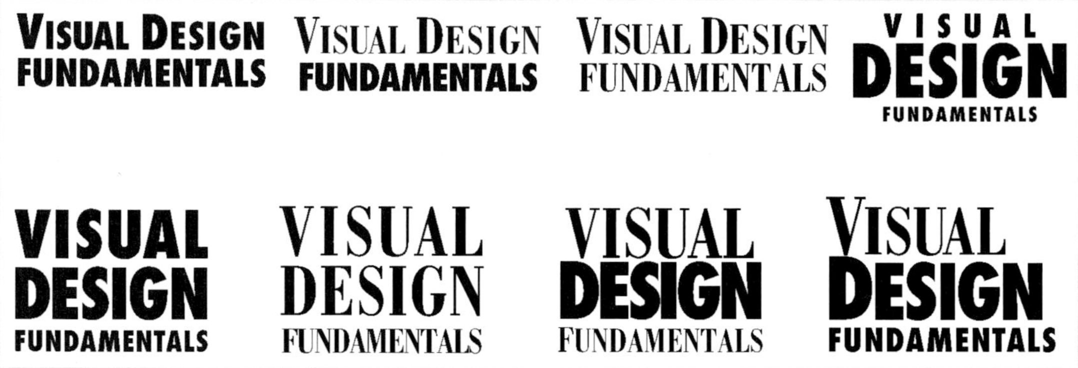

VISUAL DESIGN
FUNDAMENTALS

VISUAL DESIGN
FUNDAMENTALS

VISUAL DESIGN
FUNDAMENTALS

V I S U A L
DESIGN
FUNDAMENTALS

VISUAL
DESIGN
FUNDAMENTALS

VISUAL
DESIGN
FUNDAMENTALS

VISUAL
DESIGN
FUNDAMENTALS

VISUAL
DESIGN
FUNDAMENTALS

FIGURE 10.11   Eight examples of title designs for a book cover.

Figure 10.12 shows six book cover layouts that use one of the titles created in Figure 10.11. The top row progressively adds new information to the title. "A Digital Approach" is a description of the title so it is placed just below it and is related by being vertically lined up with the last line of the title. It is not as important so it is designed with less weight and is placed away from the main title. The middle example on the top row adds the name of the publisher and author. This type identifies people behind the book but not the subject of the book. A light, related typeface is used on top and below the title to create unity. This information is not as important to the viewer and is on the bottom of the list of information hierarchy. Thin rules (horizontal lines) help keep the loose letters from floating apart and add another unifying device to the entire design. The cover designs on the bottom row begin at the left with type that is the same cool color. Everything relates and the contrast of the light blue with the black adds some dynamics. The cover in the middle uses red to create a focal point that emphasizes the most important point of the book, "Design Fundamentals." The design on the far right uses the same information but a completely different color scheme. The colors are divided between the type in a similar way as the middle design. The black is replaced by a cream color, red replaced by purple, and the light blue replaced by dark blue. Notice how the feeling of the overall design has changed.

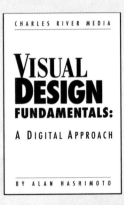

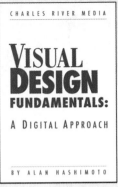

FIGURE 10.12   Six book cover layouts that use one of the titles created in Figure 10.11.

Type as an Element of Design Summary

In previous chapters the fact that type is an element of design, subject to all of the principles of design is well established. The following is a summary of concepts you should be familiar with before you begin the project related to this chapter.

1. Letters should be designed as shapes.
2. Words are made up of letters, which are individual shapes combined to form a pattern.
3. Lines of type or sentences are made of letters and words. Together they create patterns that make up paragraphs that become shapes.

The value of this shape is dependent on the typeface and how close the lines of type are placed together.

4. Shapes in patterns (repeating shapes) are not necessarily seen as individual shapes but, rather, as implied texture. These repeated shapes are visualized together and make up a larger shape (i.e., a paragraph that forms a shape).

5. Designing using pattern would be like designing using value or color. The same or similar pattern should not be restricted to one area of the composition but created so it feels like part of the entire design. You wouldn't use red or a dark value in just one corner of a design. Pattern should give the design unity. At the same time, patterned shapes should have variety. They should not be the same size. Each patterned shape should be used in an unequal amount. There should be large areas of pattern, medium areas of patterned shapes, and smaller (accents) patterned shapes. They should be distributed so there is good hierarchy (variety) and good harmony (unity).

Figures 10.13, 10.14, and 10.15 are examples of designs that use type as a shape.

FIGURE 10.13   Example of two alternative logos that combine type and shape. *Objects* © 2003. Reprinted with permission from Phillip Kesler.

FIGURE 10.14   Screen captures of a Web site that uses type as expressive shapes. *Chaos* © 2003. Reprinted with permission from Jiong Li.

FIGURE 10.15   Frames from a digitally created video using type as a design pattern to create an effective implied texture and design. *AMR-ONE* © 2003. Reprinted with permission from Anthony Romrell.

Typeface Design Project: Defining the Problem

In this project, you will research and select a typeface. Letters, words, and a small amount of information dealing with the typeface will be designed as a single composition to demonstrate the design principles of unity, variety, focal point, balance, abstraction, distortion, rhythm, repetition, and visual hierarchy using the design elements of non-objective positive/negative shapes, line, value, color, and pattern.

1. Study closely the visual characteristics of typefaces you find interesting.
2. Research their origin and find contemporary and classic examples of their usage.
3. Try to get a feeling for the typeface as individual letters, words, and text.
4. Look carefully at both lowercase and uppercase letters. Examine the unique quality of each letter and how they differ from other typefaces.
5. Using the selected typeface, design into one composition at least one letter, one word, and one short paragraph or line of type detailing some aspect of the typeface such as a visual description, appropriate usage, or history. These are just the minimum amount of elements that will make up the design. Parts of letters, multiple letters, repeated words, descriptive sentences, and multiple paragraphs can be used if they are appropriately designed into the entire composition.
6. You can use visuals other than type, but they must not dominate the design or receive more attention than the type. A background image used as a texture could be an appropriate example.
7. Non-objective lines, shapes, and textures that resemble but do not dominate the composition can be used but this is not encouraged. This project is about using type as a design element. You should not have to rely too heavily on shapes other than those found in your selected typeface to create this design project.
8. This design must reflect the feeling, style, time period, and (most important) the visual design aesthetics of the font.
9. The principles of design are very important to this project in particular, because of the non-objective nature of type. There is no recognizable subject matter used to communicate a specific meaning or feeling. This will place more emphasis on the communicative quality of how shapes, lines, value, and color are selected and organized.
10. The following are a few details and reminders concerning the elements and principles of design that should be considered in conjunction with previous information:

- Harmony. Be sure all lines, shapes, values, and colors are designed together and feel related visually and thematically. Classic letterforms have passed the test of time. Their shapes should not be manipulated and their various parts could be cropped and used to unify the letters, words, and text that make up this design project.
- Variety and Hierarchy. Be sure to have enough contrast to make this design interesting. Round or curved shapes next to sharp or angular shapes, and large and thick shapes next to small and thin shapes are just a few examples of how letterform shapes can be designed to create variety. There are at least three elements required for this project: (1) letterforms, (2) name of the typeface (word), and (3) text. To achieve successful visual hierarchy, each shape should be a different size or weight. More contrast will create more drama and dynamic relationships.
- Negative Space. Many letterforms include negative space as part of their design. Uppercase A, B, D, O, P, Q, and R, and lowercase a, b, d, e, g, o, p, and q have obvious enclosed negative space that should be considered when designing larger letters into this project. Other letters such as uppercase C, E, F, G, H, J, K, M, N, S, U, V, W, X, Y, and Z, and lowercase c, f, h, j, k, m, n, s, u, v, w, x, y, and z do not have enclosed negative shapes but negative shapes that are created through an implied line that closes off partial enclosed shapes. When designing with lines of type, remember the concept of implied line and the idea that lines of type create shapes and values through implied visual grouping of similar elements. The more distance between letters and lines of type, the lighter in value the shape they create will seem.
- Color, value, and depth. The illusion of depth can be achieved by using the following principles dealing with value and color:
  - Darker values have a tendency to recede and lighter values seem to come forward.
  - Cool colors recede and warm colors come forward.
  - Shapes with more contrast in value and color appear to come forward and put more distance between foreground and background. Conversely, shapes with less contrast seem to fall into the background and the depth between shapes seems to be very close.
- Transparency is when a shape or object clearly shows through another shape or object. A clear glass window and untinted eyeglasses or contact lenses are good examples. Translucency is when a shape or object can be seen through another shape or object but

not clearly because of diffused light. A tinted windshield and stained glass windows are examples of translucency.

11. Follow the same procedures in the value and color projects. Use thumbnail sketches, or a Photoshop collage to visualize options and alternatives. Experiment with a variety of picture frames, line directions, and value and color schemes.

Figures 10.16 to 10.18 are examples of the finished project.

FIGURE 10.16   Example of a finished typeface design project. *Bodoni Typeface Design* © 2003. Reprinted with permission from Colby Anderson.

FIGURE 10.17   Examples of finished typeface design projects. Left design: *Avenir Typeface Design* © 2003. Reprinted with permission from Trevor Harrison. Right design: *Rockwell Typeface Design* © 2003. Reprinted with permission from Fon Ulrich.

FIGURE 10.18   Examples of finished typeface design projects. Left design: *Courier Typeface Design* © 2003. Reprinted with permission from Audrey Gould. **Right design:** *Myriad Typeface Design* © 2003. Reprinted with permission from Tawnya Tate.

TUTORIAL	**DIGITAL PRODUCTION PROCESS**

FONTS AND YOUR OPERATING SYSTEM

Before we begin, there is some technical information you may need to know about fonts. A font is a file that your computer uses to create the type on your screen and your printer. There are several different types of font files. The two most common file types are True Type and PostScript fonts.

True Type fonts were created by Apple Computer as a means of allowing a typeface to be displayed at any size on screen and when printed to a laser printer.

PostScript fonts were invented by Adobe. They basically do the same thing as True Type fonts, but are handled with more power and accuracy. However, more than one file is necessary when using a PostScript font; one for the screen information and another for the printer information.

In order for PostScript fonts to be displayed correctly on your machine, an application called Adobe Type Manager (ATM) is needed. A copy of ATM Light is available for free via download from their Web site (*www.adobe.com*). Post Script font support is built into Mac OS X and Windows 2000 and higher. ATM Light is needed for all other versions of the earlier Mac OS systems, even when running in OS X Classic Mode (OS 9.2 or earlier).

The location of the fonts is particular to each operating system. Consult your computer handbook for the location of the Fonts folder within your operating system.

CHARACTER AND PARAGRAPH PALETTES

Basically all the attributes of fonts can be controlled with two palettes: the Character palette (`Window > Type > Character`; PC: control + T; Mac: command + T) and the Paragraph palette (`Window > Type > Paragraph`; PC: control + M; Mac: command + M). Normally, both palettes are docked together in the same set. To bring a specific palette to the front, click its tab within the set. Click and drag the tab out of the set to separate the palettes for use at the same time. In Figure 10.19, the palettes are shown separately.

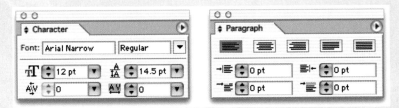

FIGURE 10.19   The Character and Paragraph palettes.

The Character Palette

The Character palette contains the attributes for individual characters. Five options can be set from this palette. These options affect the characters and how they relate to each other individually. The following is a breakdown of this palette row by row.

Font: Use the arrow at the right of these fields to open the pop-up menu and choose the typeface for the selected text. The fonts are listed alphabetically and some font sets contain their own variations in sub-menus. Scroll through the list until you find the font you want (Figure 10.20).

Font Size: A character's size is measured in points (72 points = 1 inch); the larger the number the larger the size of the character. A font is measured from its baseline to capline. Enter the number manually in the field or select a size from the pop-up menu (Figure 10.21).

FIGURE 10.20   Choose the typeface from the pop-up menu to change the selected text.

FIGURE 10.21   Change the size of the font by either entering a number in the field or selecting it from the pop-up menu.

Leading: Leading is the vertical space between the lines of text in a paragraph. Leading is measured from baseline to baseline. By default Illustrator (as well as other programs) automatically sets the leading according to the font size selected. Enter the number manually in the field or select a size from the pop-up menu (Figure 10.22).

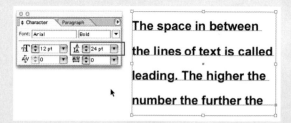

FIGURE 10.22   Leading is the vertical space in between lines of text.

Kerning: Kerning is changing the space in between two characters. This can be adjusted to help make the space between two characters seem more comfortable. The rule of thumb when it comes to kerning is that the space between each letter in the word or title should be able to have the same amount of "sand" poured in each space. Insert the pointer between the two letters to activate this option in the palette. Enter the number manually in the field or use the up and down arrows to move in increments of one (Figure 10.24).

FIGURE 10.23 Too much kerning can make the space between letters feel uncomfortable. Or the opposite, if the distance is too small.

Tracking: Unlike kerning, tracking is changing the space in between characters over a range of text. Enter the number manually in the field or use the up and down arrows to move in increments of one (Figure 10.24).

FIGURE 10.24 Tracking is changing the space in between more than two letters or a range of text.

THE TYPE TOOLS

Because the basis of this project is type, the Type tool will be reviewed. All six of the type tools are available in the menu under the Type tool icon in the Tools palette. To see all the tools at once, tear away the tools from the Tools palette by holding down the mouse button on the Type tool and dragging over to the tearoff tab and release the mouse button (Figure 10.25). A free-floating Type tools palette is the result.

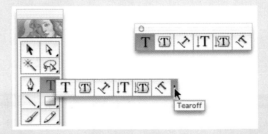

FIGURE 10.25 Click on the tearoff tab to make the Type tools a free-floating palette.

Type Tool

The basic tool in the set is the Type tool. It is used to create horizontal text. Simply click where you want the text to begin and start typing (Figure 10.26). To insert a carriage return, simply hit the Enter (Return) key, and begin typing on the next line.

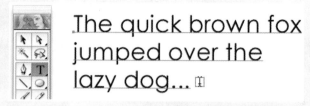

FIGURE 10.26   To place text on the page, simply click with the Type tool where you would like the text to start, and then type.

If you want to type within a specific area, click and drag out a box in which to place the text. If the text box is not the right size, resize the text box using the Selection tool (Figure 10.27).

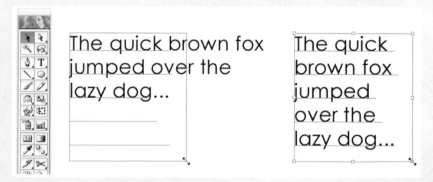

FIGURE 10.27   Resizing the text box dynamically places the text within the text box without distorting it.

If there is more text than will fit in the text box you created, a small box will appear at the right of the last visible line of text. That is a visual clue that there is more text than will fit. You can resize the text box by selecting one of the transform handles and resize the box to the desired size.

To create vertical columns of text, use the Vertical Type tool. It works in much the same way as the Type tool, but types vertically from top to bottom and the lines of text are right to left (Figure 10.28). Although not a very practical tool, it does wonders for Asian characters as well as Matrix-like type effects.

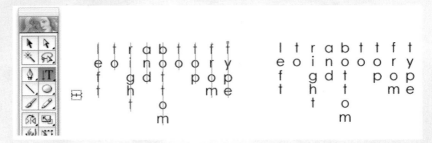

FIGURE 10.28   The Vertical Type tool is not a very practical tool, but works best for Asian languages.

AREA TYPE TOOLS

Although you can create a text box with the Type tool and place the text within this text box, you might want to place text into an odd shape and watch it flow within the space. The Area Type tool is the tool for the job.

Select the Area Type tool and click on any closed simple shape to place the insertion point into the object. Notice as you type that the text flows within the shape, automatically wrapping down to the next line as it reaches the edge (Figure 10.29). The shape can be drawn with the Shape tools or with the Pen tools. The path has to be closed. Illustrator will not allow an open path to be filled with the text. Text within a shape can be edited by using any of the Text tools to place the insertion point.

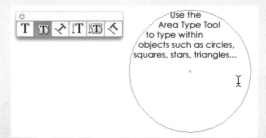

FIGURE 10.29   Using the Area Type tool, text can flow within the shape selected.

You can edit the shape in which the text is contained after the fact, using the Direct Selection and Convert Anchor Point tools (Figure 10.30). The text will automatically fit within the area. The shape in which the text is contained turns invisible when the type tool is applied to it. The path is still there, but it has no visible stroke or fill.

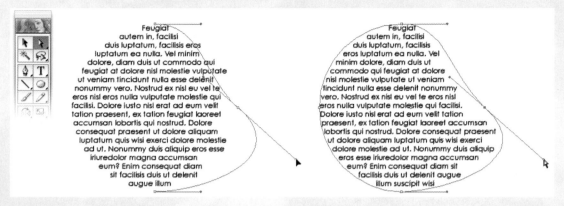

FIGURE 10.30   You can modify the points and curves of a shape with the text inside. The text will automatically reformat to fit the shape.

Keep in mind that legibility is a key issue when using blocks of text. Trying to set type inside of a star (Figure 10.31) may not read correctly. An elliptical shape would work better.

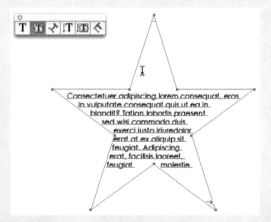

FIGURE 10.31   Placing type within the shape of a star does not read as well as type placed within other shapes.

PATH TYPE TOOLS

The Path Type tool allows you to type directly onto an open path or a closed simple path (i.e., a circle or polygon).

1. Create a new Illustrator Document. Using the Pen tool, draw an open path similar to that in Figure 10.32.

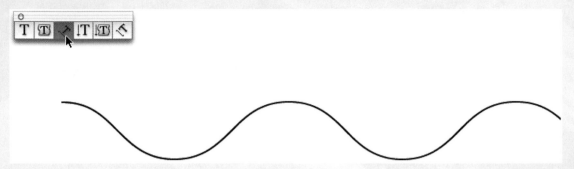

FIGURE 10.32   Create a simple path using the Pen tool.

A wavy line is drawn for this example. The path that you create can be either structured or loose. The path can cross over itself. Take note that sharp corners or sudden curves may distort the text and make it harder to read.

2. With the Path Type tool selected, click on the path near the left to set the insertion point for the text.

The point can be placed anywhere along the path. The stroke of the line the text will attach to becomes "none" so that it is not seen and does not interfere with the text type.

3. Type a basic phrase such as "The quick brown fox jumped over the sleeping dog." With the Selection tool, click outside the type area to deselect the text.

The text is displayed with the path invisible (a blue line acts as a preview). The path and type remain two separate entities, but are grouped together. The path may be modified with the Direct Selection and the Convert Anchor tools. Once in a while, the text you type may be too long for the line that you created. Add points to the line or move existing points to lengthen the line.

4. With the Selection tool, click the path and type group.

The I-beam, as identified in Figure 10.33 is the starting point of the text along the path.

FIGURE 10.33   The I-beam is the vertical line at the beginning of a line of text along a path.

5. Click on the I-beam at the beginning of the line to select it. Drag to the right to move the text along the path (Figure 10.34).

FIGURE 10.34   Move the I-beam to reposition the start of the text.

The I-beam can be moved along the path to alter the start point of the text. A colored outline is created to act as a preview of how the position of the text will be altered. Drag the I-beam back and forth until you are happy with the results.

6. Click on the I-beam and drag across the path to flip the text along the bottom of the path (Figure 10.35).

FIGURE 10.35   Drag the I-beam across the path to flip the text. The text will turn blue to give you a preview.

The text can be flipped underneath the path by dragging the I-beam across the path. Drag it back across the path to return the type to its original orientation on the path. The text is only placed when you release the mouse.

The text on the path can be edited by selecting and editing with any of the Type tools.

7. Select the words "brown fox jumped" by highlighting them with the Type tool. With the text highlighted, type "green lizard hopped" (Figure 10.36).

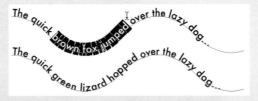

FIGURE 10.36   Highlight the text you wish to change (top) and type the new text (bottom).

Editing text is simple. Remember that if your text runs longer than the line, you can edit the path. You can also insert the point anywhere in the text to add new text.

The Path Type tool can also be used on closed paths and shapes like a circle.

8. With the Ellipse tool, draw a circle with a black stroke and a fill of "none."

By using only the stroke, you can really see the line that the text will follow. You can place the Path Type tool on a filled object, but the fill, like the stroke, will disappear when text is applied.

9. Select the Path Type tool and click on the stroke of the circle and type the phrase again (Figure 10.37).

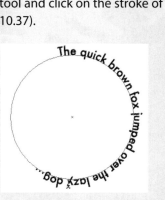

FIGURE 10.37   Type the phrase along the path of the circle.

Wherever you click on the path, this is where the text will start. If you are not happy with the results, change the start point of the line.

10. To move the text around the circle, click on the I-beam with the Selection tool and drag it around the outside of the circle.

Drag the I-beam with the Selection tool around the outside of the circle to change its start point. The change will not be made until you release the mouse button.

11. Move the I-beam across the path into the circle to cause the text to flow on the inside of the path (Figure 10.38).

\Drag the I-beam across the path to the inside of the shape to make the text flow along the inside of the path. To return it to the outside, drag back across the line.

For a shortcut to this, simply double-clicking the I-beam causes the text to flip in and out of the path. This works with either a shape or a path.

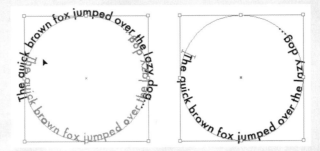

FIGURE 10.38   To cause the text to flow within the circle, drag the I-beam across the path to the inside.

The initial direction of the type along the path depends on how it was constructed. If the path is drawn from left to right, the text will flow across the top of the path. If the path is drawn from right to left, the text will automatically flow along the bottom of the path.

The path must be a non-compound, non-masking path. If you use the Pathfinder to merge two shapes together, the path must be expanded to one non-compound path. If a shape is being used as a clipping mask, the Path Type tool will not work on that path.

12. Draw two circles that overlap each other. Use the Pathfinder to add the shape areas together.
13. Select the Path Type tool and click on the compound path.

It does not work. The warning dialog states: *you must click on a non-compound, non-masking path to create text along a path*. These objects still have two paths, which share a portion of the same area. Click OK in the warning box.

14. Click on the Expand button in the Pathfinder to make the two paths one continuous path.
15. Using the Path Type tool, click on the path to set the insertion point for the text. Type some text onto the path (Figure 10.39).

As was mentioned earlier, text that is set along paths with steep and sudden angles and curves may overlap each other, making the type illegible. Add extra spaces into the text to space the characters around these trouble spots, or modify the slope of the path or the angle of the corner.

16. Add extra spaces in between the words that might overlap each other, creating illegible type (Figure 10.40).

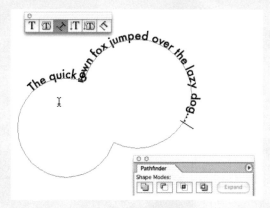

FIGURE 10.39 Because it is now one path, the Path Type tool will work.

FIGURE 10.40 Add extra spaces in between the text that overlaps.

The Path Type tool will be a great asset to you in this project. Experiment with it. See what you can do. There are some examples in Figure 10.41.

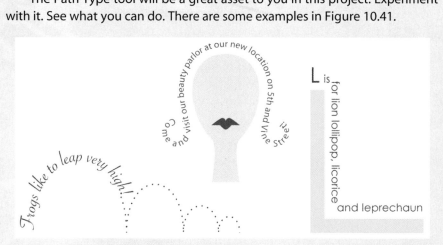

FIGURE 10.41 Examples using the Path Type tool.

As with the other Type tools, there is a vertical version of the Path Type tool called the Vertical Path Type tool. It works the same way as the other vertical tools, typing from top to bottom, right to left.

TUTORIAL

THE PROJECT: A CASE STUDY

Figure 10.42 shows the completed poster for this assignment. The same process that was taken in the other projects was taken here: research, thumbnails, roughs, composites, and finished design.

FIGURE 10.42   The final poster design for the Futura Type Poster.

RESEARCH

The most important step in this process was to research the chosen font, Futura.

Paul Renner of Germany developed *Futura* in 1928, and was one of the most prominent sans-serif typefaces created during the Art Deco period. Knowing the designer, his homeland, and the time period is a great place to start.

Look everywhere you can. Do not rely completely on the Internet. Talk to others in your class; get ideas and inspiration from them.

THUMBNAILS

From your research, sketch dozens of thumbnails. From those pick the ten best ideas and put them together (Figure 10.44). Several of them might look like good ideas at first, but as you poured over the details of the assignment read that 'non-objective lines, shapes, and textures . . . can be used but are not encouraged', then throw out all of the ones that do not meet the criteria of the assign. In the example in Figure 10.43, #1, #3, # 8, and #9 should be omitted.

After carefully reading through the requirements, #9 was chosen because it would yield the most variety.

ROUGHS

One of the good things about the Type Poster is that it can evolve once it's put into the computer. A mock-up for the rough can be made (using Illustrator) in

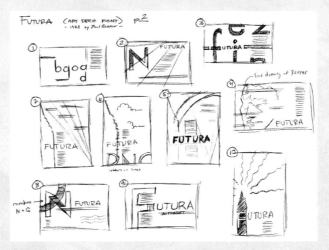

FIGURE 10.43   One of the thumbnail sheets for the poster design.

black and white (Figure 10.44). It's a simple layout using just text, without color, value, or texture.

FIGURE 10.44   The first computer-created rough of the poster.

Looking at the rough you can begin to decide where to take it. At this stage of the process, print-out a couple of the mock-ups and draw on them to gain inspiration. Look at Figure 10.45. To create a sense of unity and variety, the letter from the name of the font was duplicated and letters were reversed out of other letters to create negative shapes and keep the imagery interesting.

FIGURE 10.45   The rough is a sketched over a computer printout.

At this point, colors need to be searched. For example, using a picture of a ceramic pot from the 1920s (which was glazed with soft blues, browns, tans, and yellows), eight colors out of the photo were matched and added to the Swatches palette (Figure 10.46) in an Illustrator document. (Please refer to Chapter 9 for details on adding colors to your Swatches palette). This will be the color scheme for the poster.

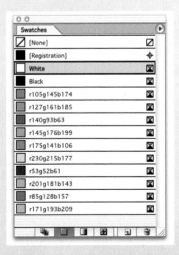

FIGURE 10.46   Color swatches
matched from reference material.

COMPOSITES

Once you have selected colors and have a rough idea, it is time to plot the letters out in Illustrator. Using color as a means of creating visual depth and coupling it with negative shapes created by reversing characters out of each other, the poster begins to come to life (Figure 10.47).

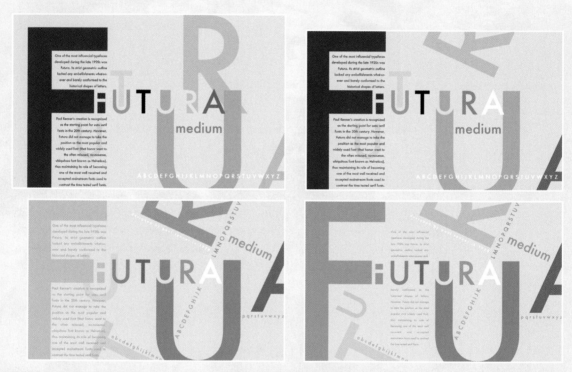

FIGURE 10.47   The first color comp of the poster (top left). Slightly modified the poster by rotating the "R" to the same angle as the left slope of the "A" (top right). More diagonals were added to complement the "R" (bottom left). Relocating the text from within the "F" helped to free up the negative space in the design (bottom right).

The design seems to be very structured with lots of verticals and horizontals. To create a strong diagonal visual, the large "R" was tilted.

Notice how there is one simple focal point and all of the colors relate. The big dark "F" seems very separate from the rest of the design. The diagonal "R" provides good variety but does not belong unless there are other diagonals. This is obviously not exact.

More diagonals, in the forms of lines of text consisting of the alphabet, can be added. By matching the left slope of the "A," all the diagonals are unified. By changing the colors of the big "F," it becomes subdued and recedes into the background color. But it still looks a visually heavy on the left side.

By moving the text out of the big "F" and aligning the margins of the text to be the total width of the small "U" and "T," the negative space breathes a little easier from not being so cluttered. The little "A" is still the focal point, as are all the elements and colors necessary to make a good basic overall design.

As you apply the design principles contained in this chapter, the project will become a little easier. Use simple transformations (scale, reflect, rotate, etc.) and the type tools to your benefit.

Frame your image carefully, as was done in the letterform and shape project. Maybe the poster as a whole is not working well but you like a certain part of it. Pick a part of the poster, crop it, and see if it can be rescued.

CREATING VISUAL DEPTH USING VALUE

In Chapter 8, value was discussed in depth. By reducing images to simple shapes and applying gray tones across the image, a sense of depth occurs.

Figure 10.48 shows the final color version on top of a grayscale version of the Futura Type Poster. The same principles apply. The darker colors tend to pop up from the light background. The lighter gray letters recede. The contrast in value allows you to focus on what's important.

FIGURE 10.48   A grayscale value study (left) of the color poster (right).

COLOR

From the color palette all but two colors were used (Figure 10.49). The colors are placed evenly throughout the design. The blues on top of the tans help the shapes come forward, as do the darker reds.

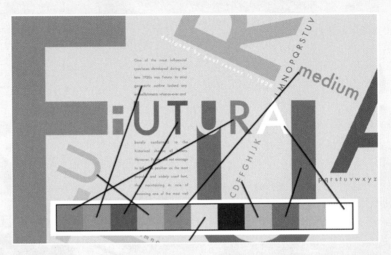

FIGURE 10.49   The color is evenly shared throughout the entire design.

It is essential to have a solid color scheme before entering the composition stage. Select the mood for the design. Should you use a palette of loud, vibrant colors? Or subdued earth tones? Or cool blues and greens? Or hot yellows and reds? Or a complimentary color scheme? Or a split complimentary? Or a triad scheme?

TRANSPARENCY

Transparency can be used in many ways. You can make objects completely solid or transparent. It can be applied to layers, groups, shapes, type, and so on. Special effects can be achieved with the click of a button.

Access the Transparency palette by selecting `Window > Transparency`. Simply select the object and use the slider to add a level of transparency to it. The lower the number the more transparent the object will become.

In Figure 10.50, the blue of the "U" was too strong on the background. Rather than pick another color, its transparency was reduced to 60%. Transparency allows the background color to come through and blends the two together. The same technique was done with the "T."

Try overlapping transparent objects to see how the colors mix. Maybe an interesting shape will appear.

PATTERN

Repetitious patterns in design can help the eye to follow a set course. Evenly spaced letters of the same basic size, color, or shape can create a pattern. The

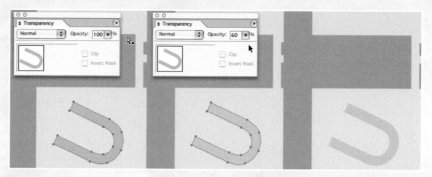

FIGURE 10.50   The transparency of the "U" is set to 60%.

diagonal alphabet creates a line, even though there are 26 separate parts to that line and two colors. It carries you right through the focal point of the poster.

In Figure 10.51, the letters in Futura help to create a strong horizontal. Are they the same color? No. Are they the same shape? No. Are they the same size? Yes. The repetition in size helps to create that visual.

FIGURE 10.51   Across the middle of the design, positive and negative shapes help to create a patterned line.

A Quick Review

The Type Poster Project uses a lot of the same techniques and skills from the project on letterform and shape. Here is a brief review of some the tools and options that will be of great benefit to you in this project.

Creating Outlines

Working with a font is one thing, but sometimes it is better to work with an outline of the character. Because this poster project requires only one font selection, once the selection is made, changing the font to outlines (a closed path) is the better road to travel. To convert a font to outlines follow these steps:

1. Create the text to be converted. Select its typeface and approximate size.

    For this example, the word "FUTURA" and its accompanying font, Futura Medium, were chosen. The font size is between 24 and 36.

2. With the type selected, choose `Type > Create Outlines` (PC: Shift + Control + O; Mac: Shift + Command + O).

 If you right-click the text with the mouse, the option to Create Outlines is contained in the contextual menu.

Grouping and Ungrouping

Once a word has been converted to outlines, the letters are automatically placed into a group. In order to select each of these letters individually, they need to be ungrouped.

1. With the text still selected, choose `Object > Ungroup` (PC: Shift + Control + G; Mac: Shift + Command + G).

 If you right-click the group with the mouse, the option to Ungroup is contained in the contextual menu.

4. For practice, with the characters selected, choose `Object > Group` (PC: Control + G; Mac: Command + G) to regroup the letters.

 If you right-click the text with the mouse, the option to Group is contained in the contextual menu.

5. Once again, ungroup the objects.

    As you work, you may want to group things together in order to move them or transform them. Remember that the Direct Selection tool can select paths and objects within a group.

Transforming Objects

One of the key components in the type poster is varying the size, angle, and orientation of objects to create unity and variety. Using the Transforming tool is crucial to achieving these principles.

1. Select the "F" (or a random letter from your own file) and grab one of the handles. While holding down the Shift key (to keep the object in proportion)

drag the handle up and to the left until the character is roughly double in size (Figure 10.52).

FIGURE 10.52   Clicking on the handles with the pointer allows you to scale the object.

Do the same with another letter, like the "U," but this time choose a different handle and go in another direction.

2. With the Selection tool, move another character slightly up from the rest.
3. Mouse over one of the handles until the pointer turns into a curved double-arrow, activating the Rotate operation. Click the mouse and rotate the object to the left or right. Release the mouse button to set the angle (Figure 10.53). Hold down the Shift key, if necessary, to constrain the angle to 45° angles.

FIGURE 10.53   Rotate the object using the handles.

4. Select another character and choose `Object > Transform > Reflect`.
5. The Reflect dialog box appears. Click the Vertical button. To see a preview of the change, click Preview. The character reflects along its vertical axis. Click OK.

All these options are available under the `Object > Transform` menu, the Tools palette, or under Transform in the contextual menu when you right-click on a selected object.

PREPARING YOUR DOCUMENT

For the other projects in this text, the document size has been kept at the default size of Letter (8$\frac{1}{2}$" x 11"). A simple sheet of paper would not be big enough for the purpose of a poster.

Document Size: Tabloid

When creating the document in Illustrator, you can either select from several preformatted sizes or set your own.

For this example a *tabloid-sized* size sheet of paper was used. Tabloid measures 17 inches wide and 11 inches high, or the same size as two sheets of letter-sized placed side by side.

1. Launch Illustrator and create a new document.
2. In the New Document dialog box, set the Artboard Size to Tabloid and the Units to Inches. Set the Orientation to Landscape (Figure 10.54). Click OK.

FIGURE 10.54 Set the Artboard size to Tabloid in the New Document dialog box.

You may choose whatever size you wish for the dimensions of your poster. Make sure that the size you choose reflects your design. To do so, simply type your measurements into the Width and Height fields of the Artboard Setup portion of the New Document dialog box.

OUTPUTING YOUR POSTER/DESIGN

Page Tiling

The setup for the document is now complete. With the Rulers turned on, you'll see that the artboard is 17 inches wide and 11 inches high. The dotted outlines that are enclosed within the space of the artboard represent the size of the paper that is currently selected in the Page Setup portion of the file. The outer line is the actual size of the paper. In this case, the default of Letter is selected. The inside line is the actual printable area of the page. They are also referred to as margins (Figure 10.55).

FIGURE 10.55   The dotted outlines show the paper's current size and printable area.

The entire image does not fit within the printable area of the Page Tile. If printed now, the output would look like something similar to Figure 10.56.

FIGURE 10.56   If you were to print, all that would print would be what was in the printable area.

If all you had access to was a printer that only printed on standard letter-sized paper, you could move the Page Tile Area around and print-out all the pieces that you would need and paste them together.

To move the Page Tile Area, locate the Page Tiling Tool from underneath the Hand Tool in the Tools palette. Use the tool to move the printable area around the page. The pointer is connected to the lower-left corner of the tile area (Figure 10.57). Move the area and print. Then move the area again and print. Repeat this process until the entire area has been printed. The result should be something like Figure 10.57. Trim and mount the pieces to mat board or foam core for stability. This is passable for Roughs and Comps, but not for finished pieces.

FIGURE 10.57 You can move the printable area around the page with the Page Tile tool (right). Take the pieces of the design and trim and mount them together (left).

If your printer is capable of printing on Tabloid paper, set the printer to print Tabloid in the Page Setup area (`File > Page Setup`). The printable area should be similar to that shown in Figure 10.58 (left), with the result looking like Figure 10.58 (right).

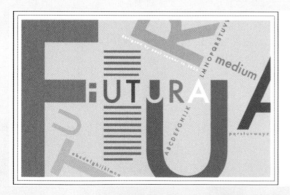

FIGURE 10.58 With the paper size set to Tabloid the entire design will fit within the printable area (left). The result of outputting the design on a printer capable of Tabloid prints (right).

All printers are different and have their own way of doing things. It would be difficult to try to explain every detail of the printing process because there are so many variables that go into printing. If you have any questions, contact you teacher, local print shop, or service bureau.

SUMMARY

Much of what we know about the history of civilization and the accomplishments of past cultures is through their ability to share ideas, tell stories, and record events. All of society's realities and ideals are preserved and made available through the development of devices and systems to communicate and record this information. Design for communications has always been a reflection of a culture's beliefs, political structure, art, and technological advances. Letterforms are the most widely used visual form of sharing information. This is why this book is concerned with the structure and variations of these designs. Can you look back through history and give examples of the relationship and visual similarities between the transportation design and type designs of that period? How about examples of industrial design and type designs? Can you find examples of interior design or architecture that reflect the shapes, colors, and forms of the more popular typefaces of that period?

If visual information design is directly related to a society's beliefs and technical advancements, what would be the characteristics of a typeface you would create for your present technically advanced social group? What would a typeface of the future look like?

11

DESIGN PROJECT SEVEN: DIGITAL MONTAGE/COLLAGE

INTRODUCTION

This last project is a culmination of the design theories and content contained in this book. All the elements and principles of design will be incorporated into one composition. Realism, in relationship to other designed shapes such as non-objective, stylized, and abstract shapes, will be encouraged and theme will be used as one of the unifying elements.

Up to this point, only the basics of the paint program Photoshop have been explained and incorporated into projects. This final project will use Photoshop exclusively for the finished design. The basic tools and techniques that make up this powerful program will be covered in the production process section.

Learning the ins and outs of Photoshop and how to create the final project will be involved. The elements and principles of design have been discussed and projects concerning each of these have been completed. Therefore, there will be fewer new concepts dealing with design theory, less conceptual demands, and more space dedicated to the digital production process.

CONTENT

The Basic Problem Defined

Combining imagery from at least three to five different sources, a single composition will be created. Photographs, illustrations, typography, and any traditional or digitally created imagery can be used for this project. The design principles of unity, variety, focal point, balance, abstraction, distortion, rhythm, repetition, and visual hierarchy will be demonstrated using the design elements of shapes, line, value, color, pattern, and texture. The final design can use realism, be an abstraction, or be a stylization.

Background Information

In terms of visual design, a *montage* is a collection of separate images that are designed into one related composition, each retaining its original identity. All these individual items form a relationship between each other as one design but the individual parts are still recognizable.

A *collage* is a work of art that uses visual materials that were not originally created by the artist for that particular piece. These materials, textures, patterns, and objects retain their own original identity but also become part of a new design that may or may not have the same atmosphere, meaning, or emotional content as the original source from which it was taken.

Both of these types of designs are good examples of Gestalt theory. They are similar in that they combine elements from different sources into one composition and these elements retain their own integrity becoming recognizable parts of a whole design. They differ in how the original pieces are gathered or created for the final design. In a montage, the original images are created beforehand with the intention of becoming part of a final design. A collage uses images that existed before the conception of the final design with no intention of becoming part of a larger design. Materials used for collages are often found objects or textures. Found objects can be any objects that can be scanned or attached to the design; textures refer to the surface quality of shapes or objects. They might include a sheet of rough sandpaper or a smooth piece of silk.

This final project can technically be a collage or a montage or both. If photographs or other visuals are created separately with the intention of being used for this project, this is a clear example of a montage. If the materials used are all selected photographs or other visuals not originally intended for this design, it is an example of a collage. The project could contain elements of both. Photographs could be taken and combined with found objects, fabric, or printed material.

Figures 11.1 to 11.6 are a few examples of montage or collage designs. Figure 11.6 is an example of the project detailed in this chapter.

FIGURE 11.1   Example of a painting that uses a collaged page of type in the background. *Peace* © 2003. Reprinted with permission from Brisida Magro.

Figure 11.2 shows examples of collage and montage. The design at the top left is created using photographs of leaves and manipulating them using Photoshop. The image on the top right combines scans of applied textures and faces to create a digital collage. If you look closely at the visual on the bottom left, you will notice it is made up of a combination of other photographs manipulated and designed in Photoshop. The design on the lower right is an interactive menu page using transparency to create a relationship between the dinosaur background and the interface navigation system in the foreground.

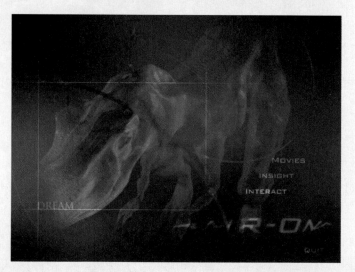

FIGURE 11.2   Example on the top left shows a scan of leaves. The example on the top right shows how the scan is used in a collage. The example on the bottom left is a digital montage that combines several scans. *Leaves* © 2003, *Three Faces* © 2003, and *Half Moon* © 2003. Reprinted with permission from Jim Godfrey. The example on the bottom right is an interactive interface design that uses a montage. *AMR-ONE* © 2003. Reprinted with permission from Anthony Romrell.

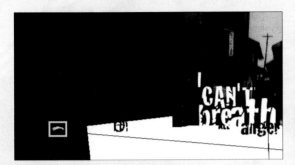 

FIGURE 11.3   Example of two pages from a Web site. These pages combine textures and typography to create a spontaneous digital collage. *Chaos* © 2003. Reprinted with permission from Jiong Li.

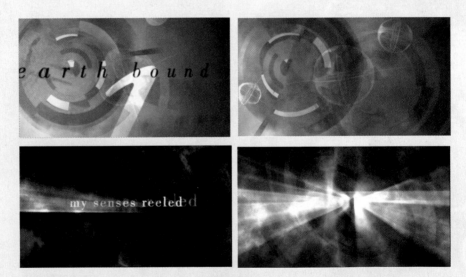

FIGURE 11.4   Example of a collage and a montage. Selected digital video frames illustrate the layering and design that is found in compositing type and non-objective shapes. The motion and design of the shapes and type seem calculated but the translucent patterns and textures that are created by the overlapping motion of the shapes seem to occur at random. *Selected frames from* digital video *"Floyd"* © 2003. Reprinted with permission from Anthony Romrell.

FIGURE 11.5   Example of a montage. A calculated combination of images characterizes the top illustration. The bottom two designs incorporate non-objective shapes that represent symbols related to mathematics. *Chemicals in America* © 2003, *One* © 2003. and *Two* © 2003. Reprinted with permission from Alan Hashimoto.

FIGURE 11.6   Example of three photographic montages. The original images were digitized slides taken from a traditional 35mm camera. *Bellinzona* © 2003. *Morcote* © 2003. *Luzern* © 2003. Reprinted with permission from Robert Winward.

Conceptual Process and the Project Details

The following is a summary of procedures that are involved in the conceptual process of creating this project. Most of these steps are mentioned in Chapter 10.

1. Select several themes that seem interesting. Theme is a topic or subject matter that gives meaning and continuity to an entire project.
2. Research these themes and try to find as many different approaches to visually communicate their content.
3. Narrow your choices to one theme and begin collecting and/or creating images that will support your idea and make your design interesting.

4. Get a feel for the subject matter and try to visualize an appropriate style that will convey your idea.

5. Select and/or create quality images that can be combined and output at a high resolution (at least 300dpi).

6. In addition to photographs, illustrations, and type, non-objective shapes, lines, patterns, and textures can be incorporated into the final design.

7. Following are a few details and reminders concerning the elements and principles of design that should be considered in conjunction with previous information:

   • Be sure all lines, shapes, values, and colors are effectively combined, and feel visually and thematically related.

   • Classic letterforms have passed the test of time. Their shapes should not be manipulated, but their various parts could be cropped and used to unify the letters, words, and text that comprise this design project.

   • Variety and hierarchy: Be sure to have enough contrast to make this design interesting. Round or curved shapes next to sharp or angular shapes, and large and thick shapes next to small and thin shapes are just a few examples of how letterform shapes can be designed to create variety.

   • Color, value, and depth: The illusion of depth can be achieved by using the following principles dealing with value and color:

     Darker values have a tendency to recede and lighter values seem to come forward.

     Cool colors recede and warm colors come forward.

     Shapes with more contrast in value and color appear to come forward and put more distance between foreground and background. Conversely, shapes with less contrast seem to fall into the background and the depth between shapes seems to be very shallow.

     Transparency and translucency: Transparency is when a shape or object can be seen right through another object or shape. This makes the portion of the shape or object in the foreground almost invisible. Translucency is when a shape or object can be seen through another object or shape. This makes it possible for the shape or object in the foreground to be seen at the same time.

8. Similar to the value, color, and typeface assignment, the best way to visualize all of these elements together is by viewing all the reference material at once and creating thumbnail sketches combining all of

the material. This is a quick way to visualize a variety of options and analyze the relationships between separate elements. Position, proportions, and scale of each visual may be studied in relation to each other. Changes may be made early to save time and energy. Once the source material can be visualized together as a thumbnail sketch, the shapes and values can be analyzed. Color choices can then be researched, and decisions can be made.

9. Experiment with various picture frame proportions.
10. Experiment with different values and color schemes.

TUTORIAL

DIGITAL PRODUCTION PROCESS

PREPARING THE PROJECT

In preparing for the project, the first step is to pick a topic. The next step is to find material to support your topic. This research is crucial to the success of your project. Material can include images taken with a digital camera (although you can also scan photographs), fabric, textured surface, illustrations, type, and a variety of other things.

FIGURE 11.7   Source files for the montage.

From your source materials (Figure 11.7), create thumbnail drawings of the montage. These drawings (like the ones for the color project) can help you compose on paper, instead of wasting time using the computer.

FIGURE 11.8 Samples from the thumbnails for the montage.

From your thumbnails, create several rough drawings, paying attention to the placement and size of each image (Figure 11.8). When completed, you can begin to scan the images and objects and build them on the computer.

FIGURE 11.9 Rough layout of the montage.

The final result should be close to your original rough drawing (Figure 11.9). You can take liberties in this design later when using the computer. As you begin to put the pixels together, you might see something that does not quite work right. Feel free to fix it.

To put this montage together, Photoshop will be used. It is important to note that Photoshop is a very robust software application. This tutorial was created with the intention of introducing you to several tools that will be important in your completion of the project. Please experiment and see what works for you. There are many secondary options and tools. Feel free to try them out and change their options.

FIGURE 11.10   The final montage.

Document Setup

When creating new document in Photoshop, there are a few more options to consider then when creating a new document in Illustrator. (Refer to Figure 11.11 for the following steps.)

Figure 11.11 has been edited and the video preset sizes have been removed.

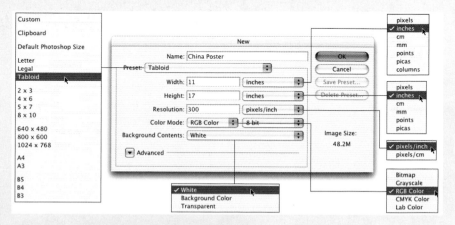

FIGURE 11.11   A break-out diagram of the New document dialog box.

1. Launch Photoshop.

    If you have not already done so, launch the program.

2. From the top menu choose `File` > `New` (PC: control + N; Mac: command + N).

This opens the New document dialog box. This dialog box is divided into two sections: Image Size and Contents.

3. Name your file accordingly.

At this point in the process, give the file a name. It can be changed later when you save the file. It is good practice to name your images up front so that as you work on multiple new images, you won't become confused as to which is which.

4. From the Image Size section, click on the Preset Size drop-down menu.

This drop-down menu houses several preset file sizes as they relate to standard paper, photograph, screen, video and metric paper sizes.

5. Select Tabloid.

When the Tabloid option is selected, the Width and Height fields are changed to match the selection. There is not an orientation option in this dialog box, so if you wish for the Tabloid size to be landscape (horizontal) instead of portrait (vertical), you will have to type the dimensions in manually (or rotate the canvas 90° after the file is created).

6. Set Width and Height units to inches.

The default unit of measurement in Photoshop is the pixel. To change the unit of measurement, select the drop-down menu at the right of the Width and Height fields and select inches.

7. Set the Resolution to 300 pixels per inch (ppi).

Resolution is the number of pixels per inch. The higher the resolution, the better the image quality. Photographs printed in magazines can be anywhere from 300 to 2400 ppi. This results in a higher-quality print but the file sizes are large. Images for the Web and screen presentation only need to be the standard 72 ppi (the same as your screen resolution) and only require a minimal file size.

As you modify the dimensions and resolution of the image in the New document dialog box, the Image Size number at the top of this section changes. This number is an approximation of the size of the file. An image that contains more pixels will result in a larger file size. For example, an image that is 1" by 1" at 144 ppi is four times as large as an image that is the same size but with a resolution of 72 ppi (Figure 11.12).

8. Set the Color Mode to CMYK.

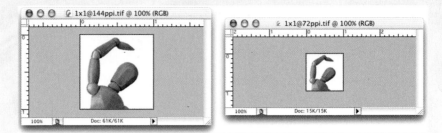

FIGURE 11.12   The size relationship of two images: 1" by 1" @ 72ppi (left) and 1" by 1" @ 144 ppi (right). Notice that the image on the right, according to the total number of pixels, is four times larger than the image on the right.

For images that are going to be printed, select CMYK. For images that will be displayed on the Web or on screen in a presentation, RGB is appropriate. Because this project is a poster that will output on a color printer, select CMYK.

9. In the Contents section choose Transparent.

Your selection in this area affects the background layer in your document (Figure 11.13). If White is selected, the background is filled with white. Background Color fills it with the current color in the Background Swatch. The Transparent option creates a file with one transparent layer (Layer 1).

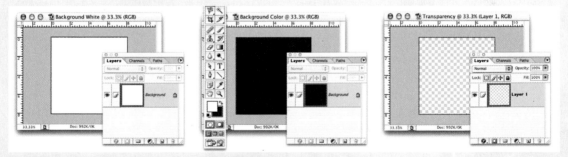

FIGURE 11.13   The results of the different options from the Contents field: (left-right) White, Background Color, and Transparent.

10. Click OK.

The file that is created looks like the one in Figure 11.18. It is 11" wide, 17" high, and has a resolution of 300 ppi. There is no background layer, but a transparent first layer. The grey and white checkerboard in the background represents transparency.

Saving and New Image

Once a new image has been created, you should save it right away. Save your file using the following steps:

1. Choose `File > Save As` (PC: control + shift + N; Mac: command + shift + N) from the top menu.

   The Save As dialog box is quite simple (in spite of all the options).

2. Select the proper file type from the Format drop-down menu (Figure 11.14).

FIGURE 11.14   Breakout view of the Format options in the Save As dialog box.

The file type is very important. In Chapter 4, a few of the different file types were discussed. The following are some of the more important file types associated with Photoshop.

Photoshop Document (.psd): This is the default option for most users. This file type in no way compresses any information. The individual layers and their properties will be maintained. The file size of this format is large due to the fact that the file is not compressed in any way.

Photoshop EPS (.eps): The file is saved as an Encapsulated PostScript and can only be printed correctly on PostScript printers. White areas are saved as transparent areas. The vector data (fonts, shapes, etc.) is made available for other applications that the file is imported into. If the file is saved as an EPS and is opened back up into Photoshop, the vector elements will rasterize.

TIFF Format (.tif): This type of file can be easily used in bitmap, page layout, and image-editing programs and on multiple operating systems. Layers can be saved in the TIFF format, but the file size is larger. The option to flatten the layers is given in a prompt if the File Handling subset of the Preferences is set. This file type is excellent for printing.

BMP or Bitmap (.bmp): The native graphics format for Windows users. It is often used in software for presentations or for use in the operating system itself. This image file type is best used with PowerPoint Presentations and some 3D software applications.

PICT File (.pct): The native file format for the Apple Macintosh OS. They are used on Macs they same way BMPs are used on Window machines. These images may not display correctly on a PC.

Depending on the file type chosen, the other options in the Save and Color areas of the dialog box may become available.

3. Select the location in which to save the file.

Save the file to your projects folder, hard drive, zip disk, or wherever you store your files.

4. Click the Save button to complete the command.

After you have saved the file once, you can save the file again by using File > Save or the keyboard shortcut (PC: control + N; Mac: command + N). Remember to save often. If you wish to save the file under a different name every so often so as to see the progress you make, or to keep an original before changes are made, use the Save A Copy feature, which works in much the same way, but does not overwrite the original file.

Color Correction

Most of the images that you scan from photographs or take with digital cameras are not correct color-wise. They tend to be too dark or too light, or have some sort of colorcast (namely bluish or greenish casts). The process of "fixing" the color of an image is called *Color correction*.

Although some scanners and cameras have software that corrects the image as it scans or captures the picture, it is better to make these corrections in an editing program such as Photoshop.

The image in Figure 11.15 was taken with a digital camera under normal indoor light. As can be seen on the left side of the image, if the flash is off this particular camera places a bluish tint over the entire image, washing out the lighter colors. To make the image obtain a truer color and contain a full range of values, some changes must be made to the image.

LEVELS

In the value chapter, levels were explained as they pertain to grayscale imagery. When using the Level Command on a grayscales image you are modifying the image's tonal range: the levels of black and white within the image. On

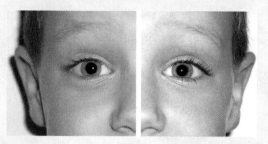

FIGURE 11.15 The left side of the image is untouched. The right side of the image has been corrected.

a color image, using the Level Command adjusts the color balance of the image.

The Levels dialog box allows you to adjust the image by changing the levels of its shadows, midtones, and highlights. This can be achieved manually through the Levels dialog box or automatically by using the Auto Levels command.

Use the following exercise to color correct the image.

ON THE CD

1. Open the image *11face.psd* from the *Photo Montage* folder on the CD-ROM.

   Notice that the image has a bluish cast over it.

2. Show the Info palette by selecting `Window > Info` (Figure 11.16)

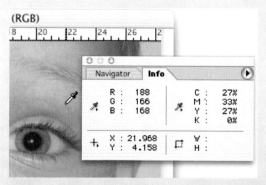

FIGURE 11.16 The Info palette returns the properties of a pixel (color, placement, etc.) as the cursor passes over it.

The Info palette is divided into four quadrants. The top two quadrants show information about the color of the pixel. The bottom two show position and height and width of the current selection.

The upper-left quadrant tracks the actual color values of the pixel that the current tool is hovering over within the image. By default it loads the numbers for red, blue, and green channels in the image. When combined, these three levels produce a color. Remember that "0" means that the pixels are black and that "255" means they are white. If you mouse over the area in between the eyes, the software returns the values of 214, 205, and 206 (respectively), or a light gray color.

3. Open the Levels Command by selecting `Image > Adjustments > Levels` (PC: control + L; Mac: command + L).

The Levels dialog box looks a little complicated. The Channel options take up most of the dialog box. There are three major parts of this area (Figure 11.17).

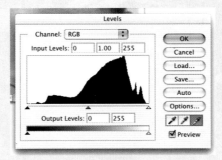

FIGURE 11.17   The Levels dialog box allows you to manually color-correct the image.

The pop-up menu next to Channel allows you to view the histograms of the channels individually (R, G, and B) or together (RGB). The channels can be modified individually for better control over color correction. To increase the overall redness of an image, select and make changes to that channel.

The Input Levels sliders allow you to manually set the dark and light points of the image. Dragging the sliders resets the points of each Input Level. For example if you set the Input Level's black triangle to 10, all the pixels to the left of the slider will be remapped to 0 (or black). Likewise, moving the white arrow to the left will cause the pixels to the right to become 255 (or white). The levels in-between will remap the histogram accordingly to help even out the tone of the image. The Input Level's gray arrow sets the midpoint of the levels. Setting it to the right darkens the image by decreasing the percentage of levels between 50% and 255 (white). Alternatively, moving it to the left lightens the image by increasing the number of levels between 50% and 255 (white). You may also input the numbers into the fields (black, gray, and white arrows) to move the sliders.

The Output Levels are modified in the same way, but the results can only be seen when printed. If after printing your image you notice that the darks are dark enough, slide the black triangle to the right and remap the output level. Like with the Input Levels, the Output Levels can also be typed into the fields (black and white arrows).

4. Click on the Preview box.

By selecting the Preview box, the changes made to the inputs will be reflected in the image.

 The changes will not be made until the OK button is pressed. To reset the dialog box, press Alt (PC) or Option (Mac) to temporarily change the Cancel button to Reset.

5. Select the White Point eyedropper tool from the right of the dialog box (Figure 11.18).

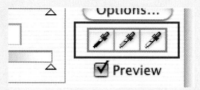

FIGURE 11.18 The eyedroppers in the Levels dialog box control the (l-r) black point, midtones, and white point.

Using the White Point eyedropper tool from the lower-right corner (under the buttons), you can physically set the White point of the image. Click on the icon to select it.

6. Click on the lightest area of the image, which is around the white part of the eye.

With the tool selected, mouse over the area of the image around the eyes. As you move over the whites of the eyes the RGB reading in the Info palette will reflect the levels in each. The closer the numbers get to 255, the whiter the area. The average around the eyes is somewhere around R: 215, G: 235, and B: 250. When you are close to those numbers, click to select it. The white point (255) has been set. Notice the image lightens up and the bluish tint begins to drop from the image.

7. Select the Black Point eyedropper tool from the lower-right area of the dialog box.

The Black Point eyedropper is two to the left of the current tool.

8. Click on the darkest area of the image. In this case, it's the pupil of the eye.

Like the White Point eyedropper, the Black Point eyedropper remaps the black (0) of the level. Clearly the darkest part of the image is the pupil. The numbers for this area should be around R: 25, G: 28, and B: 35. When the darkest part of the image is found, click with the tool to set the black (0) point.

The image really pops from the dull, bluish image that it was before. The eyes have become green and the hair has become brown. The skin tone has improved.

9. Move the grey Input Level slider to the left until it reads 1.20.

Moving the grey Input Slider changes the contrast of the lights and darks of the image, remapping the midtones to achieve a better continual tone of the image.

10. Click OK to set the change.

Figure 11.19 shows the final color-corrected image. If you are not happy with the change, select Edit > Undo (PC: control + Z; Mac: command + Z) to return to the state before the Levels were changed.

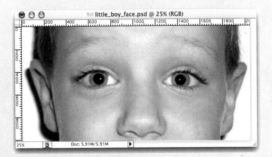

FIGURE 11.19   The final color-corrected image.

11. Undo the Levels Command by selecting Edit > Undo.

Auto Levels

Using Auto Levels allows the computer to recalculate the image by automatically setting the new Black point and White point of the image.

1. Select Image > Adjustments > Auto Levels (PC: control + shift + L; Mac: command + shift + L).

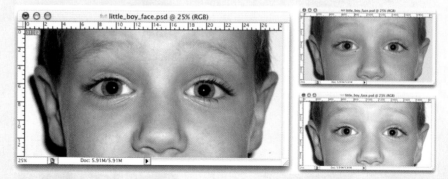

FIGURE 11.20 A comparison of all the images (Auto Levels [left], Original [top right], and manually leveled [bottom right] shows that Auto Levels is not necessarily the best way to go.

The result of the image is pretty good. Tighter control of the color of the image can be achieved through the Levels Command. The image that was autocorrected is a little darker through the midtones. In Figure 11.20, the difference between the auto-corrected version (left) and the manually corrected version (bottom right) was that the gray Input Slider was controlled to change the contrast to something more to our liking. You can further modify the image by opening the Levels dialog box and moving the gray Input Point to change the contrast of the image.

Overall, its better to color-correct the image manually rather than to let the software do it for you automatically.

Color correct all of your images before you begin to create the montage. Although the Level Command only affects the current selected layer, it becomes a tedious task to try to do it within the montage. However, you might want to further modify an image after it has been placed within the montage to unify it with the other images and elements.

Combining Images from Separate Files

Because this project is a montage, you will need to combine multiple images into one Photoshop file. The result of combining images is one file with multiple layers. Each of the layers can be moved and edited independently from the original. There are many methods that can be used to accomplish this.

LAYER OPTIONS

A layer can be moved from one file to another using the Duplicate Layer command from the Options menu in the Layers palette.

1. From the *Chapter 11* folder on the CD-ROM, open files *11empty.psd* and *11eggs.psd*.

To open files, select File > Open and navigate to the *Chapter 11* folder on the accompanying CD-ROM. Repeat this command for each file. Because the CD-ROM is a read-only media, copies of the file will be opened. A dialog box may appear prompting that the files are "read only." You will have to save the files to your hard drive to keep them.

2. View the Layers palette by selecting View > Layers.

The Layers palette may already be viewable. It is almost always coupled with the Channels and Path palettes. They will appear as tabs in the palette window.

3. With the *11eggs.psd* active (in front), select Duplicate Layer from the Options menu in the Layers palette (Figure 11.21).

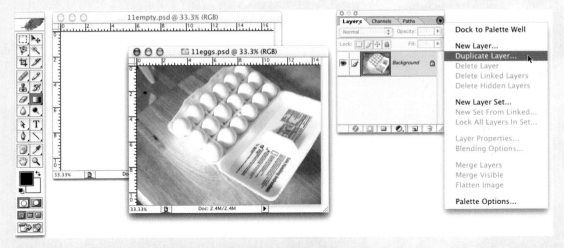

FIGURE 11.21   Select Duplicate Layer from the Option menu in the Layers palette.

The Options menu is under the arrow in the upper-right corner of the Layers palette. The Duplicate Layer dialog box appears.

4. In the Duplicate Layer dialog box, in the As field name the layer "eggs."
5. From the Destination area choose *11empty.psd* (Figure 11.22).

From the drop-down menu, choose the destination for the file. The names of all of the files that are currently opened will be reflected in this menu. Choose the appropriate file to which you wish to duplicate the layer. If you

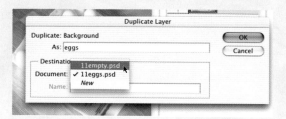

FIGURE 11.22   From the Destination menu choose the file to which you would like to copy the layer.

want it to open up into a new image, select *New* and give the file a name in the field below.

6. Click OK.

The *eggs* layer is added to the *11empty* file. The layer is automatically centered in the file and is in its own layer (Figure 11.23).

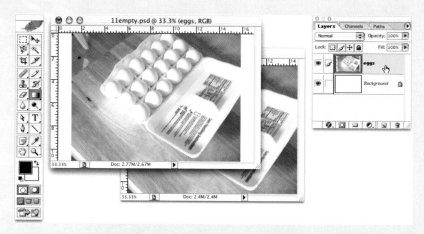

FIGURE 11.23   The resulting placement for the new layer is centered in the destination document.

The Move Tool

1. With the *11empty.psd* file still active, choose `Edit > Undo Duplicate Layer` (PC: control + Z; Mac: command + Z) to undo the last command.
2. With the *11eggs.psd* active, select the Move Tool (V).

The Move Tool is the located in the first row, second column of the Tool palette. It is represented by a black triangle with a plus sign to its lower right. Use the V key to toggle to this key. Click on it to select it.

If you mouse over a tool long enough, the name of the tool will appear as will the shortcut key, in this case it is V for the Move Tool. The shortcut key for simple tools will be shown in parentheses at the name of the tool.

3. Click on the image in the window and, while holding down the mouse button, drag the image from *11eggs.psd* file to the *11empty.psd* file (Figure 11.24).

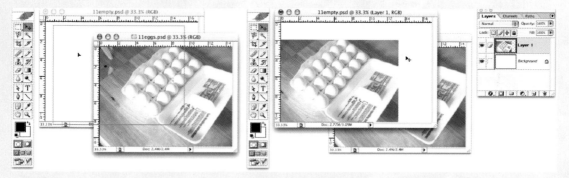

FIGURE 11.24   A preview box shows that a layer is being moved from one file to another. The new layer is placed where it was dropped, not centered like in the previous method.

A rectangular preview box shows you the size of the object being moved from one file to the other. If both files are viewable at the same time (as seen in Figure 11.24), you can drag and drop layers back and forth between them. You can also drag the layer from the Layers palette to the new file. The layer is dropped where you put it, unlike the Duplicate Layer command, which automatically centers the layer. To place the layer in the center of the destination file, use the Shift key as you drag and drop.

4. From the top menu bar selected `Edit > Undo Drag Layer` to undo the previous command.

This removes the new layer (*Layer 1*) from the *11empty.psd* file.

5. As in Step 3, drag the layer from one image to the other while holding down the Shift key. Release the mouse button before the Shift key to place the file in the center.

The new layer (*Layer 1*) is centered in the destination file.

1, 2, 3: SELECT ALL, COPY, AND PASTE

Images can also be combined using a simple series of select, copy, and paste commands.

1. With the *11empty.psd* file still active, choose `Edit > Undo Drag Layer` (PC: control + Z; Mac: command + Z) to undo the last command.
2. With the *11eggs.psd* active, choose `Select > All` from the top menu.

By choosing `Select > All`, a marquee is drawn around the entire perimeter of the canvas. This marquee is a box with a dashed line that "marches" around the selection. The area on that layer within the box can now be copied.

3. Select `Edit > Copy` (PC: control + C; Mac: command + C) to copy the image to the clipboard.

The area within the marquee is now stored in the clipboard.

4. Bring the *11empty.psd* file to the front by clicking on its title bar.

To call attention to the focus on the destination file, bring it to the front by clicking on the title bar (where the name of the file is). The Layers palette changes to reflect the active file.

5. Select `Edit > Paste` (PC: control + V; Mac: command + V) to paste the image from the clipboard into the *12empty*.psd file.

The copied image is pasted into the center of the destination document in its own layer.

Layers

Layers make using Photoshop easier.

Layers help you to work on individual elements of an image without affecting the others. When there is no part of an image on the layer, the images behind come through. You can combine parts of images on each layer using a variety of different techniques, some of which will be discussed later.

Like in Illustrator, layers in Photoshop can be renamed, reordered, hidden, locked, and made to be transparent.

RENAMING LAYERS

There are two ways you can rename layers in Photoshop.

The first and easiest way to rename a layer is to simply double-click the name of the layer in the Layers palette and type the desired name (Figure 11.25).

The second method of changing the name of a layer is to go through the Options menu and choose Layer Properties. The resulting dialog box enables you to not only give the layer a name but also a color label (Figure 11.26). These color labels can be useful when creating images that have many layers. Layers with photographs could be one color, effect layers could be another, text layers another, and so on.

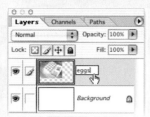

FIGURE 11.25   Renaming a layer is as easy as double-clicking on its name.

FIGURE 11.26   Rename the layer in the Layer Properties dialog box, and even assign it a color.

Changing the Stacking Order of Layers

Like in Illustrator, the hierarchy of layers is the same: the top-most layer appears in front, while the bottom-most layer is in the back. The Background layer (if there is one) is the very back of the layer hierarchy.

To change this order of layers, simply drag the layer in the Layers palette to its new place in the order.

ON THE CD

1. In the folder Chapter 11 on the CD-ROM, open file *11layers.psd*.
2. Click on the "eggs" layer and drag it in between the "cookies" layer and the "dough" layer (Figure 11.27).

FIGURE 11.27   Drag the layer in between the correct layers to reorder them.

It is that simple. The layer is now between the "cookies" and "dough" layers.

Palette Options

Some people complain about the size of the thumbnail image to the left of the layer name, but few know that it can be remedied. There are actually four different sizes for thumbnails: None, Small, Medium, and Large.

To access this option, choose Palette Options from the Options menu in the Layers palette.

HIDING AND SHOWING LAYERS

Layers can easily be hidden and shown, with the click of a button. It may become necessary as you work, to hide a particular layer and concentrate on a certain area.

To hide a layer, simply click on the Hide/Show layer (eye) icon to the left of the layer (Figure 11.28). To show it again, click again. If you try to modify the layer while it is hidden, a dialog box will appear telling you that the layer is hidden.

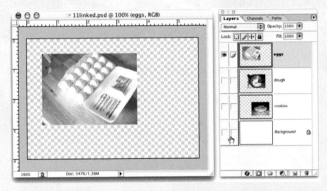

FIGURE 11.28   Hide the layer by clicking on its eye icon. If there is no eye symbol it is already hidden.

LINKING LAYERS

There is no such thing as grouping in Photoshop, at least the way that you understand it. In Photoshop, it is called Linking.

ON THE CD

1. In the folder Chapter 11 on the CD-ROM, open file *11linked.psd*.
2. Click on the "eggs" layer in the Layer palette to select it.
3. Click on the empty space to the right of the eye icon on the "dough" layer to link it to the "eggs" layer (Figure 11.29).

You can link a second layer to the active layer by clicking the area to the right of the eye icon. Clicking results in a little chain icon that lets you know a link has been made. Another layer can be added to the "chain" by clicking on its linking area as well.

4. With the Move tool, move the image around within the document window (Figure 11.30).

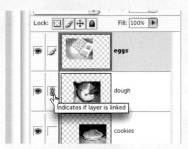

FIGURE 11.29   As shown, click the empty space next to the eye icon to link the layer to the selected layer.

FIGURE 11.30   Linked layers are moved when the active layer is moved, regardless of where it is in the stacking order.

When layers are linked, they can be moved together.

5. Click on the link next to the "dough" layer to unlink the layers.

To unlink a layer, simply click on the chain icon to clear it. The layers will remain linked until you break the chain.

LOCKING

There are four locks that can be placed on layers: locking transparent pixels, locking image pixels, locking position, or locking all of them (Figure 11.31). By first selecting the layer to be locked and then clicking on the desired lock icon at the top of the Layers palette, the layer will be locked. The following is a description of each lock:

Lock Transparent Pixels: By checking this box, transparent pixels within that layer cannot be painted on or affected. Only pixels that already contain information (color) will be able to be affected. This helps when touching-up edges of selections.

Lock:

FIGURE 11.31   The four Locks: (l-r) Transparent
Pixels, Image Pixels, Position, and All.

Lock Image Pixels: Just the opposite of the previous attribute, this locks the
colored pixel so that only the transparent ones can be colored.
Lock Position: This setting keeps the layer from being moved. The layer can
be painted and modified in other ways, it just cannot be moved.
Lock All: This setting locks the layer from being affected in any way. You cannot move it, resize it, color it, or change its levels. If a layer is part of a linked
group, all the other layers in the chain are affected as well.

Use this exercise to become familiar with locks.

1. Using the *11linked.psd* file, hide all the layers except for the "eggs" layer by
clicking on their eye icons.
2. Select the "eggs" layer and click on the first lock button, which is Lock
Transparent Pixels.
3. Using the Paint trush Tool (B) paint on the "egg" layer.

You will not be able to paint on transparent pixels, only on pixels that already contain some color information (Figure 11.32).

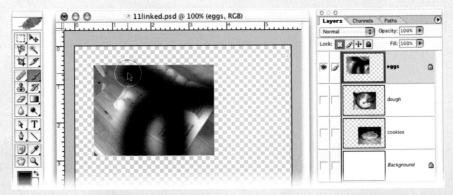

FIGURE 11.32   Only pixels that are already colored will be colored when this attribute is
locked.

4. Hide the "eggs" layer and show the "dough" layer.
5. Select the "dough" layer and click on the second lock button, which is Lock
Image Pixels.
6. Use the Paint Brush tool (B) to paint on the layer.

With the Lock Image Pixels button checked, it is not possible to paint on existing pixels. A warning dialog box (Figure 11.33) appears, stating "could not use the brush tool because the layer is locked."

FIGURE 11.33   A warning dialog appears to tell you that you cannot complete the operation due to the image being locked.

7. Hide the "dough" layer and show the "cookies" layer.
8. Select the "cookies" layer and click on the third button, which is Lock Position.
9. Using the Move tool, attempt to move the image in the document window.

A warning box appears informing you that locked layers cannot be moved.

10. With the "cookies" layer still active, uncheck the Lock Position button and click on the fourth button to Lock All.

You cannot do anything to the layer. You cannot paint on it or move it, or edit it in any way. This becomes quite useful as you begin to get things just the way you like them. If a layer is completely locked, a black lock appears to the right of the name of the layer. If one of the other locks is engaged, a gray lock occupies that space.

OPACITY

A layer's opacity governs the degree of transparency a layer has. As a layer becomes more transparent, the layers underneath it begin to come through. This can create some really interesting effects when creating your montage.

There are two forms of opacity in the Layers palette: Layer Opacity and Fill Opacity.

Layer Opacity: Affects the entire layer including any layer effects (drop shadows, inner glows, etc.) it might have.

Fill Opacity: Only affects those pixels that were originally painted on the layer, not the effects or modes.

Figure 11.34 shows the differences between the two. As you create your montage, experiment with these two sliders, you might be surprised how powerful they can be. There may be part of an underlying image you would like to have creep through, or you may want to use some line work or type without it being too overpowering in the design. Lower its opacity. See what happens.

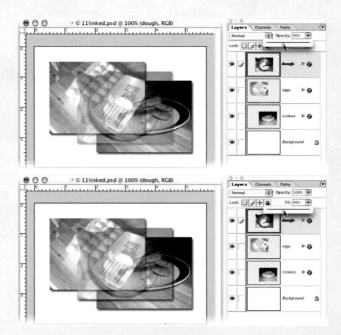

FIGURE 11.34 The top image has a Layer Opacity of 40% and the drop shadow that is applied to the layer is also affected. However, the bottom image has a Fill Opacity of 40% as well, but only the pixels that were originally drawn on the layer are affected.

Masking

In your montage there might be just part of one image that you want to include. Instead of erasing (removing pixels) from the image, it is possible to simply block it out and make it transparent. The concept of masking is just that, blocking out parts of the image from view, while maintaining the integrity of the image.

Making is quite simple. It consists of two parts: the layer and an attached mask (Figure 11.35).

A mask is a grayscale overlay on top of the layer image. The area on the mask that is white is opaque and whatever is black is transparent. The varying levels of gray result in different opacities of the layer. The closer to black the shade of gray is, the more transparent it becomes.

FIGURE 11. 35   The original image (left), the mask (middle), and the result of the mask applied to the image (right).

Follow these simple steps to add and modify a layer mask to an existing layer.

ADDING A LAYER MASK

ON THE CD

1. In the Chapter 11 folder on the CD-ROM open the file *11addmask.psd*.

FIGURE 11.36   In this exercise, you will mask out the little girl in the background.

The image is of a little boy holding a cookie sheet with the dough on it and a little girl looking on (Figure 11.36). You will be eliminating the little girl from the picture, leaving behind only the boy and cookie sheet. This can be done with a simple mask. It is first necessary to convert the background to a layer so that a mask can be applied.

2. Double-click the Background Layer to convert the background to a layer. Give it the name "boy with cookie sheet" and click OK.

Like double-clicking a layer to name, a background layer can be converted into a regular layer the same way. The New Layer dialog box appears. There are several options for this layer; it is only necessary to name the layer.

3. With the layer now selected, choose `Layer > Add Layer Mask > Reveal All` (Figure 11. 37).

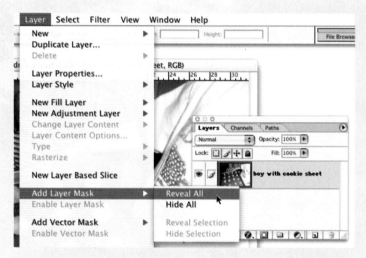

FIGURE 11.37   The location of the Reveal All command, which adds a mask to a layer.

The layer mask has just been added. In Figure 11.38 the thumbnail for the layer is visible on the left with the mask thumbnail to its right.

FIGURE 11.38   The mask appears as an empty thumbnail next to the layer's preview thumbnail image.

PAINTING ON A MASK LAYER

To make areas of the mask transparent and opaque, you must use the Paint tools to apply colors to the mask.

4. Select the mask thumbnail by clicking on the second thumbnail.

To select the mask layer, so that it can be painted on, simply click on the mask thumbnail next to the image thumbnail in the layer.

The Brush

The Brush is used to apply color pixels to a layer, whether it be a normal layer, a layer mask, or so on. The color comes from the Foreground Color swatch.

5. From the Tool palette select the Brush tool (B).

The Brush tool is the second icon in the second section of the Tool palette (Figure 11.39). When the Brush is activated (selected) the Options bar changes to its set of attributes. The second drop-down menu houses the brush sizes. There are several types of brushes from which you may choose. Because the images in this montage are 300 ppi, a larger brush will be needed.

FIGURE 11.39   The location of the Brush tool in the Tool palette.

6. Make sure the Options bar appears at the top of the screen (under the top menu). If it is not visible, choose Window > Options (Figure 11.40).

FIGURE 11.40   The Options bar for the Brush tool.

The Options bar will dynamically change according to which tool is se-lected. These options can be used to make accurate measurements or set specific properties for that tool. The Info palette will also reflect the current measurement for a selected item.

7. From the Options bar, set the brush to the Soft Round 200-pixel brush (Figure 11.41).

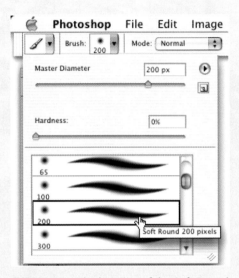

FIGURE 11.41   The location of the Soft Round 200 pixel brush is in the Brush Preset Picker in the Options bar.

To select the Soft Round 200 pixel brush, scroll down through the list of brushes until the number beneath the brush is 200.

8. Set the Foreground Color to white and the Background Color to black by clicking on the Default Foreground and Background Colors icon (Figure 11.42).

FIGURE 11.42   Click the icon shown to set the default colors to the swatches.

The Default Foreground and Background Colors icon is to the lower left of the main color swatches in the Tool palette. Clicking on this icon resets the foreground color to black and the background color to white.

9. Set the Foreground Color to white by clicking on the Switch Foreground and Background Colors icon (Figure 11.43).

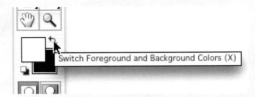

FIGURE 11.43   Click the icon shown to switch the Foreground and Background colors.

The Switch Foreground and Background Colors icon is to the upper right of the main color swatches in the Tool palette. Clicking on this icon switches the foreground color to the background color and vice versa. In this case, white will become the foreground color and black will become the background color.

10. Paint over the face of the little girl with black to make it transparent (Figure 11.44).

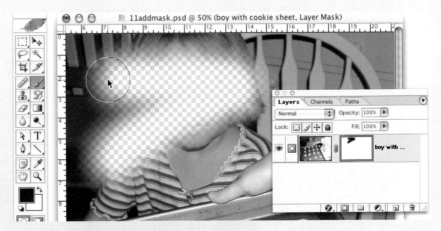

FIGURE 11.44   Paint with black on the mask to make pixels transparent.

Whatever is painted with black on the mask will become transparent without erasing the pixels. They are merely masked out. If a mistake is made, either undo the brush stroke or paint with white.

11. Click the Switch Foreground and Background Colors icon to switch the colors back, making white the Foreground Color.
12. Paint with white where you painted with black to see the face restored to the layer (Figure 11.45).

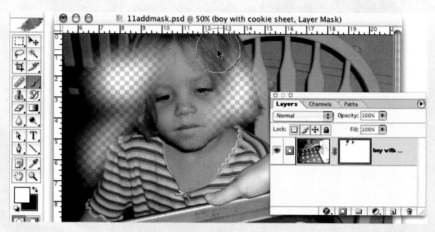

FIGURE 11.45   Paint with white to restore the opacity of the pixels.

Painting on the mask with white reveals the area that may have been covered up with black. Notice that the image returns as you paint over it.

13. From the Swatches palette (Window > Swatches), choose 50% Gray (Figure 11.46) and paint with it on the image.

FIGURE 11.46   Select 50% Gray from the Swatches Palette to replace the Foreground Color swatch (left). Painting with different shades of gray result in varying levels of opacity (right).

Painting with a varying percentage of gray results in a semitransparent image being revealed. Cool effects can be achieved by doing this. You will also notice that if you use a soft brush, the edges of the brush leave behind a gray "halo," allowing the original to show through slightly. To avoid that, choose a hard-edge brush.

Disabling a Mask

To temporarily turn off the effects of the mask of a certain layer, simply disable the mask.

14. From the top menu choose `Layer > Disable Layer Mask` to disable the mask (Figure 11.47).

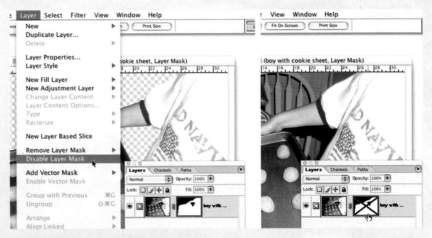

FIGURE 11.47   Disabling the mask allows you see the entire image, without deleting the mask. A giant red "X" covers the thumbnail to signify that it is disabled.

The mask thumbnail is still there, it just has a big red "X" through it, letting you know that it has been disabled. The mask has not been deleted, simply hidden.

15. To re-enable the mask, choose `Layer > Enable Layer Mask`.

The mask is then reapplied to the image. Editing the mask can continue if necessary.

Deleting a Mask

When it comes to removing a Layer Mask from a layer, there are two results that can come of it.

When a mask is deleted from a layer, to leave the layer unaffected choose `Layer > Remove Layer Mask > Discard`. This removes the mask and leaves behind the entire image. The area that was once transparent is made opaque and the mask is discarded.

If you would like the Layer Mask to be removed, but the layer to take on the transparent properties of the mask, choose `Layer > Remove Layer Mask > Apply`. The mask is removed, but the pixels that were once transparent are now deleted, leaving only the object on the layer. Those discarded pixels cannot be retrieved.

16. Discard the current layer mask by selecting `Layer > Remove Layer Mask > Discard`.

Painting on a mask is often not the best way to make a mask. However, using a series of tools to select the areas can make the process easier.

Making Selections

Rather than painting the areas of layer transparent, you can use the Selection tools to select areas of an image and then apply the Layer Mask to that area. There are three major types of tools: Marquee tools, Lasso tools, and the Magic Wand tool.

MARQUEE TOOLS

The Marquee tools are used to create selections based on predefined areas: rectangles, ellipses, and single-pixel rows and columns. By default, the selection box is created from its corner.

ON THE CD

1. In the Chapter 11 folder on the CD-ROM open the file *11selections.psd*.
2. Select the Rectangular Marquee tool (M) and simply click and drag a box around the plate of cookies (Figure 11.48).

Figure 11.48 Use the Rectangular Marquee tool to draw boxes around areas you wish to select.

Holding down the mouse button and dragging the mouse creates a selection border around the desired object. Hold down the Shift key during the initial selection to keep it constrained to a square (or a circle if using the Elliptical Marquee tool).

Using the Rectangular Marquee tool to select the round plate is not going to work. The Elliptical Marquee tool is the better tool for the job.

3. Select the Elliptical Marquee tool from the Tool palette by clicking and holding on the Rectangular Marquee tool until the sub-menu pops up, then choose the second tool in the menu (Figure 11.49).

FIGURE 11.49   The Elliptical Marquee tool is hidden under the Rectangular Marquee tool.

The Elliptical Marquee tool lies in a sub-menu underneath the other marquee tools. Single Row and Single Column are also in that menu.

You can use the "M" key to toggle between the four tools.

4. Click and drag from the upper left of the plate (as seen in Figure 11.50) and drag down and to the right until the border surrounds the plate.

FIGURE 11.50   Start the ellipse from the top-left edge of the plate. By default, the marquee tools draw from the corner.

The border surrounds the plate on all sides, but according to where you started to drag, the border may not be aligned correctly around the plate.

Adding the Alt (PC) or Option (Mac) key to the command makes the tool draw from the center out.

5. With the Elliptical Marquee tool still selected, while holding the Alt or Option key, click in the center of the plate and drag outward (Figure 11.51).

FIGURE 11.51   Using the Alt or Option key allows you to draw from the center out.

This makes selecting the plate a little easier. Keep trying until you feel you have gotten the hang of it. After a selection has been made, you can use the same tool to move the border of the selection (Figure 11.52).

If the Move tool (V) is used, the area within the border will be moved.

FIGURE 11.52   With the Move tool still active, use it to reposition the selection border, not the contents.

6. Deselect the selection by choosing `Select > Deselect`.

The Single Row and Single Column marquee tools select a 1-pixel row or column when used. These tools do not have a wide variety of uses, but they can be used to sample single lines from an image to create a pattern or other element. Experiment with them at your leisure.

Options for the Marquee Tools

When the Marquee tools are selected, the Options bar changes in order to house the several different settings for this tool (Figure 11.53). The set of four icons on the left controls the relationship between the current selection and the next selection (Figure 11.54).

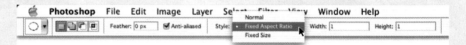

FIGURE 11.53   The Options bar changes to show the options for the Marquee tools when they are selected.

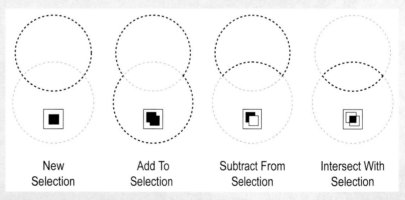

| New Selection | Add To Selection | Subtract From Selection | Intersect With Selection |

FIGURE 11.54   There are four different options for selections that can be made using the Options bar.

New Selection: By default if you draw one border and then draw a second, the first disappears. Each click-and-drag results in a new selection.

Add to Selection: The area of the next selection is added to the current selection.

Subtract from Selection: The area of the next selection is subtracted from the current selection.

Intersect with Selection: The area that the first and second selection share (in which they overlap) is result of this action.

Feather: When a pixel number is entered into this field, the resulting selection's edges are blurred to give the selection a soft edge (Figure 11.55). When working with high-resolution images, this number needs to be higher than when using this setting for a low-resolution graphic.

FIGURE 11.55   The Feather option gives a blurred edge to selections that are made.

Anti-Aliased: When this box is checked, the jagged edges of the selection are blurred into the background image to keep from getting a hard line when the selection is moved, deleted, or other wise modified (Figure 11.56).

FIGURE 11.56   When the Anti-Aliased button is unchecked, the resulting selections have a hard edge (top), when compared to selections made when it is checked (bottom).

Style: This drop-down menu contains the following settings as they relate to this tool.

Normal: Your dragging determines the size of the selection.

Fixed Aspect Ratio: This is a set height-to-width ratio. If you wish to make a selection based on the proportion of your screen, then a "4" would be in the width and a "3" in the height, giving you a ration of "4:3."

Fixed Size: This is an absolute pixel measurement. You specify the border's height and width.

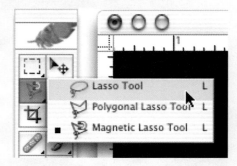

FIGURE 11.57   The Lasso tools.

LASSO TOOLS

There are three Lasso tools to choose from: the Lasso tool, the Polygonal Lasso tool, and the Magnetic Lasso tool (Figure 11.57).

FIGURE 11.58   Selections that are made with the Lasso tool are made freehand; the selection is made wherever you draw.

The Lasso tool is the easiest of the three to use. The tip of the lasso is the icon's hot-point (i.e., center). To use the Lasso tool, click-and-drag around the edge of the object. Whatever is contained with in the border is selected (Figure 11.58).

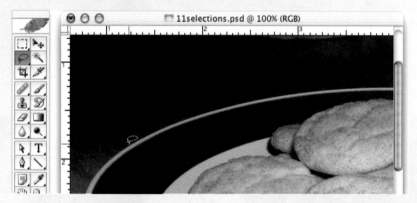

FIGURE 11.59 Place the Lasso tool along the left edge of the plate as shown.

1. With the *11selections.psd* still open, select the Lasso tool from the Tool palette.
2. Place the point of the Lasso tool along the top-left edge of the plate (Figure 11.59).
3. With the mouse button pressed, drag to the right along the edge of the plate.
4. Continue around the plate until you come back to the point of origin. Release the mouse button to complete the selection.

You have to be very steady when using the Lasso tool. If at any time you make a mistake, simply click off to the side to delete the selection. It takes patience and a steady hand to master this tool.

The Polygonal Lasso tool works a little differently than the Lasso tool. Whereas the Lasso tool traces using a path, the Polygonal Lasso tool makes selection based on polygons (points and lines). Figure 11.60 shows the tool in action. In this particular montage there is no need for this tool, but it may come in handy for you. The Lasso tool can dynamically change to the Polygonal Lasso tool and back when you hold down the Alt (PC) or Option (Mac) key when using the Lasso tool.

You create the path by moving the tool and clicking where you want that particular line to go. Click on the start of the path or double-click to snap the path closed.

The Magnetic Lasso Tool

The Magnetic Lasso tool calculates the difference in the contrast of light and dark pixels by automatically creating a selection between the two (Figure 11.61). As the tool travels around the edge of these objects it automatically

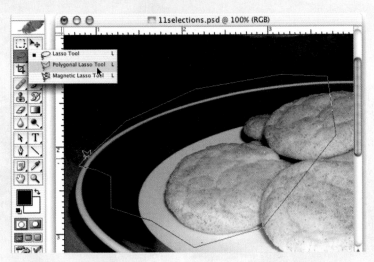

FIGURE 11.60   The Polygonal Lasso tool draws using the point and click method of straight lines.

FIGURE 11.61   An example of how the Magnetic Lasso tool differentiates between the light and dark pixels to create its path.

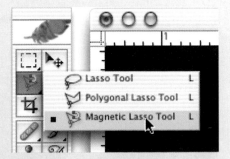

FIGURE 11.62   The location of the Magnetic Lasso tool.

places insertion points along the path of the selection. There is no real need to remain accurate as the software does all the work.

1. Select the Magnetic Lasso tool (L) from the Tool palette by selecting the third icon under the Lasso tool (Figure 11.62).
2. Place the tip of the Magnetic Lasso tool along the same edge of the plate and, while holding down the mouse button, move the tool to the right, roughly along the same path as the edge.

Notice how the selection path snaps in between the dark pixels of the background and the light pixels of the plate. Also notice the inserted points

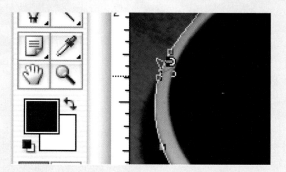

FIGURE 11.63   When the path is closed, a small circle will appear to the lower right of the tool.

along the path of the selection. Continue to complete the selection by going around the plate. As you reach the underside of the plate, follow along the path between the shadow and the table. When the tip of the tool reaches the first inserted point a small circle will appear next to the tip (Figure 11.63). This signifies the completion of the path. Double-click the mouse to complete the path.

With the path completed, it is replaced with the (marching ants) border.

A Feather can be set before the selection is made by setting the number in the Options bar, or after the fact by choosing Select > Feather.

3. From the top menu choose Select > Feather. Set the Feather to "5," and click OK.

The Feather dialog box appears. Set the desired number for the feathering in the field and click OK.

4. Hide the selection by choosing View > Extras (PC: control + H; Mac: command + H).

This operation hides the border from view. However, the object is still selected.

FIGURE 11.64   The selection is removed from the file, leaving behind a soft edge.

5. Choose `Edit > Cut`.

The selected area is cut from the document and placed in the clipboard (Figure 11.64). Notice that the edge of the selection is soft, not jagged. This is the result of the feathering.

6. Undo the last action to restore the cut portion of the image.
7. Choose `Select > Deselect` to clear the selection.

The options for the Magnetic Lasso tool appear in the Options bar. The three most important options are Width, Edge Contrast, and Frequency (Figure 11.65). The Width option tells the tool how many pixels around the tip it is allowed to select when creating the path. The Edge Contrast is the percentage of

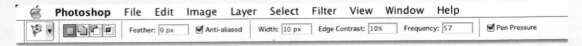

FIGURE 11.65   The Options bar for the Magnetic Lasso tool.

light and dark pixels that control the lasso's sensitivity. A high number chooses edges that contrast sharply, whereas a lower number chooses the lower-contrast edges. The Frequency is the number of insertion points the lasso places along the paths. Together these three options can make selecting objects very easy.

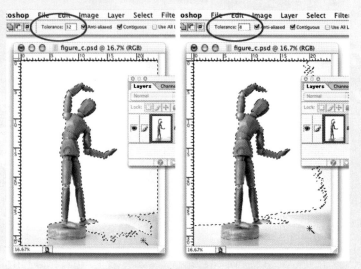

FIGURE 11.66   The Tolerance in these images is different. Notice how the one with the higher Tolerance (left) includes more pixels.

Magic Wand Tool

The Magic Wand tool selects similar colors that are adjacent to the selected pixel. For example, if you click on a light-colored pixel, all the other adjacent consistently light-colored pixels will be selected.

The number of pixels selected is controlled by the Tolerance, which is located in the Options bar (Figure 11.66). The higher the number, the more pixels will be included in the selection. Add the Shift key when clicking to add more pixels to the selection.

Using Selections and Masks Together

CONVERTING A SELECTION INTO A MASK

Earlier in the chapter a layer mask was attached to a layer first and then painted on to create the transparent and opaque areas. Although this is an easy way to do it, there is another way that may be a little more accurate.

Once a selection is made using the Selection tools, it is easy to convert that selection into a mask.

Using the Magnetic Lasso tool made selecting the plate of cookies a snap. Making the outside area transparent is even easier.

1. Using the Magnetic Lasso tool (L), create a selection around the plate of cookies in the image.

2. Double-click the Background layer to change it to a normal layer.

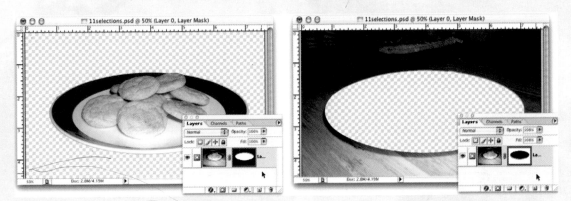

FIGURE 11.67   The result of the Reveal Selection command on the plate of cookies (left). The result of the Hide Selection command on the plate of cookies (right).

Make sure that you have the options set correctly when selecting the plate. Close the selection by ending at your starting point.

3. With the selection active, choose `Layer > Add Layer Mask > Reveal Se-lection`.

A mask is created and the area that was outside the selection has been made transparent (Figure 11.67). If there are any inaccuracies or blemishes in the mask, simply use the Brush tool to clean up the mistakes.

FIGURE 11.68   An image (left) can be flipped horizontally (middle) or vertically (right).

If you had chosen Hide Selection instead, the area within the selection would have become transparent. See Figure 11.67.

Transformation Tools

As in Illustrator, Photoshop has its own set of Transformation tools. Transformations such as Scale and Rotate can either be performed on certain selections or entire layers.

FLIPPING LAYERS

Sometimes objects fit into the design better when they are flipped (reflected across an axis). Layers can be flipped horizontally (left and right) or vertically (top and bottom) (Figure 11.68).

ON THE CD

1. From the Chapter 11 folder on the CD-ROM, open file *11transform.psd*.

In the file there are several layers. In this exercise you will flip the layer "cookies" and place it in the lower-left corner of the page.

2. Select the layer "cookies" to activate the layer.
3. From the top menu, choose `Edit > Transform > Flip Horizontally`.

The "cookies" layer flips across its y-axis. It doesn't matter that it was flipped; there are no visual clues that would even cause suspicion. But beware of flipping images that contain words, symbols, signs, tags, and so on. Things that appear unusual tend to jump out at you first and that could be very bad. Move the "cookies" layer into the lower-left corner of the document. It will be positioned correctly in a moment.

SCALE

Some images that you prepare will be a little large and may need to be scaled down.

4. Unhide the layer "boy with cookie sheet" and select it.

Show the layer above by clicking on the first empty square in the layer "boy with cookie sheet." Then select the layer by clicking on it. Make sure you select the thumbnail, and not the mask.

5. From the top menu, choose `Edit > Transform > Scale`.

There is no shortcut specifically for the Scale command. By choosing it from the Edit menu, a bounding box appears around the contents of the layer. When the box appears, notice that the Tool Box Options appear at the top of the screen.

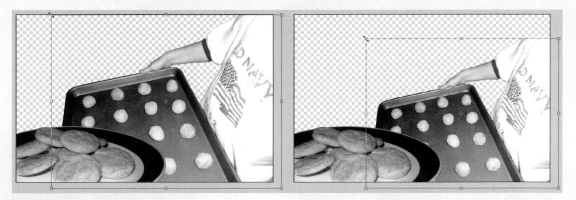

FIGURE 11.69   Using the Shift key keeps the file proportioned correctly.

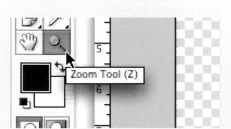

FIGURE 11.70   The location of the Zoom tool in the Tool palette.

FIGURE 11.71   Use the Info palette or the Options bar to check the current percentage of the scale.

FIGURE 11.72   The Cancel and Commit buttons are on the far right of the Options bar.

6. Place the mouse over the top-left corner of the bounding box and, while holding down the Shift key, move the handle down and to the left (Figure 11.69).

The bounding box is larger than the image. Use the Zoom tool (Z) to zoom in and out (hold Alt or Option to toggle it) so that you can see the entire bounding box (Figure 11.70). Holding down the Shift key as you scale the image constrains the height and width of the scale, just as it has in other operations.

7. Scale the image until the measurement in the width and height reads approximately 90% (Figure 11.71).

There are two buttons at the end of the Options bar; they are Cancel (Esc) and Commit (PC: Enter; Mac: Return; Figure 11.72).

By clicking on the Commit button the transformation is set. If the change is not what is wanted, click on the Cancel button. Nothing is permanent until either the Cancel or Commit buttons are clicked.

FIGURE 11.73   Click the link symbol to maintain the aspect ratio of the scale.

8. Click on the Commit button to set the transformation.

Depending on the speed of your computer's processor and the size of the file, Photoshop renders the transformation, rewriting the pixels in the layer to match the change.

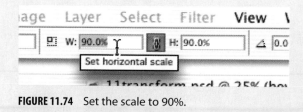

FIGURE 11.74   Set the scale to 90%.

9. Undo the transformation by selecting Edit > Undo Free Transform to reset the image.
10. Choose Edit > Transform > Scale again.

Rather than drag the handles of the bounding box, the percentage of the Scale can be typed manually into the Options bar.

FIGURE 11.75   Position the image before committing to the transformation.

11. Click on the link symbol in between the width and height fields of the Options bar (Figure 11.73).

    Clicking this symbol maintains the aspect ratio of the Scale. If you type one number into the width, that same measurement will be reflected in the height field.

12. Type 90% into the width field (Figure 11.74).

    By typing exact numbers into this box you can gauge the size of the image a little better. Change the number over and over again until the size is right.

13. Move the image to the right and down behind the contents of the "cookies" layer as shown in Figure 11.75.
14. Click on the Commit button to set the new scale.

ROTATE

To use the Rotate command, the steps are similar to those for using the Scale command.

1. Click on the eye icon of the "dough bowl" layer to unhide the layer.
2. Choose `Edit > Transform > Rotate`.
3. Mouse over any one of the corner handles and click and drag clockwise until the spoon on the left is pointing straight up (Figure 11.76).

FIGURE 11.76 Rotate the image so that the spoon points to the top of the screen.

4. Click on the Commit button to set the transform.

You can also type a number into the Angle field of the Options bar to rotate an object.

There is a really simple shortcut that will allow you to do several different transformations at once, and that is the Free Transform command (PC: control + T; Mac: command + T).

5. Undo the last transform by choosing `Edit > Undo Free Transform`.
6. From the top menu choose `Edit > Free Transform`.
7. Using the handles, scale the image as usual.
8. Rotate the image by placing the cursor just outside of one of the handles until the rounded arrow appears, then click and drag to rotate the object.

You may also type the measurements into the Options bar. Then click on the Commit button to confirm the transformation.

Notice that there was no selection made prior to doing the Transformations. If a layer is selected, then the entire contents of the layer are affected. If an area of the layer is selected it can be transformed separately from the rest of the contents of the layer. That information is "hovering" over existing pixels. However, when the Commit button is clicked, the pixels are placed on top of those pixels.

Continue the process of making selections, applying masks, and transforming the objects to create your montage. Feel free to experiment with all the other tools and menus and see what else you can do with this robust program.

Good luck!

SUMMARY

Now that you know everything about design, there is an easy test for you to take. Go back to an art museum or gallery you visited before you read this book. Take another look at one of the works of art you remember. Does it look the same? Can you analyze it visually and determine why you either liked or hated it? Do you feel differently about it now? Take some time when you go shopping or driving around and pay special attention to a label, store sign, or billboard. Can you analyze it visually and determine why you either liked or hated it? You should be able to see design more clearly and appreciate great design that you may have previously passed by. You may also wonder why there are so many poor designs in the world.

In the Summary section of Chapter 8, the following statements and questions were asked: As you make your design decisions, a personal style will begin to emerge. A preference for certain subject matter is only a superficial beginning. What types of compositions do you prefer: asymmetrical or symmetrical, closed form or open form? Did you use mostly curvilinear or rectilinear shapes for this project? What is the dominant line direction? Do you have a preference for designs that emphasize unity or variety? Will you be experimenting with low key or high key values for future designs? Will you be using mainly realistic, stylized, abstract, or non-objective shapes in your compositions?

Are you any closer to answering these questions? Can you look back and see if there are any similarities to your project solutions?

If you put in the time and energy to complete the projects in this book and thoroughly studied the theories and concepts, you have a fundamental background in the field of design. The information and projects were designed for the person who looks at the computer as a creative tool and has the desire to see more than function in everyday design. The reading and projects were not easy. They are reflective of the work you will face as a designer. Design isn't always fun but if you try to follow the ideals discussed in this book you will always find it challenging.

ABOUT THE CD-ROM

The CD-ROM included in this book contains the files used with the tutorials in the latter chapters of the text. Follow the directions within the tutorials for opening the files.

To access these files you will need the correct software. For files with the extension *.psd* or *.tif* you will need Adobe® Photoshop® (Version 7.0 or later), and for files with the extension *.ai*, Adobe Illustrator® (Version 10.0 or later) is required.

The files are contained within chapter folders for those chapters with tutorials only (i.e., Chapter 8 will have the files associated with the value tutorial).

- **Tutorial Folders**
    - Chapter 4
    - Chapter 5
    - Chapter 6
    - Chapter 7
    - Chapter 8
    - Chapter 9
    - Chapter 10
    - Chapter 11

Feel free to use the files to help you to learn the concepts within the tutorials.

- **Demo Folder**

This folder contains trial versions of Adobe Photoshop 7 and Adobe Illustrator 10 for Windows for your convenience. Macintosh trial versions of the software can be downloaded for free from the Adobe Web site at *www.adobe.com/products/tryadobe/main.jsp*.

SYSTEM REQUIREMENTS

The following are the minimum system requirements for the effective use of Illustrator 10 and Photoshop 7.

WINDOWS

- Intel® Pentium® III or 4 processor
- Microsoft® Windows® 98, Windows 98 Special Edition, Windows Millennium Edition, Windows 2000 with Service Pack 2, or Windows XP
- 128 MB of RAM (192 MB recommended)
- 800x600 color monitor with 16-bit color or greater video card
- CD-ROM drive (8x or higher)

MACINTOSH

- PowerPC® processor (G3, G4, G4 dual, G5, or G5 dual)
- Mac OS software version 9.1, 9.2, or Mac OS X version 10.1.3 (or higher)
- 128 MB of RAM (192 MB recommended)
- 800x600 color monitor with 16-bit color or greater video card
- CD-ROM drive (8x or higher)

INDEX